THE 8TH AIR FORCE WON THE WAR IN EUROPE

By August C. Bolino

Kensington Historical Press
PO Box 221
Fenton, Michigan

The 8th Air Force Won the War in Europe

Copyright © 2018 August C. Bolino
All Rights Reserved

ISBN-13: 978-1732301009

Without limiting the rights under copyright reserved above, no part of this publication may be reproduced, stored in or introduced into a retrieval system, or transmitted, in any form, or by any means (electronic, mechanical, photocopying, recording, or otherwise) without the prior written permission of the above author of this book.

Interview with General Robin Rand

I wrote this book because I was asked to write it by General Robin Rand.

On August 6, 2016, the last day of the bomb group meeting in Oshkosh, Wisconsin, General Rand, who is in charge of the Air Force, called for a special meeting of all veterans who had served in the war of the skies in Europe. He gave each of us a framed copy of a commendation for our service, and he printed at the bottom "Thank you for your sacrifice," and he wrote in long hand "Thank you for winning."

When he had handed out all of the commendations and said his goodbye, he headed toward the exit door, which was behind me. He headed toward me and asked, "How many missions did you fly?"

I said, "Thirty."

"And you have a Distinguished Flying Cross?"

I said, "Yes."

"And how did you earn it?"

I paused for a moment, then I answered. "The two leading planes in the group were shot down, and all planes scattered in the sky. I called the pilot and asked him, "What are we going to do?"

He did not waste a second. "We are going to regroup, and we are going to kick the sh-- out of those gunners down below."

I looked at my map, and I used my fingers which told me how to get to the target. "Try fifteen degrees," I told him.

In ten minutes we were over Liege, Belgium, and all bomb bay doors opened at the same time. We destroyed some of the city and all the factories behind it."

General Rand seemed to be satisfied with my answer, and he continued with his queries. "You have written some books, haven't you?"

"Yes," I said. "Sixteen are printed."

Then he cut in, "Can you write a history of the 8th Air Force?"

"Sure," I said.

Then he shouted a command, "Well, do it."

And this is it.

TABLE OF CONTENTS

Introduction		9
Part I	Some Early Pioneers	11
	America in World War I	12
	Jimmy Dolittle	14
	Edward F. Rickenbacker	15
	Billy Mitchell	16
Part II	Creating the Army Air Force	21
	Henry H. "Hap" Arnold	21
	Chapter 1 The Growth of the Air Force	25
Part III	Getting Sworn In	29
	Chapter 2 Reporting to Nashville, TN	31
	Chapter 3 Navigation at Monroe, LA	33
	Chapter 4 Joining a Crew at Pyote, TX	38
	Chapter 5 Going Overseas from Dyersburg, TN	42
Part IV	Joining the Fray at Knettishall, England	46
	Chapter 6 An Early Easy Mission	59
	Chapter 7 Not So Easy Missions	62
Part V	Some Mission Reports	67
	Chapter 8 A Friendship Out of the Blue	72
	Chapter 9 Tailgunner Regains Memoir	75
Part VI	Victory in Europe	78
	Chapter 10 The B-17 Flying Fortress	78
	Chapter 11 Some Famous B-17s	87

	Chapter 12 Destroying the German Oil Industry	99
	Chapter 13 Our Fighter Escorts	108
	Chapter 14 Our Two D-Day Missions	111
	Chapter 15 Our Monthly Leaves	121
	Chapter 16 Some Lucky Missions	126
	Chapter 17 The 388ths Most Disastrous Mission	128
	Chapter 18 A German Prison Camp	130
	Chapter 19 A Mission to Russia	135
	Chapter 20 Death Bombers	137
	Chapter 21 Bombing Peenemunde	141
Part VII	The Success of Strategic Bombing	148
	Chapter 22 The End of the War in Europe	159
	Chapter 23 The War in Asia	161
	Chapter 24 Merciful Missions	162
Part VIII	Flying Home	167
	Chapter 25 Atlantic City to Hollywood	169
	Chapter 26 Denver, CO	172
	Chapter 27 Leaving Santa Ana, CA	173
	Chapter 28 Gunnery at Las Vegas, NV	176
	Chapter 29 Parachutes at Shreveport, LA	178
	Chapter 30 Leaving Fort Smith, AR	180
Part IX	Casualties, Honors, and Awards	181
	Chapter 31 Caring for the Wounded	188
	Chapter 32 We Lost a Long Time Friend	190
	Chapter 33 The "Greatest Generation" Honored	193
	Chapter 34 Honoring Our Dead	201
Part X	Museums and Monuments	208
	Chapter 35 The Air Force Academy	227
Part XI	The 388th Bomb Group Association (H)	231

Chapter 36 A Special Meeting	234
Chapter 37 What Does Legacy Mean?	236
Chapter 38 Historically Speaking	239
Chapter 39 Some Correspondence	241
A Sweet Letter from a Daughter	241
The Story of "Tom"	244
"The Little Girl"	245
A Tree and a Friend	246
After 56 Years – The Puzzle	249
A Letter from the Boss to	
First Lt. Julian M. Carr	251
Return to Knettishall	252
Bibliography	254
About the Author	258
Other titles by August C. Bolino	259

THE 8ᵀᴴ AIR FORCE WON THE WAR IN EUROPE

INTRODUCTION

The roots of the Army Air Forces were found when the idea of strategic bombing at the Air Corps Tactical School was argued by Brig. General Billy Mitchell that resulted in his later court-martial. Despite many who resisted the growth of the Air Corps, it made great strides in the 1930s. A major step toward a separate air force came in March 1935, when command of all combat air units within the Continental United States was placed under a single organization called the *"General Headquarters Air Force."* (GHQ)

During the 1930s, the commanders of GHQ Air Force argued over how the air arm should be developed, but when war began, Congress enacted the First War Powers Act allowing President Franklin D. Roosevelt to reorganize the executive branch as he thought necessary. He responded with an Executive Order 9082, on February 28, which changed Henry Arnold's

The bombing at Pearl Harbor caused a major reorganization of the aviation branch in its history, by developing a unified command of all air elements and giving it total autonomy and equality with the ground forces. This resulted from the successes of the British Royal Air Force and the German *Wehrmacht's* military air arm, the *Luftwaffe*.

While other nations had separate air forces, the AAF remained a part of the Army until a defense reorganization in the post-war period resulted in the creation of an independent United States Air Force in September 1947. But when World War II ended, the Army Air Forces had become almost an independent service, but it was still a subordinate agency of the War Department.

The leaders of the AAF developed policies for rotating combat crews between different theaters, and on July 1, 1942 the

9

War Department established a one-year tour of duty for all AAF combat crews, but this policy was unrealistic and never put into effect, and on May 29, 1943 it changed the regulations for assignment of replacement crews.

The first combat operation by members of the 8th Air Force Bomber Command (as it was then known) occurred on July 4, 1942 when 6 USA crews borrowed RAF A-20 Havocs from the British (the British called them Bostons,), and flew a low level mission to German airfields in Holland. Six aircraft left England and only three came back. The First Official Mission of the 8th Air Force, using Boeing B-17 Flying Fortresses, occurred on August 17, 1942 when they attacked *Rouen / Sotteville* marshalling yard in France with 12 aircraft. All returned safely. A leading problem was that the 8th AF Bombers required up to two hours to assemble three bomber divisions before heading over to *Festung Europa*.

Part I Some Early Pioneers

Daedalus and Son Fly to Escape

Daedalus is mentioned in the story of *Theseus* as the inventor and scholar whose ingenuity and intelligence was unmatched by any other. Daedalus constructed wings for Icarus. Daedalus and his son, Icarus, spent their days locked up in a tower, unable to escape by land or sea. All the ships leaving the island were carefully monitored by King Minos, who was determined to not let Daedalus escape. So the inventor decided that if he could not escape by sea, then he would escape the island of Crete by riding on the winds.

Daedalus collected the feathers of the numerous birds that roosted in his tower prison. He constructed a set of wings that could be worn by a man by using candlewax and thread to hold the feathers in place. He then constructed wings for his son Icarus, who had been cast away in the tower as well. When the wings were complete the father and son prepared to jump from the tower and fly to freedom. Before they did so, Daedalus warned his son not to fly too low to the sea, as the mist would dampen his wings and cause him to fall. He also warned the young boy not to fly too high as the warmth from the sun would melt the wax that held the feathers and cause him to fall to earth.

Daedalus and his son leaped from the tower and soared across the land and out to sea. The farmers and herders stopped their work and looked up at the duo flying like birds. The citizens of Crete thought that the pair were gods, never before had they seen such a miraculous sight.

The two flying men traveled at peace for some time. They passed the islands of Samos and Delos and eventually flew past Lebynthos. All the while they were careful not to fly too low or too high, however.

AUGUST C. BOLINO

The Wright Brothers

On December 17, 1903, Orville Wright piloted the first powered airplane 20 feet above a wind-swept beach in North Carolina. The flight lasted only 12 seconds and covered 120 feet. This was the culmination of all the experiments dating from 1896.

The brothers began their experimentation in flight in their bicycle shop in Dayton, Ohio. They selected the beach at Kitty Hawk as their proving ground because of the constant wind that would lift their craft. In 1902 they came to the beach with their glider and made more than 700 successful flights.

They began with glided flight, then they moved to powered flight. Because no automobile manufacturer could supply an engine powerful enough for flight, they designed and built their own. All of their hard work, experimentation and innovation came together that December day as they took to the sky and forever changed the course of history. The brothers notified several newspapers prior to their historic flight, but only one - the local journal - made mention of the event.

Americans Who Flew in World War I

American fliers reached Europe in September 1917 without any aircraft. They used British and French planes. Most of them flew SPADS.

The first American trained pilot to become an ace was Lt. Douglas Campbell, who shot down five German aircraft by the end of May 1918. He was a member of the celebrated 94th 'Hat in the Ring' Aero Squadron, which created the bulk of American aces in World War.

Pilots who scored five or more aerial victories were classified as "air aces." They served with the Aeronautique Militaire. The following were some of the American Aces:

| Paul Frank Baer | Lieutenant | Escadrille N.124 (Lafayette Escadrille) | |

THE 8TH AIR FORCE WON THE WAR IN EUROPE

		Escadrille SPA.80 103d Aero Squadron	
Frank Leaman Baylies	Lieutenant	Escadrille SPA.73 Escadrille SPA.3	12 victories (3 shared) Killed in action: 17 June 1918
James Dudley Beane	Lieutenant	Escadrille SPA.69 22d Aero Squadron	6 victories (4 shared) Transferred to Air Service, United States Army, August, 1918
Charles John Biddle	Major	Escadrille N.124 (Lafayette Escadrille) Escadrille SPA.73 13th Aero Squadron 103d Aero Squadron	
Thomas Gantz Cassady	Captain	Escadrille SPA.157Escadrille SPA.163 28th Aero Squadron 103d Aero Squadron	9 victories (5 shared); 3 unconfirmed. Transferred to Air Service, United States Army, July, 1918
James Alexander Connelly Jr.	Adjutant	Escadrille SPA.157 Escadrille SPA.163	7 victories (5 shared); 2 unconfirmed.
Charles Gossage Grey	Captain	Escadrille SPA.93 Lafayette Flying Corps 213th Aero Squadron	5 victories (3 shared) Transferred to Air Service, United States Army, March, 1918

Lansing Colton Holden Jr.	Lieutenant	Escadrille N.461 95th Aero Squadron	7 victories (1 shared)
Gorman DeFreest Larner	Captain	Escadrille SPA.86 103d Aero Squadron	
Gervais Raoul Lufbery	Major		
Edwin Charles Parsons	Lieutenant	Escadrille N.124 (Lafayette Escadrille) Escadrille SPA.3	8 victories (2 shared)
David McKelvey Peterson	Major	Escadrille N.124 (Lafayette Escadrille) 103d Aero Squadron 94th Aero Squadron 95th Aero Squadron	

Jimmy Doolittle

Lt. Col. Jimmy Doolittle accepts a medal from the skipper of the USS Hornet, Capt. Marc A. Mitscher (U.S. Air Force photo)

THE 8TH AIR FORCE WON THE WAR IN EUROPE

James Harold Doolittle was an American aviation pioneer. As a Reserve officer in the United States Army Air Corps, Doolittle was recalled to active duty during World War II. He was awarded the Medal of Honor for personal valor and leadership as commander of the Doolittle Raid, a bold long-range retaliatory air raid on the Japanese main islands, on 18 April 1.

In July 1923, after serving as a test pilot and aeronautical engineer at McCook Field, Doolittle enrolled at the Massachusetts Institute of Technology, and in March 1924, he conducted aircraft acceleration tests at McCook Field, which became the basis of his master's thesis and led to his second Distinguished Flying Cross.

In 1942 he was awarded the Medal of Honor for personal valor and leadership as commander of the Doolittle Raid, a bold long-range retaliatory air raid on the Japanese main islands, on 18 April 18, 1942, four months after the attack on Pearl Harbor.

Doolittle died on September 27, 1993 at age 96. He was buried at Arlington National Cemetery.

Edward F. Rickenbacker

Edward Rickenbacker was born in Columbus, Ohio, to Swiss German-speaking immigrants. From childhood, he loved machines and experimented with them. He was encouraged by his father's words: "A machine has to have a purpose."

In what was to signify the major element of his life, he came close to dying in several episodes. He began with horse-drawn carriages, and he ended with airplane crashes.

According to W. D. Lewis's *Eddie Rickenbacker: An American Hero in the Twentieth Century*, his father died after a fight with another man in Columbus. Rickenbacker had to find jobs to help support the family, but he was always learning about machines. He tried to learn about some complicated machines, but he had to enroll in a correspondence course in engineering. He began with automobiles, as he was employed as a salesman with the Columbus Buggy Company.

In 1917, when the United States entered World War I, the first American aviation combat force was created as the Air Service, which was part of the American Expeditionary Force (AEF). Major General Mason Patrick commanded the Air Service, with Brigadier General Billy Mitchell as his deputy. This unit in France provided tactical support for the U.S. Army, especially during several battles. Captain Eddie Rickenbacker was one of the aces. A major development was the removal of this combat force from the Signal Corps and was put under the United States Secretary of War. An assistant secretary was created for the Army Air Service, but with the end of the First World War, the AEF's Air Service was dissolved and the Army Air Service was removed from active duty. In 1920, the Air Service became a branch of the Army and in 1926 was renamed the Army Air Corps. During this period, the Air Corps began experimenting with new techniques, such as air-to-air refueling and it was involved in creating the first all-metal monoplane bombers, the martin B-10.

Rickenbacker was also an avid golfer, often playing at the Siwanoy Country Club course near his home. He is one of a very select few Club members who were granted honorary lifetime membership at Siwanoy.

Rickenbacker became well known as a race car driver, competing in the Indianapolis 500 four times before World War I, and earning the nickname "Fast Eddie." Rickenbacker joined the Maxwell Race Team in 1915 after leaving Peugeot. After the Maxwell team disbanded that same year, he joined the Prest-O-Lite team as manager and continued to race improved Maxwells for Prest-O-Lite.

Billy Mitchell

In the 1920s Americans were fascinated with new airplanes, but they were captivated by all the stunts that were done in many small towns. These involved women walking on wings while the pilot completed stunts. This was also the time when air mail developed. The slogan was, "The mail must go through," so these pilots learned how to fly in bad weather and good.

THE 8TH AIR FORCE WON THE WAR IN EUROPE

General Billy Mitchell, the deputy director of the Air Service, was involved in a battle to take control of coastal defense away from the Navy. He insisted that his planes could sink battleships any day, which he proved with a series of tests that ended with the sinking of the *Ostfriesland*. Mitchell lost his self-control in 1925 when he accused the Navy of "incompetency, criminal negligence and almost treasonable administration of the national defense."

Because of his loss of self-control, he received a highly publicized court martial. But he continued to state his theory that air power alone would suffice to win the next big war. He was convicted in court, and he resigned. He was a popular hero to Americans, and his outcry forced the War Department to strengthen the Air Corps. Mitchell's main approach was to demand that air power had to be autonomous—it had to be controlled by fliers who knew new technology, new tactics and new strategies. He feared that the Armies and the Navies would waste precious assets in trying to assist old-fashioned armies and navies. Until he died in 1936, Mitchell continued to make speeches urging that the Government establish a separate Air Force.

Pre-invasion bombing of Pointe du Hoe by Ninth Air Force bombers

But the Air Corps was set aside by civilians like Charles Lindbergh, Howard Hughes or Amelia Earhart. In 1934 President Franklin Roosevelt, who became a firm believer of airpower, suddenly turned the delivery of air mail over to the Army Air Corps. He did this despite the fact that there were many crashes by inexperienced Air Corps pilots in mediocre planes with poor navigation equipment gear, and this seemed to remove the Air Force claims that in wartime it could perform miracles.

When World War II began in 1939, Roosevelt began in 1940 to expand the role of the Air Corps. He called for a program of 50,000 planes per year, sending the best new models to Britain for its war against the *Luftwaffe*.

In 1935, the Boeing B-17 was under contract, but the Air Corps was commanded by Frank Andrews, Oscar Westover, and followed by Henry H. ("Hap") Arnold. The effect of this change was to split the Air Force into two parts--both of which were commanded by major generals.

In 1937, the B-17 Flying Fortress made its first appearance. In a very impressive feat of navigation; three B-17s intercepted the Italian passenger liner *Rex* at sea. This mission told the Air Corps and the American public that these bombers were ready for strategic bombing.

Major General Carl A. Spaatz took command of the Eighth Air Force in London in 1942; with Brigadier General Ira Eaker as second in command, he supervised the strategic bombing campaign. In late 1943, Spaatz was made commander of the new U.S. Strategic Air Forces, reporting directly to the Combined Chiefs of Staff. Spaatz began daylight bombing operations using the prewar doctrine of flying bombers in close formations, relying on their combined defensive firepower for protection from attacking enemy aircraft rather than supporting fighter escorts. The doctrine proved flawed when deep-penetration missions beyond the range of escort fighters were attempted, because German fighter planes overwhelmed U.S. formations, shooting down bombers in excess of "acceptable" loss rates, especially in combination with the vast number of flak anti-aircraft batteries defending Germany's major targets. American fliers took heavy casualties during raids on the oil refineries of *Ploieşti*, Romania, and the ball-bearing factories at *Schweinfurt* and *Regensburg*, Germany, and it was the loss rate in crews and not materiel that

THE 8ᵀᴴ AIR FORCE WON THE WAR IN EUROPE

brought about a pullback from the strategic offensive in the autumn of 1943.

The Eighth Air Force had attempted to use both the P-47 and P-38 as escorts, but while the Thunderbolt was a capable dogfighter it lacked the range, even with the addition of drop tanks to extend its range, and the Lightning proved mechanically unreliable in the frigid altitudes at which the missions were fought. Bomber protection was greatly improved after the introduction of North American P-51 Mustang fighters in Europe. With its built-in extended range and competitive or superior performance characteristics in comparison to all existing German piston-engined fighters, the Mustang was an immediately available solution to the crisis. In January 1944 the Eighth Air Force obtained priority in equipping its groups, so that ultimately 14 of its 15 groups fielded Mustangs. P-51 escorts began operations in February 1944 and increased their numbers rapidly, so that the *Luftwaffe* suffered increasing fighter losses in aerial engagements beginning with Big Week in early 1944. Allied fighters were also granted free rein in attacking German fighter airfields, both in pre-planned missions and while returning to base from escort duties, and the major *Luftwaffe* threat against Allied bombers was severely diminished by D-Day.

The Air Force became a significant part of winning the war in World War II. President Franklin D. Roosevelt called for a very enlarged air force based on long-range strategic bombing. In 1941, the Army Air Corps became a part of the new U.S. Army Air Forces (AAF), in Circular 59, effective March 9, 1942, the newly created Army Air Forces gained equal voice with the Army and Navy on the Joint Chiefs of Staff and it achieved complete autonomy in 1947) in favor of a streamlined system of commands and numbered air forces for decentralized management of the burgeoning Army Air Forces.

The reorganization merged all aviation elements of the former Air Corps into the Army Air Forces. Although the Air Corps still legally existed as an Army branch, the position and Office of the Chief of the Air Corps was dissolved.

In the Pacific Theater of Operations, the AAF provided major tactical support under General George Kenney to Douglas

MacArthur in the Southwest Pacific theater. Kenney's pilots invented the skip-bombing technique against Japanese ships. Kenney's forces claimed destruction of 11,900 Japanese planes and 1.7 million tons of shipping. The first development and sustained implementation of airlift by American air forces occurred between May 1942 and November 1945 as hundreds of transports flew more than half a million tons of supplies from India to China over the Hump.

Part II Creating the Army Air Force

Henry H. "Hap" Arnold

Henry Arnold was born in 1886, and he was a graduate of West Point in 1907. His first assignment was to the 29th infantry, then to the Signal Corps in in 1911, where he met the Wright Brothers, who taught him how to fly. In 1912 Arnold set an altitude record of 6,540 feet. When War I began, he was sent to Panama to establish an air service there. When Billy Mitchell was tried in 1925, and he was found guilty, Arnold believed in the potential of an Air Corps.

During the 1930s, the commanders of GHQ Air Force argued over how the air arm should be developed, but when war began, Congress enacted the First War Powers Act on December 18, 1941 allowing President Franklin D. Roosevelt to reorganize the executive branch as he thought necessary. He responded with an Executive Order 9082, on February 28, which changed Henry Arnold's title to Commanding General, Army Air Forces, effective March 9, 1942.

General of the Army Henry H. "Hap" Arnold

The bombing at Pearl Harbor caused a major reorganization of the aviation branch in its history by developing a unified command of all air elements, giving it total autonomy and equality with the ground forces. This resulted from the successes of the British Royal Air Force and the German *Wehrmacht's* military air arm, the *Luftwaffe*.

The leaders of the AAF developed policies for rotating combat crews between different theaters, and on July 1, 1942 the War Department established a one-year tour of duty for all AAF combat crews, but this policy was unrealistic and never put into effect, and on May 29, 1943 it changed the regulations for assignment of replacement crews.

The first combat operation by members of the 8th Air Force Bomber Command (as it was then known) occurred on July 4, 1942 when 6 USA crews borrowed RAF A-20 Havocs from the British (the British called them Bostons), and flew a low level mission to German airfields in Holland. Six aircraft left England and only three came back. The First Official Mission of the 8th Air Force, using Boeing B-17 Flying Fortresses, occurred on August 17, 1942 when they attacked *Rouen / Sotteville* marshalling yard in France with 12 aircraft. All returned safely. A leading problem was that the 8th AF Bombers required up to two hours to assemble three bomber divisions before heading over to *Festung Europa*.

Each base usually had a local pub nearby, and every US base had an Officer's Club and an Enlisted Club on the base. But combat flying was not fun. Each crew had to follow all SOPs (Standard Operating Procedures). As one example, the procedures for landing were very particular: each group was required to get them all back onto the ground quickly without running into other planes in the pattern. Planes with wounded aboard landed first, then all undamaged planes, and finally seriously damaged planes landed last so that if they crashed, the runway would not be closed. One pilot had a flight training procedure for his co-pilot: "Gear up, flaps up, shut up."

After each mission there was always an intelligence briefing. Each crew member was to report what he saw. This combat report provides information on what planes were shot

THE 8TH AIR FORCE WON THE WAR IN EUROPE

down, how many parachutes were open. Later, the 8th Air Force learned that not all aircraft that were shot down were not destroyed. Some were repaired and used by the *Luftwaffe* for behind the lines work.

Memorial for the 384th BG (H) in the form of stained glass in the Parish Church of St. James the Apostle at Grafton Underwood, Northants, England.

There are such memorials at almost every base where the 8th Air Force was stationed. There are also memorials in many of the churches near where American units were stationed.

This is the Eighth Air Force shoulder patch that was worn on the left side of the uniform by members of the United States Army Air Forces during World War II

Flak was always the first sign that we were over German occupied territory. The German anti-aircraft gunners were probably the best in the world. When we flew at 25,000 feet, they were on the ground preparing to load a 5 or 6 inch shell. They would set it for our altitude and when the shell reached it, they hoped that it would explode at the bomb bay doors. If it did not hit the bomber, it would explode and scatter hundreds of pieces of flak – each was about one inch long. Its jagged end was meant to disable any airman inside a bomber. If he was hit, there is no first aid at 65 below zero. He would probably die in the air.

German fighters rarely intercepted bombers on the way in over the ocean, but they would pursue them over the ocean on their way home – unless there were escorts about.

The mission of "The Mighty Eighth" was to safeguard America's interests through strategic deterrence and global combat power. The Eighth Air Force mission was to be capable of deploying its power against enemy threats from anywhere, any time. The 8th Air Force motto was "Peace Through Strength."

The Eighth Air Force team consisted of more than 16,000 Regular Air Force (e.g. active duty) Air National Guard and Air Force Reserve professionals operating and maintaining a variety of aircraft capable of deploying air power to any area of the world. The air power includes the heart of America's heavy bomber force: the B-17 Flying Fortress and the B-52 Stratofortress. The Mighty Eighth's B-17 force for each bomb group was 36 planes configured as lead, high and low squadrons. The B-52 force consisted of 76 bombers assigned to two active duty wings, the 2d Bomb Wing at Barksdale AFB, Louisiana and the 5th Bomb Wing at Minot-AFB, North Dakota, and one reserve wing, the 307th Bomb Wing at Barksdale AFB, Louisiana. The B-2 force consists of 20 bombers assigned to the active duty 509th Bomb Wing along with the Missouri Air National Guard's associate 131st Bomb Wing at Whiteman AFB, Missouri. The B-1 force consists of 62 bombers assigned to the active duty 7th Bomb Wing at Dyess AFB, Texas and the 28th Bomb Wing at Ellsworth AFB, South Dakota.

THE 8TH AIR FORCE WON THE WAR IN EUROPE

Chapter One
The Growth of the Army Air Force

The peak size of the AAF during the Second World War was over 2.4 million men and women in service and nearly 80,000 aircraft by 1944, and by "V-E Day", the Army Air Forces had 1.25 million men stationed overseas and operated from more than 1,600 airfields worldwide. This produced a 1945 *Wehrmacht* joke that most flyers knew. "When we see a silver plane, it's American, a black plane, it's British. When we see no plane, it's German." But no matter what the joke, the 8th Air Force Combat Losses in Europe were heavy.

There was a higher percentage of being killed, wounded or captured while flying in the 8th AF than if you were in the infantry in the front line. There were 47,000 casualties, of which 26,000 were killed. The statistics would be even higher if only the front line regiment combat personnel were counted and not the whole division. A US division was 16,000 or so personnel with only 3,600 being the front line combat troops.

In February, 1944 the American air attacks were a prelude to the invasion of France. The B-17's attacked railroad junctions, airfields, ports and bridges in northern France and along the English Channel coastline. In addition, fighters from both Eighth and Ninth Air Forces mounted strafing missions at airfields and rail networks. By the time of D-Day, on June 6, Allied fighter pilots had damaged or destroyed German air fields, hundreds of locomotives, and thousands of motorized vehicles, and many bridges.

The P-51 Mustang began service in Europe with the British in early 1942. But the Allison V-1710 engine was inadequate at higher altitudes, so they switched engines with the Rolls Royce, two speed, two stage supercharger that improved performance, and by using a four-bladed propeller, rather than the three-bladed one, the performance was more improved. It could achieve a level speed of 441 mph at 29,800 feet, which was over 100 mph faster than the Allison-engine. With these improvements, The USAAF had an aircraft that could compete on equal terms with the *Focke-Wulf* 190 and the models of the *Messerschmitt* 109.

In January 1944, Major General Jimmy Doolittle made a major change in policy that saved many bombers. He required escorting fighters to remain with the bombers at all times. Later that year, American fighter pilots began flying far ahead of the bombers that were in combat box formations, thereby "clearing the skies" of any *Luftwaffe* fighter planes heading towards the target. This strategy effectively disabled the twin-engined *Zerstörergeschwader* heavy fighter wings and their replacements, single-engined *Sturmgruppen* of heavily armed FW 190s. The chief result was that the *Luftwaffe* was almost absent over the skies of Europe after D-Day as the Allies were able to achieve air superiority over the continent. The presence of larger formations of Allied heavy bombers, mostly the growing numbers of B-17s and B-24s attacking enemy targets, was overwhelming for the German fighter force. It could not sustain the losses the Eighth Air Force bombers and fighters were inflicting on it. By mid-1944, Eighth Air Force had reached a total strength of more than 200,000 persons, and it is estimated that more than 350,000 Americans served in the Eighth Air Force during the war in Europe. At peak strength, Eighth Air Force had forty heavy bomber groups, fifteen fighter groups, and it could send out more than 2,000 four-engine bombers and more than 1,000 fighters on a single mission to multiple targets. The above results were very costly, because these heavy bomber groups of the Army Air Corps in World War II had more casualties than the U.S, Navy and the Marines combined.

On May 29, 1944 35,000 Boeing employees gathered to sign their names on the 5,000th Flying Fortress "5 Grand." It signified that U. S. airpower had reached a new and impressive level. At the same time, the Lockheed plant at Burbank, California had just produced its 13,000th war plane—mostly P-38s.

In January 1945, the *Luftwaffe* attempted one last major air offensive against the Allied Air Forces. Over 950 fighters had been

THE 8ᵀᴴ AIR FORCE WON THE WAR IN EUROPE

sent west from the Eastern Front for "*Operation Bodenplatte.*" The entire German fighter force in the West, comprising combat aircraft from some eleven *Jagdgeschwader* (day fighter wings), took off and attacked 27 Allied airfields in northern France, Belgium and the southern part of the Netherlands in an attempt to cripple Allied air forces in the Low Countries of Europe. It was a last-ditch effort to keep up the momentum of the German Army (*Wehrmacht Heer*) during the stagnant stage of the Battle of the Bulge (*Unternehmen Wacht am Rhein*).

The operation was a total loss, as the *Luftwaffe* suffered over 300 Luftwaffe aircraft were shot down, mostly by Allied Anti-Aircraft guns. The Allied Air Forces were replaced within weeks. The operation failed to achieve air superiority, even temporarily, and the German Army continued to be exposed to air attack.

First seen by Allied airmen during the late summer of 1944, it wasn't until March 1945 that German jet aircraft started to attack Allied bomber formations. The history of this development goes back to ancient Greece in the year 60 when a Greek scientist built a small jet engine that was powered by steam. It was expanded by Sir Isaac Newton in 1687 when he developed jet propulsion by utilizing his third law of motion.

On March 2, when Eighth Air Force bombers attacked the synthetic oil refineries at *Leipzig, Messerschmitt ME* 262s attacked the formation near Dresden. The next day, the largest formation of German jets ever seen, most likely from the *Luftwaffe's* specialist 7th Fighter Wing, *Jagdgeschwader 7 Nowotny*, made attacks on Eighth Air Force bomber formations over Dresden and the oil targets at Essen, shooting down only three bombers. The *Luftwaffe* jets were too few to have any serious effect on the Allied air armadas that were now sweeping over the *Reich* without opposition. A lack of fuel and available pilots for the new jets greatly reduced their effectiveness.

While other nations had separate air forces, the AAF remained a part of the Army until a defense re-organization in the post-war period resulted in the creation of an independent United States Air Force in September 1947. By the time that World War II ended, the Army Air Forces had become almost an independent service, but it was still a subordinate agency of the War Department.

Part III Getting Sworn In

My official beginning of World War II began on August 31, 1942, but there were events that preceded it. When the Japanese bombed Pearl Harbor on December 7, 1941 President Franklin Roosevelt asked the Congress to establish a draft of all males who were 18 years or older. He also asked it to finance the construction of 50,000 airplanes.

When the draft began, the President went on the radio each day to announce which numbers had been chosen. I believe my number was 358, so I listened for that number to be called. One day in August I heard my number, so I told my mother, "Ma, I am going to enlist in the Army Air Corps, because I did not want to walk across Germany in the mud."

She answered, "I don't want you to bomb Italy, because I have cousins there."

I told her that we would be bombing Germany, not Italy.

The next day I went to 10 Commonwealth Avenue in downtown Boston, Massachusetts where I took the written examination to qualify. I barely got in because I had taken three years in the Evening Division at Northeastern University, which was equal to two years in days. The questions were the usual math and English type. For example, if a ladder was 20 feet long and was placed at a 30 degree, angle how far away from the house was it? I was elated to pass.

After the written examination, I was given a physical exam along with about a hundred others. When they took my pulse, it was very low and not qualifying, so the medic told me to go out in the hall and run around, which worked well. I went next to main area for the rest of the examination. As I went through the commands given by the officer, he pointed at me and yelled, "You, stand aside." I waited as the exam was completed and then I was questioned about my crooked right arm. I told the officer that it was broken recently and that it would straighten out in time.

Later, I was told that I would have to wait to be called on active duty, so I continued working at the Charlestown Navy Yard. It was during this wait that the Coconut Grove fire occurred. It was the day of the Boston College-Holy Cross football game. BC was heavily favored, but Holy Cross won by a score of 55 to 12. Boston College had planned a large celebration at the Coconut Grove--a favorite nightclub in Downtown Boston. That victory celebration never took place. Vito Salerno, a graduate of Holy Cross, came down from Worcester for the game. He and I went downtown to celebrate his victory.

The Coconut Grove was jammed, so we went instead to the Tic Toc--a block or two away. As we sat drinking and talking, someone came in and yelled, "The Coconut Grove is on fire." We hustled over and saw the flames high in the air. Because I was already sworn in to the Air Force, I volunteered to carry out the dead, but I was turned away.

The results of the fire were unbelievable. The rear door was locked with a chain and a heavy lock. The only exit was a revolving door in the front. The people tried to push from both sides and no one got out, except a couple of persons who jumped out the second story window. There were 498 persons behind that door, including cowboy film star Buck Jones (one of my boyhood idols) who was there with his girlfriend, not his wife. In fact several persons who died were girlfriends.

The only good news that came out this calamity was that the City of Boston and many other cities passed laws requiring that all exits had at least two doors.

THE 8TH AIR FORCE WON THE WAR IN EUROPE

Chapter Two
Reporting to Nashville, TN

I was finally called to active duty and ordered to Nashville, Tennessee for classification. All new recruits were told to report to South Station for the train ride south. Since my father was working twelve hours a day, seven days a week as a chef and my mother was working in a textile factory--a real sweat shop--my uncle Tony drove me to the station. As I walked to my railroad car, Tony began weeping (he was such an old, gentle softie), and I couldn't keep my eyes dry so I said goodbye with a hug and boarded the train. When we got to Richmond, Virginia, the train stopped and about a hundred young cadets came on board. Talk about culture shock. They laughed at our Boston accents, and we couldn't understand a word they spoke. Of course, later we inter-mixed and became good friends.

When we arrived in Nashville, we were taken to our barracks and issued GI stuff. My loving mother had bought me a beautiful leather bag to carry my clothes in. When we got our GI issue, everything we had of a civilian nature was thrown into a big trash container, including my new luggage.

The official name of the place was the U.S.A.A.C. Psychomotor & Classification Center. The barracks were of wood construction with tar-paper sidings, and they were heated by stoves that burned soft coal, making the air difficult to breath. The buildings were set along a creek that overran the banks when it rained, which was a regular occurrence. We had outdoor latrines and lousy food, which was eaten out of mess kits.

While we awaited our tests, we were quarantined, which meant that we could not use the PX, or the movie theater. I started to miss Boston and my family. When the tests began, they involved some reading and hand coordination tests (if you tried to put a square peg in a round hole you probably failed). I got a 95 for pilot training, a 95 for navigation training and a 75 for bombardier. I don't know if that means that I am uncoordinated, but in any case an officer called me and said, "Mr. Bolino, we are sending you to navigation school."

I answered, "But I joined up to be a pilot."

He replied, "We are sure you can pass navigation school, because you have taken a lot of courses in mathematics. We cannot waste the government's money since it will cost $50,000 to train you as a navigator."

I had to make one final decision. I was given a choice of B-17s or B-24s. It was then that I remembered a conversation that I had with my mother. She told me when I joined the Army Air Corps that she did not want me to bomb Italy, because she had several cousins there. Since the B-24s were flying out of *Foggia*, Italy, I chose B-17s.

While I was waiting for orders to go to flying school, I came upon one bar, the Brass Rail, that was particularly interesting, because in it there were literally hundreds of hats from every branch of military service, including several from foreign groups. I learned quickly that no liquor was sold in bars in Tennessee. Each patron brought his own bottle and paid for setups. I also learned in those bars that girls in Tennessee married early. One I spoke to one she claimed that she was fifteen years old (she looked much older), and she had three children.

Each weekend we went to the Hermitage, Andrew Jackson's home. At that time it was a restaurant, where magnificent filet mignons were the specialty. Because I had never had one before I had to give one a try. The taste was unbelievable. I asked a waiter how they were made. He answered, "The steak is wrapped in bacon and seared." While we ate, we listened to the music of Francis Craig and his orchestra. Their big hit was "Near You," which later became the theme song of the Milton Berle Show.

Chapter Three
Navigation at Monroe, LA

We finally got orders to board a train to Selman Field, on the outskirts of Monroe, Louisiana. It was an unbelievable place, in the north-central part of the state, east of Shreveport. In the summer, the temperature was 95 degrees and close to 100 percent humidity. If you put on a clean uniform at 5:00 p.m., it would be dripping wet by 5:10 p.m.

The Virginians and the Bostonians considered each other "weird," but the cultural shock wore off eventually. I had never met a southerner before and I know they had never met a Bostonian. They were more accustomed to the humidity of the place, which fostered the growth of all kinds of insects. On my first trip to town, I headed for the local hotel and as I walked toward the door I had to step on hundreds of big black water beetles to get into the lobby, which was also full of beetles. They were everywhere on the sides of buildings and inside. It was a shock for a person from Massachusetts, where few bugs could survive the cold winters. But you just stepped on them and went on.

When I settled in at the base I was told to report to the Major's office. I could not understand why he would want to see me. I entered his office, I saluted, and said, "Cadet Bolino reporting as ordered." It was "Dutchy" Holland, my track coach at Mechanic Arts High School. He walked over, said welcome and hugged me. I was one of his favorites on the track team because I was one of the smallest members, and he was delighted when I earned my letter as a senior. Selman field was the only time that we chatted "man to man."

On a typical day, we began with reveille at 06:00, then breakfast at 07:00, then a quick inspection and classes began at 08:00. At the end of each hour, we had a ten-minute break. At

11:00, we had PT (physical training). These sessions were particularly rigorous, and we sure sweated because of the heat. We began with a series of exercises, including Ju Jitsu. Then we headed to the obstacle course--several walls to climb over or crawl under, some chinning bars and simulated parachute jumping into a sand pit. Then came the killer: we had to complete a run around the entire airfield--distance of about five miles. When you finished you headed right to the mess hall for lunch. The longer it took you, the less time you had for lunch, because the next class began at 1:00 p.m. Since I had been on the track team I usually finished among the first two or three. Some walked the entire distance and had to forego lunch.

Lunch was a ritual. We sat 8 to a table, 4 on each side. When we were given the command to sit, we had to eat a square meal. This meant taking a forkful of food raising it to mouth level and then putting it in your mouth. It was up and over for every mouthful. The food was terrible. We called it grits and grease.

At 13:00, we went back to classes until 16:00, when we mustered for retreat. By then the heat was blazing and several cadets fainted as they marched. The rule was that you could not fall out of formation to help, so they just lay there until the flag had been lowered and put away. We had thirty minutes for supper, time to cleanup before going to our evening classes. At 22:30 taps were sounded, and we fell into bed exhausted.

We started school slowly, but then it became almost a round-the-clock operation. The first week, we concentrated on learning navigation theory. Then we learned how to use particular pieces of navigation equipment. Later in the program, we were awakened at 02:00 to study star formations and the constellations. It did not matter when we marched, we sang the Air Corps song:

> Off we go into the wild blue yonder,
> Climbing high into the sun;
> Here they come zooming to meet our thunder,
> At 'em boys give her the gun!
> Down we dive spouting our flames from under,
> Off with one helluva roar,
> We live in fame or go down in flame,

THE 8ᵀᴴ AIR FORCE WON THE WAR IN EUROPE

Nothing will stop the Army Air Corps.

On weekends, the Cascade Bar was the favorite watering hole in Monroe. It was always packed with cadets from Selman Field and the WACS from the nearby college at Southwestern Louisiana. The guys and gals were always pairing off, but I did not participate in these episodes because I always felt there was something wrong with a soldier dating a soldier, especially since some of these WACS looked like football players.

I remember well my first flight. Before we took off, we were all excited, but as soon as we got in the air, I realized that I had to start doing navigational things, and I had little time to even look at the ground. It seemed more a job than that glorious moment in the song that said "Off we go into the wild blue yonder." We had to apply all the things we had studied in the afternoons, and the glamour evaporated very soon.

Beech AT-7 Trainer 1943

Our plane was an AT-7 trainer, a twin-engine plane, which had a pilot and a copilot and three navigators-trainees, who sat at their work stations. The mission was a three-legged route. Each cadet taking turns directing the pilot to a pre-determined checkpoint, the last leg being the base. While one cadet was directing the pilot to certain headings the other two cadets followed along, determining the plane's location, one using pilotage and the other using instruments. After each leg, the three changed positions, so that each would get experience at all three navigational systems.

Later on during evening flights, we were expected to use celestial navigation, which is why we were awakened all those nights to study the constellations. We were expected to make diagrams of the stars and their relative positions in the sky. We got to know the dippers, Orion and the sisters, and all the other highlights of the sky. We were also introduced to the theory of navigating by radio compass, but in practice we could not use it over enemy territory because this would disclose our location. But when I was flying in combat, I often set my radio to *Berlin*, because that station often played big band sounds from Glenn Miller, Benny Goodman and Artie Shaw. They used this for propaganda purposes, but I used it to relax the crew and to get a relative fix on my position.

One last item. Some cadets went out at night to catch giant frogs in the bayous. They would rent a rowboat and head out quietly in the darkness. When they arrived at a designated place, they flashed their spotlight in the water and the giant crabs came up to the boat and were easily taken by net. They told us that restaurants were paying them a dollar for each crab, which was enough in 1943 to buy a large steak dinner.

We were treated one night when Bob Hope brought his Pepsident show to our airbase. His group included Frances Langford, the vocalist, Jerry Colonna, the comedian, and the Les Brown band. The show opened with his usual monologue of jokes about life in the military and Monroe in particular. When the radio show ended, he said, "Now we can tell some real jokes," and he proceeded to spew out a long list of rather adult jokes. This session last over two hours, and, of course, we loved it.

I can never forget walking the line. It happened because my mother's birthday was October 3, 1901, and since I was about ten years old I always bought her a present. My problem at Selman Field was I couldn't get leave to go into town to buy her something, so I decided to gamble. I would jump the fence and come back unnoticed. The plan was working well until I got off the bus that was returning to the base. An officer must have recognized me. He asked for my name and number, and I was confined to the

THE 8ᵀᴴ AIR FORCE WON THE WAR IN EUROPE

base until graduation, which was three weeks away, and I had to walk the line on Saturdays.

This was a kind of Air Force torture. I had to wear full dress with parachute and gas mask and walk a designated line (about a quarter mile) for four hours. Even in October the temperature was 90 degrees, and extremely humid. I survived the ordeal and graduated with my class 43-14 in October 1943. I did not realize at the time that because I left the base without orders, I was AWOL (absent without leave), and if it is war time you can be shot.

I did graduate on time, and when I walked away from the ceremony, the first officer I saw was named Cope. When he was not around, we often sang as we marched "There is no hope for Cope the dope." I gave him a $1 bill, which was the custom, and I called him a few names which I can't disclose here. For reasons which I could not understand, he did not seem to like me and he picked on me as we marched. His favorite complaint was, "You are bouncing, Bolino." I was happy to head out of town.

Chapter Four
Joining a Crew at Pyote, TX

The next base was Rattlesnake Bomber Base in Pyote, Texas. It was about six miles from Pecos, which still had the hitching posts on Main Street for tying up horses. Our whole crew was assembled there for what was called phase training. We flew Flying Fortresses (B-17s), and I met my crew:

Pilot: Daniel Glenn Houghton, he enlisted in Chicago. He signed on for a second tour as a captain. He always said that, "No German was ever going to shoot him down," but he was killed on the sixth mission of his second tour. His wife's name was Dora.

Co-pilot: Julian Monroe Carr, he enlisted at Broadsmith, TX. He also signed on for a second tour, but before he could fly a second time he broke his wrist, so he was sent to Atlantic City, NJ. He spent most of his life flying as a commercial pilot for Dow Chemical. Tex was an expert banjo player. He died in January, 2000. His wife's name was Mary.

Navigator: August C. Bolino, I signed up in Boston, MA. Spent most of my life as a Professor of Economics. My wife's name was Thora, but everyone knew her as TJ. She died on July 23, 2015.

Bombadier: Charles Max Kemp, 21 Apple Rod, Southhampton, New York, 11968-2346, (631) 287-3347. Wife's name: Jane. She died in 2005.

Radio: Kenneth L. Fitz, 1122 Wells Dr., Madison, IN, 47250, (812) 273-1667, died 1992. Wife's name: Dorotha.

THE 8TH AIR FORCE WON THE WAR IN EUROPE

Engineer: Robert Vogt, enlisted at St. Paul, MN. Was trained at Amarillo Army Air Field. Wife's name: Doris.

Tail gunner: Harry Knoll, enlisted at Eden, New York, died June 22, 1988. His wife's name is Eunice.

Ball turret: Robert Kerns, enlisted from Portland, OR. Currently living in Richland, WA.

Waist: John (Jack) Hollister of Oklahoma City, OK. Lost one eye in combat but stayed in Air Force for twenty years. He died in 1999. Wife's name: Rose "Pat."

Photo: Patrick O'Keefe, enlisted at Milawaukee, WI. Was selling real estate in Orlando, FL.

    Like all crews in the Air Force, our ten members were from many places and they had many backgrounds. Everything in the 8th Air Force begin with the pilot. Our pilot was Daniel Glenn Houghton. He was from Chicago and was married when he signed on. He was tall and handsome and a pretty good pilot. If he had a fault it would have to be called braggadocio. I believe he did say one that he went to Northwestern University, but I investigated that claim and the school has no record of him.
    Our co-pilot was Julian Monroe Carr. Born on August 17, 1921 in the north-central Texas town of Rising Star, Carr enlisted in the Army Air Corps at age 19 and asked to be assigned to a bomber after receiving his wings.
    The crew christened our plane the "Wolf Wagon" and painted a caricature on its nose of a leering wolf with his tongue hanging out.
    "We were a very close team, very similar to an athletic team, except that it was life or death," Carr had said on a videotape he made in 1998 for a ninth-grade class at Bryan High School, taught by his granddaughter, Denise Carroll.
    Carr was part of a crew that made it through 30 missions, eluding flak and German fighters without a single death and with only one injury. A 20 mm anti-aircraft shell once set a left wing

ablaze, Carr recalled on the videotape. He said he shut off the fuel to those two engines and plunged the aircraft into a steep, 10,000-foot dive to blow out the flames.

On another mission, he said, anti-aircraft fire knocked out an engine and his plane lagged behind the others on the return to base. Carr said his lone bomber was an inviting target, but his crew shot down three fighters and damaged two others.

Carr met and proposed to his wife, Mary, while on a 30-day leave in Texas after completing 15 missions. They were married December 30, 1944, after he returned to the United States.

Carr, who was discharged a major, received the Distinguished Flying Cross, the Air Medal and a number of other decorations. As a civilian, he trained Air Force pilots for the Korean War before beginning a career as a corporate pilot that lasted 30 years.

I had tried for many months to find our co-pilot, Julian "Tex" Carr. I had almost given up when a friend from Texas said to me, "Try the Motor Vehicle Department. If he drives you will find him there." It cost $4, but it was worth it. When the annual meeting was scheduled for San Antonio on September 16-19, 1998, I telephoned Tex and he said he would meet us there.

He made it, but he was not too well. He could hardly walk and his hands shook. But the six of us had a great emotional meeting. There was Tex and Mary, Charles Kemp and Jane, and TJ and I.

We learned a lot about Tex whom we had not seen for 54 years. He had flown as a commercial pilot for several years, then he switched to making custom homes, but our biggest surprise was that he traveled all over the United States as a member of the Bayou Banjo Club. Its membership totaled 31. He was one of the stars, and his picture is on the wall where the group plays. Sadly, when he could no longer move his fingers he had to cease playing.

When I telephoned his wife in 1998, she said that when he learned about this information he hugged her and cried. He said, "I have found my boys." Our bombardier and I attended a reunion in San Antonio with the three other surviving members.

"We were relying on each other, and with teamwork we pulled through," Carr told the Bryan High School students.

THE 8TH AIR FORCE WON THE WAR IN EUROPE

Julian Carr died on January 23, 2002 at his Conroe, Texas home after suffering a stroke according to his daughter Barbara Carr Hasara.

Our bombardier, Charles Max Kemp, was born in Iowa, but resides at 21 Apple Rd., Southhampton, New York, 11968-2346; (631) 287-3347. Wife's name: Jane. She died in 2005. Max was a fanatic bridge player. He had a partner after his wife died, and they won many contests. He is most proud of his granddaughter who was valedictorian of her high school class, which gave her a scholarship at Tufts University in Boston.

When NBC Correspondent Tom Brokaw authored his book, *The Greatest Generation,* Honorary Chief Inductee and retired Air Force Technical Sergeant Jack Hollister was the type of person he was talking about. Sergeant Hollister graduated from high school at the age of 17 and enlisted in the U.S. Army Air Corps in September, 1942. He trained as an aircraft mechanic working on P-47 and B-17 aircraft. In August 1943, Sergeant Hollister completed gunnery school and deployed to *Knettishall*, England, with the 388th Bomb Group Heavy. On only his fourth combat mission, Sergeant Hollister earned the Distinguished Flying Cross for actions over *Liege*, Belgium. He flew 28 combat missions before being wounded in July 1944, during action over *Mantz*, France. Sergeant Hollister's other decorations include the Purple Heart, the Air Medal with one silver and two bronze oak leaf clusters, the Occupation Medal for the Berlin Airlift, and a Citation from Queen Wilhimena of Denmark, for rescuing people from floods in Denmark and The Netherlands.

After the war, Sergeant Hollister continued to work in aircraft maintenance until his retirement in 1962. Both he and Rose (Pat), his lovely wife of 56 years, were lifetime AFSA members.

In January 2001 Jack developed breathing problems, and he died on March 16, 2001.

Chapter Five
Going Overseas From Dyersburg, TN

Dyersburg was known as the "Overseas Replacement Training Center." It was where crews flew high altitude in close formations to prepare for combat. It was up the Mississippi River 77 miles from Memphis. Each day we would simulate what we would find in Europe. One day we started out in very tight formation heading for New Orleans. When we got over Baton Rouge, somehow one Fortress flipped over on top of another. Both planes crashed.

When we returned to base we learned that several persons had been killed. I talked to one who survived. He said as the plane plummeted to earth upside down he tried to open the escape hatch, but apparently he was pulling when he should have pushed. He didn't how he escaped. It was a miracle. When a crew had a crash, the Air Corps had a policy of trying to get the survivors into the air as soon as possible, but this person (whose name escapes me) refused to fly again so he was washed out of the cadet program.

When we were not flying, we took trips to Memphis. We went by Greyhound bus and got off downtown near the best hotel in the city, the Peabody. We made the rounds of the local bars looking for girls.

After we had been there for several days, I was called into the Colonel's office where he told me that I was going to be an instructor and I would not be going overseas for a while. So I called my home and told my mother that I would be home soon. I took the trains for Boston and I tried to enjoy my leave time but every place was deserted, so I just sat in a bar ever night talking mostly to older women.

When my leave was over I started out in my 1938 Oldsmobile It was a real car--four door, straight eight cylinder

THE 8TH AIR FORCE WON THE WAR IN EUROPE

engine and big whitewall tires. My Uncle Tony, when he learned I was coming to get the car, had it tuned up. He got me some good used tires because he worked for a roofing company. The roads weren't good, so it was a slow trip. When I got to Virginia, south of Washington, DC, I fell asleep. The car went down an embankment and I awoke unhurt. A farmer came over, got his tractor and towed me back onto the road, and I continued on to Tennessee.

It took me about twenty hours to get to the officer's club. When I entered I was told that I was late, and I was being shipped out. Sure enough, when I checked the duty roster, I was assigned to the Eighth Air Force, England. I had to get rid of the Oldsmobile. I found a group of persons playing poker, so I walked up and asked, "How much will you bid for my 1938 Oldsmobile?" Floyd Buzzi, who had just won a pot, offered me $225. I said sold and joined my crew to Fort Dix, New Jersey.

The trip overseas was an episode. During the last three weeks of training, I spent most of my time learning to navigate a Flying Fortress across the Atlantic Ocean by way of *Belem*, Brazil and *Morocco*, Africa. Then came the puzzling part. We were ordered to Fort Kearny, Nebraska on our way to Camp Kilmer, New Jersey.

I did not learn until much later why we were sent to Nebraska to get to New Jersey. When the Union Pacific Railroad was constructed westward to join up with the Central Pacific Railroad in 1869, the Federal government made loans to finance construction. One clause in the agreement stated that the military would be able to ship troops over these lines free in perpetuity (this provision was cancelled after World War II).

Painting of the Mauretania. Photo by A. Bolino.

AUGUST C. BOLINO

From New Jersey we took a bus to a New York dock and boarded the *Mauretania*--a Cunard liner that was built in 1939. I was told that in peacetime it carried 1,500 persons, but we went across the Atlantic with 14 or 15 thousand military on board. The stateroom we were in had 100 persons stacked five high, with no room even to get out of bed. We had each brought several bottles of bourbon because we heard that it was very scarce in England. We packed these in our B-4 bags, and we had a very interesting time going over. We played bridge and the rest of the time was spent waiting for our meals. We only got two per day, so as soon as we finished breakfast, we headed for the dinner line which was always one to two thousand persons long.

The North Atlantic in February was incredible. When we were about half way over, the waves hit over the bow against the bridge, which was probably a hundred feet above the water. There were always thousands of persons throwing up. The flyers numbered only 105, and of course we didn't get sick because the Flying Fortress was a much rougher ride than any ship. The good news is that there were one hundred nurses on board, so only the officers could fraternize with them. Unfortunately, there were guards posted all around them at all times so nobody accomplished much. But as that song said, "I can dream, can't I."

The weather was not the only problem. Several times on our crossing we would hear a message on the ship's intercom, with the captain declaring, "Sub sighted." This meant that we could take evasive action. We didn't travel in a convoy because the *Mauretania* was faster than any submarines. We were making about 25 knots.

To prepare us for these eventualities, the Captain called for constant lifeboat drills, but we decided not to participate because temperature of the water was in the low 30s and we thought it would be useless to evacuate into a lifeboat in the Atlantic Ocean.

We reached *Liverpool* on Palm Sunday, 1944 and headed to the classification center at Stone prior to joining our bomb group. I met a man I knew only as Mike. About 7:00 p.m. we met at a local pub. After a night of drinking Half and Half beer, we started back to the base. We waited hours for a bus until a British woman came

THE 8TH AIR FORCE WON THE WAR IN EUROPE

by.

"Are you Yanks waiting for a bus?" she asked. When we answered yes, she told us that the buses stopped running at eight or nine. We had no choice but to walk the six miles to the base. At about the halfway point we decided to rest a while on the highway. We both fell asleep. I was awakened by something hitting my toes. The six o'clock bus came by and all the passengers asked if I was alright. I told them I was and then I asked, "Where's Mike?" They looked puzzled at my question, and they looked under the bus and found him badly hurt. He had fallen asleep with his head towards the highway. I never saw him again, and I have always wondered if he survived.

AUGUST C. BOLINO

Part IV Joining the Fray at Knettishall, England

Knettishall, which is in East Anglia, was a farming region until it was converted into a number of flying fields for the British and later for Americans. Before the Yanks took it over, it was an RAF fighter base about six mile from the train station at *Thetford*-- located about 35 mile north of *Cambridge* and about 75 miles from *London*. We located it from the air at Splasher 5 and Buncher 10---- our navigation aids. There was one oddity for me: it was in Suffolk County, England and I was born in Suffolk County, Massachusetts.

The Villages which numbered a handful of persons was converted into thousands of crews that were prepared to battle the *Luftwaffe* in the air. But before they could begin they had to read booklet about how to behave.

A Handbook for New Arrivals

This booklet has been issued to help you become familiar with the 388th Bombardment Group – your new home. We should like to feel, however, that is more than just a book of "Do's and Don'ts." And when you've finished reading it, we know that you will take as much pride in the accomplishments of your new Group and its facilities, and feel, as we do, that you are now a member of one of the best, if not the very best, Heavy Bomb Groups in the United Kingdom. We speak with the background of almost two years of fighting, working, and playing together – and the lessons learned in well over 250 operational missions against the enemy.

In the few hundred words allotted to us, we can only touch upon the highlights – on what has been an interesting, exciting,

THE 8TH AIR FORCE WON THE WAR IN EUROPE

and unforgettable experience in all our lives.

It was on a pleasant summer day in July 1943 (yes, the summer can be very pleasant in England!) that the ground echelon arrived on this base, following our advanced party. Within two weeks after setting down here, all our crews having landed from the flight across the North Atlantic, we were set for operations. Two weeks later, we flew our first mission on the 17th, to Amsterdam. Our missions from that day to this have included trips to Norway, Russia, Italy, North Africa, and of course, to our favorite bombing range, Germany. The Presidential Citation which you are entitled to wear as long as you remain a member of the 388th was earned by the Group for its part in the shuttle mission to North Africa, bombing the Messerschmitt Plant at Regensburg on the way. Of the 60 aircraft lost by the Eighth Air Force on that August 17th, 1943, the 388th lost one plane, but its crew was picked up out of the Mediterranean, wet, but unharmed.

We have borne our brunt of attacks by the enemy and have had our losses, which is inevitable, but we boast of an enviable record in the few crews missing in the missions flown. Our total of e/a (enemy aircraft) destroyed exceeds, by far, the score against us, and it was climaxed last May 12th (1944) when, in our attack against the synthetic oil plant at *Brux*, the 388th alone was credited with destroying 30 enemy aircraft for the loss of only one B-17 crew, subsequently reported P/W's in Germany (and don't underestimate the present strength of the *Luftwaffe*. It still packs a nasty wallop or two – but you'll get more of this from your Gunnery Officers and the S-2's.).

The distinct honor of leading the Eighth Air Force Heavies over the beaches of Normandy on D-Day fell to our young CO, Lt. Chester C. Cox, when he led the 388th, the 45th Combat Wing (to which we belong), the 3rd Air Division (both the Wing and the Group are members of this higher echelon) and the Eighth Air Force, in support of the men who were storming the beaches of France, 18,000 feet below. Too, this Group was one of the few to drop aid in support of the Marquis in France in the early days before and after D-Day; we participated in the first shuttle mission from this country to Russia (if you want to spend an interesting evening, get one of the old crews to tell you about their experiences on this mission)[1].

388th Bomb Group (H) 45th Combat Wing 3rd Bomb Division and 562nd Bomb Squadron patches

Our pride in the 388th organization also embraces the so-called "extracurricular" activities we enjoy on this base. Without doubt, you will find here the finest equipped theater in the 3rd Division, and many say, the finest in the Eighth Air Force. We take pride in this theater, and we hope you will treat our red plush seats with some consideration and kindness, for since the Germans stopped blitzing London, we have been unable to purchase new seats (this is the manner in which we bought the original chairs!) You have a finely stocked library of over 10,000 volumes; a complete gymnasium with a regulation-size boxing ring; and both the lower-graders and the upper-graders have their own recreational facilities and their own clubs.

You would expect to find rules and regulations in any town back home of 3,200 people. Well, we have the same rules and regulations here, too. Some men call this "chicken"----We tell you, and know, that these little rules, while they may be

---

[1] This handbook was produced by the 388 Collection, Hillside Farm, Suffolk, England target study for our Bombardiers and Navigators. These are just a few of our accomplishments from an operational standpoint. Also, not only generally known, personnel from this Group pioneered many of the "secret weapons" now being used against the Japs in the Pacific – security prevents us from telling you anymore.

THE 8ᵀᴴ AIR FORCE WON THE WAR IN EUROPE

annoying to one or two rugged individualists, in the long run make for a smooth and pleasant life. We know you'll comply.

We are proud of our own 388th Band, "The Gremlins", a dance orchestra that has played up and down England, which "wowed 'em" in London, and recently made broadcasts over FAN and BBC. The Boys will be playing for your dances, too. Another thing that we talk about is the fact that our Group was first in the Eighth Air Force Bond-Selling Contest last summer, when we topped every group in all Commands, with a total bond subscription of over $233,000 (our original quota was set for $80,000).

We could go on for pages recounting our deeds and exploits. We know, however, that in a short time you, too, will have the pride in the 388th that we have. Your Commanding Officer and Staff are all young men--young in years, but with a background in the Air Corps, and in this war, second to none. And it is a good thing for all that you will be working with these young men, for then your problems will be more readily understood and appreciated. The esprit between the ground and air personnel on this base is excellent. Both groups of men have an appreciation of the work each is doing. For you air crew members, just realize that the ground personnel of this base were intended to operate and maintain a group of only 36 aircraft. Today, with no increase in personnel and plus an increase in the number of missions run, we now maintain double that number of aircraft. All that takes a lot of teamwork and effort, night and day, in good weather and bad. We merely present this in case anyone feels inclined to forget this fact when he first arrives.

Many of the things we have told you so far, and many of the things you will read in the following pages, are intended for you alone. We should like to be able to tell you that you are free to send this booklet back to the folks so that they may have a better idea of how you will be living for the next few months, but for security reasons (here comes that S-2 Officer again!), you will just have to write those things the censor permits.

In closing, may we welcome you to the 388th. We know that when this war is won, and you are back home again enjoying white shirts, cokes, and all the little things that spell "home," you will look back to your days of membership with the 388th Bomb Group and feel pride in the fact that you were once a member of the best Group in the Eighth Air Force—the best Air Force in the whole U. S. Army.

Lt Col Chester C. Cox, Lt Col Ben L. McLauchlin, Major Donald C. Samuel, Captain Samuel L. Clark, W/C Charles W. Oakes, M/Sgt Raymond Robinson, Lt Col Gilbert E. Goodman, 1st Lt Jerry J. Rosenthal, Major Ivan M. Willson, 1st Sgt Lloyd J. Lon.

Our base is not unlike other bases in the ETO, in that you will find it to be an American island so to speak, surrounded on all sides by a friendly, but nevertheless, foreign power. While remaining on the station you are safe from criticism, except that which you would normally expect to find among the neighbors anywhere. To this, as long as you conduct yourself properly and do your job, you can afford to remain aloof. It is natural. But once you step a foot off the base, you immediately take on an additional responsibility whether you are aware of it or not. You become less an individual and more a personality, a representative of America.

By your actions and your talk, you and your nation is judged. The impression you create in the minds of the British with whom you come in contact is a lasting one. Before the war, the British knew very little about your country. They imagined a great deal. A lot of it was colored by their second-hand knowledge of Hollywood, which was inevitable. America, in Technicolor, is often represented as a place where, if you apply yourself diligently enough through eight reels, you can marry Ginger Rogers in the ninth and retire to a Spanish-type ranch house, complete with swimming pool and stable.

Well, perhaps. At the same time, now that we are grown up, we have to admit to ourselves that this is the exception rather than the rule. Until we settled down in England, the British had no way of knowing that such happy circumstances were anything but average. They are great film-goers; by degree they have learned that Hollywood doesn't represent America, any more than does Chicago. But you do! You are real, cut from the same cloth as themselves; we're fighting the same war and for essentially the same reasons. Neither nation could afford to be dictated to by an ex-paperhanger whose delusions about a superior race seemed comic to begin with, and tragic only later. It's true the beer we get over here doesn't taste much like the beer made in St. Louis or Milwaukee, but England is in its sixth year of total war; we're lucky to find any beer at all.

There are differences in heating, plumbing, and a lot of things--no one has to point them out to you. But then, there are differences in our own country, too, which we are very apt to ignore. Not every bedroom in America has a bathroom attached, though some do. Yet the first home-owner would hardly have the bad taste to go around boasting about the number of bathrooms in his home; if he did, his one-bathroom friends would drop him flat, or knock him on the head. Well, beer and bathrooms, though important in themselves, are not the issues in this war. The issue is broader and a bit more fundamental: -- To be able to live decently, in a world free from want and anxiety and fear. These are the things England, Russia, America, China, and a host of small nations are fighting for--objectives they hope to perpetuate in the post war world. With your help, maybe they can.

The point is simply this: -- Don't brag. America is a pretty great nation, capable of holding its own without any cheap pub brawls undertaken in an effort to prove it. We represent a great nation and wear its uniform. Our pride in this responsibility can best be shown by the way we look, the way we act, the way we talk among our friends over here, and especially among the strangers we encounter.

In English towns and cities you will find American MP's. In most cases you will find them helpful, strict, and just; if you have a question, don't hesitate to ask it. They are no more eager to run you in than you are to get tangled up with the law; all you have to do is to cooperate in little things. When leaving the station, be sure your pass is in order and properly signed. Don't overstay your leave; plan ahead; arrange your train or bus schedules accordingly. The penalty for overstaying leaves in a war zone is understandably sever. This station's attitude in such matter is anything but lenient.

Then how does one escape the critical eye of the MP's away from the station? -- There is nothing to it, nothing that could not be expected of the soldier anywhere--see that your pass is in order to begin with, and carry it with you at all times. Wear the correct uniform and wear it properly. Wear your dog tags around your neck. Keep your uniform clean and pressed, and your shoes shined.

If you remember to do these things, your behavior is likely to be much the same as it would be back in the hometown, with family and friends looking on. And that is as it should be.

There are many Negro troops in this theater of operations, wearing the same uniform as ourselves and serving the same cause. It automatically follows that they are governed by similar regulations; they must abide by the laws that govern us all. Our association with them, either in line of duty or otherwise, should be that of soldier to soldier. Their associations with civilians, on the other hand, concerns us not at all.

Remember compliance with directives and orders, whether verbal or written is of course, mandatory. (It is well to note that Tannoy announcements are all official; if such an announcement directs you to attend a class or formation, it is the same as being ordered to do so personally). On this station, under no circumstances will the Commander tolerate either refusal or failure to obey an order, whether issued by a commissioned offer or a non-commisioned officer. Where there is a refusal to obey a direct order, trial by General Courts-Martial usually results.

On the subject of military justice, it may interest you to know that the 388th Group is among the lowest in the 3d Division, from the standpoint of disciplinary violations requiring reference to trial by courts-martial. Here are a few legal aspects to bear in mind; incidents involving minor breaches of military discipline, such as simple drunkenness unaccompanied by any disorderly conduct, or, an altercation between two persons where the principal damage inflicted is too much talk, can, if committed on the base, usually be corrected without resorting to courts-martial. On the other hand, even minor offenses committed away from the station, and particularly within the presence or hearing of British citizens, necessitates trial by courts-martial. Misconduct towards,

THE 8TH AIR FORCE WON THE WAR IN EUROPE

or disrespect to a British citizen, inevitably leads to such a fate.

This station considers every case on its individual merits. It will not tolerate any act of larceny, no matter how insignificant the value of the item taken. Nor will it look the other way when any person attempts to settle his personal grudges by using a knife or any other weapon. Two members of this station are now serving a total of seven years at hard labor because they resorted to this last-named offense.

Remember, if you are tried by a court-martial, your case will be heard according to American military law. Sentences imposed under American law are often much more severe than those imposed by the British for identical offenses. For example, under British law, carnal knowledge of a girl of fifteen can be treated as a misdemeanor; under American military law it becomes an offense punishable by a sentence of hard labor for a term of up to fifteen years. This you might want to know: in England, sixteen is the age of consent, and it is no defense whatsoever for the girl to have told you that she was of age.

I was delighted to be assigned to a base of B-17s. They were one of the most well-known and durable bombers of all time. They were famous for the long daylight bombing raids over Europe in WWII. While it lacked the range and bomb load of its contemporary B-24 Liberator, the B-17 became the more famous of the two due to the many tales of B-17s bringing their crews back home despite heavy damage. With up to thirteen machine guns, the B-17 seemed to be a genuine flying "fortress in the sky." However, bomber losses reached the unacceptable point in 1943 in the face of stiff German opposition, and the B-17s welcomed the introduction of long-range fighter escort before they could continue their war against the Reich.

The 388th Bomb Group (H) was activated December 24, 1942 at Gowan Field just outside of Boise, Idaho. It moved to Wendover Field, Utah in February 1943 and to Sioux City AAF, South Dakota that May. It was officially assigned to the Eighth Air Force, Army Air Corps, in June 23, 1943. Seventeen crews landed on that day. Colonel William B. David was the Commanding officer. On July 8 the ground crew arrived. After hostilities ended in Europe, the 388th BG relocated to Sioux Falls AAF, South

Dakota, and prepared to deploy to the Pacific. When the war in the Pacific ended, the group was inactivated on August 28, 1945. The 388th Bomb Group (H) had existed for 32 months, and then was no more.

Our base was typical. It had housing for four squadrons, the 560th, 561th, 562nd and 563th. It included a briefing room, a mess hall, a chapel, an officer's club and a non-commissioned club. The planes were serviced on concrete areas near the runways (where the crew chiefs operated). We lived in Quonset huts that had pot-belly stoves on each end of double-decker bunks in between. The latrines (toilets) were on the ends of buildings. We left all our personal stuff and money lying around when we went on missions.

If a crew was shot down, we went through the personal stuff that was to be sent home to "make sure that nothing embarrassing could be sent to parents or loved ones." We usually divided up the wearable stuff. I remember one pilot who had a beautiful pair of leather boots hand-made in London and he was shot down soon after. The boots fit only one person.

We spent our evenings in the officer's club. In the center of the club was a chicken wire fenced area, which had thousands of packages of chewing gum that the flyers did not consume on their flights. Because of this, there was probably no gum on the home front. Gum was just one part of our daily ration on a mission. We also got a small box of cigarettes, some cheese, and a piece of chocolate.

At first, I could not stand the taste of scotch whiskey, but since there was no other choice, I learned to like it. Over the bar, there was a small two-colored flag. If the green flag was showing, a mission was on, and most people retired to get a few hours sleep. Red meant no mission.

I remember our Saturday night dances. We would send three trucks (lories as the Brits called them) to the neighboring towns and bring back fifteen young girls who would serve as dancing partners. They were very anxious to come to the base because we served a very large dinner, and most of them were on very severe rations during the war.

When my wife and I visited the American Air Museum in

THE 8TH AIR FORCE WON THE WAR IN EUROPE

London several years later we were astonished at the rations that the Brits lived on during World War II. There was a table about three feet by four feet which illustrated the ration for a family of four for a month.

And our band was first rate which was assembled when our crew men brought their instruments to the base. After an evening of eating, drinking and dancing the girls got back on the trucks for the ride home. This function had to wrap up early, because we often had a mission that evening for the morning. On one occasion, our pilot was fairly drunk, so we loaded him into the airplane and put him on full oxygen for a quick sobering up.

One young lady came to a dance and stayed in an enlisted man's barracks for 31 days. The sergeants loved it because she cleaned the barracks and might have performed other duties.

In a typical bombing mission, we were awakened by a sergeant sometime between 5:00 or 6:00 a.m. We headed to breakfast for powdered eggs, cereal, etc. Then went to pre-briefing. There were separate briefings for navigators, bombardiers and pilots. At the pre-briefing I was given the latest weather report, the intelligence reports about anti-aircraft guns (which were shown on the daily maps) and I was briefed about the main and alternative targets. I was told that there were over 300 British spies in Germany who spoke perfect German and who had short-wave radios, which they used to send information to London concerning the movement of antiaircraft guns. This is why each day I received a new map indicating where these guns were moved. This is why we never flew a straight line to our target.

AUGUST C. BOLINO

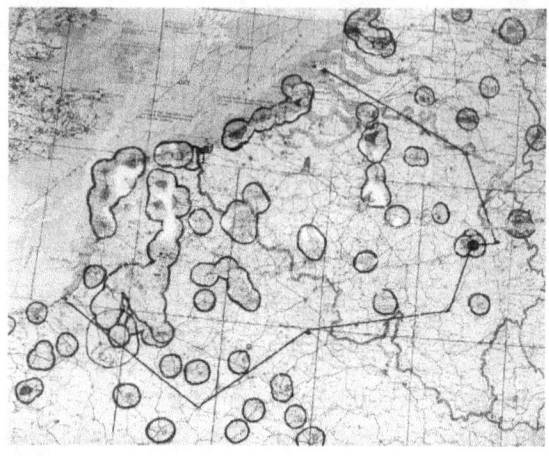

This is one of the maps that each navigator received before a bombing mission. The circles are anti-aircraft guns. Each diagram was different because all guns were moved each day. Fortunately for us, British spies used short-wave radios to send any changes to the London headquarters.
Photo provided by A. Bolino

    The next step was the main briefing, when all the crews reported to the auditorium for final instructions. At the front was a bunch of weather maps and there was a very large screen covering the front wall, which covered the route of the daily mission. We were told about codes for the day (for example "Yellow-Yellow), the order of takeoff, ditching procedures. When the briefing officer came in he pulled a cord that uncovered the rout of the mission for that day.

    From there we took jitneys to our planes. The sergeants entered the B-17 by way of the rear door, but we had to hoist up into the front hatch. It was then that I realized why we did so many chin-ups in flying school. We were loaded down with heavy, fleece-lined flying suits, flak suits and parachutes.

    The planes took off in twos and when airborne we circled the field getting to altitude. It was a perilous part of the mission, because there were 97 British and American airfields in East Anglia and it was dark or foggy or both. When we got to 10,000 feet, I gave the "put on oxygen mask" command. At the prescribed altitude we headed out to the English Channel or the North Sea. While over water we test-fired our guns. If there was

THE 8TH AIR FORCE WON THE WAR IN EUROPE

a malfunction we were supposed to fix it in flight.

The remainder of the trip was getting to the target and scanning the sky for enemy aircraft (we called them bandits). As navigator, I kept a log of any encounters (How many aircraft? What type? Any shot down? Any Fortresses out of control or exploded? Any parachutes?) When we got to the IP (the initial point of the bomb run), the pilot turned the plane over to the bombardier, who flew it using the Norden bombsight. It was a fairly small box with two white lines—one being stationary. The other moved, and the bombardier had to set it to determine when the bomb doors would open and the bombs would drop out.

I used to kneel behind Max Kemp, our bombardier, as he worked the wheels of the sight. When the crosshairs reached the target, the bombs were released automatically. The next command came from the pilot, "Let's get the hell out of here," as we banked quickly for the return voyage. This was the worst part of the mission because if you had any mechanical problem and you couldn't keep up with the group, you became a straggler, and this was when the *Luftwaffe* would pounce for the kill. The only hope was to dive towards the ground and fly low enough so the fighters couldn't shoot at you.

We all feared bailing out of the Fortress. The proper procedure was to stick your head in the hatch and fall out head first. If you went out feet first you probably would hit your head on some part of the airplane. If the plane had to ditch in the North Sea or the English Channel, we were to throw out everything that moved because these objects would become flying bombs when the plane hit the water. We were to crouch down with our heads in our laps. When the plane stopped in the water, we were to evacuate in less than a minute--the time it would take for a B-17 to sink.

When we were on the return part of our missions and we felt safe, Max and I used to sing--Max imitated Frank Sinatra, and I sang blues numbers, imitating Jimmy Rushing of the Count Basie band. I sang stuff like "Saint James Infirmary" and "Sent For You Yesterday and Here You Come Today."

After the flight we went immediately to debriefing. The Red Cross girls gave us coffee and donuts, and we gathered for the questions about fighters, our planes that went down and German planes destroyed. The Red Cross girls were loved and hated. They greeted us warmly, gave us donuts with a smile and were generally very pleasant. But some chose to take on other duties: they sold their wares. One in particular went home with hundreds of dollars she had earned. The men resented her, but we appreciated what the other girls did for us.

When members of a crew went to a Pub, they often fell in love with a British girl. When the Americans were finished with their missions, they struggled to take home their English girlfriends. When the war was over, the total number of English brides was 45,000.

Chapter Six
An Early Easy Mission

"Fighting Fortress Crew's Grateful When Mission Over France is Easy"
By Price Day, a Sunpapers War Correspondent

Somewhere in England, Jan. 14, 1944. (By Cable-Delayed)

The Ambulances at this base had nothing to do today. No returning Fortresses dropped red flares asking landing priority because of wounded aboard. The only lights were from the ground- -pairs of flares to assist the big ships home through the dusk. Today every ship that went out from here came back. Unlike last Tuesday's, the day's mission was a milk run, with prompt delivery just inside the "rocket" or "invasion" or, as the Germans call it, "reprisal" coast of France.

"It wasn't anything," the twenty-year old pilot of the fortress "The Princess Pat," Lieut. Arthur B. Pack of the 4300 block of Cleveland Ave., Baltimore, reported.

Standing before his locker, a Nissen hut, with a cup of rich cocoa, Pack pointed out the importance of the word "the" in the name of his ship-"I think it adds distinction to it" –and expressed the hope that there wouldn't be powdered eggs for dinner.

Little Flak, No Fighter

Lieutenant Pack's navigator Second Lieutenant Robert S. Izak, of Lonaconing, Md., his map case under his arm, agreed that today had been uneventful; a little flak, no enemy fighters, excellent protection by the escorting Mustangs, Thunderbolts and

Lightnings.

The two young officers moved toward the briefing room, for interrogation. Other men drifted in and grouped themselves by crews and stood quietly. Walter V. A. Harrison, ambulances at this base had nothing and intelligence officer, who before them also stood quietly talking. All looked solid and chunky in their heavy clothes. Some still wore once-white parachute harnesses and bright yellow "Mae West." life jackets.

In a few minutes they followed Lieutenant Pack's crew to sit around tables and tell their composite stories to intelligent officers.

Expected Early Mission

All day the men left behind on the ground had anticipated that the mission would be an easy one. But "easy" in bombing terminology is a relative term. Indeed, well before the Forts were due to return small knots of men gathered on the edge of the field, watching the skies, now and then saying a few words through the roar and rattle of the giant bulldozer trying to worry a few drops of water out of a small seas of thin black mud across the road from headquarters hut.

The men who never take part in combat but who are indispensable to any mission's success waited as eager as any.

Baltimoreans in Group

Among them were two Baltimore staff sergeants. William H. Helfrich of the 3000 block Brendan Avenue, who once worked at Maryland Drydock Co., and Bernard Thanner, of the 2600 block of Chesterfield Ave., a meat cutter before he entered the army. Sergeant Thanner is an operation draftsman. Sergeant Helfrich is assigned to group operations. Major Walter V. A. Harrison, intelligence officer, who before the war had his law office at 100 St. Paul St. in Baltimore, interrupted his discussion of the beauties of the base's new rustic bar to watch a plane coming in over the far end of the field.

THE 8TH AIR FORCE WON THE WAR IN EUROPE

Too High For Landing

"Bring her down, boy," he said to himself, but the plane was too high at that moment.

The pilot took it around the field once again and then made a beautiful three-point landing.

By now it was almost dark. In the briefing room the flight surgeon, Major James R. Bell, who studied medicine at the University of Maryland, stood smoking his pipe, his back to the stove which heated a small area of the large hut.

"The more days like today, the better," he said, inhaling deeply and nodding his head.

Grateful For Outcome

Today's mission, however, though important, will create no big splash in the communiques or newspapers, and no one cared. Everyone knew they had done their job well and were grateful for the bloodless outcome. Every man also knew that most missions would neither be as easy as today's, nor as "rugged" as some others. Either way, the bomber crews are ready and eager to take them as they come.

AUGUST C. BOLINO

Chapter Seven
Not So Easy Missions

When a B-17 crew reached Germany, the quiet of the first hours was replaced by chaos and intensity. A single error by any one of the crew could result in calamity.

Regensburg: A Shuttle to Africa

It took place on August 17, 1943, when 21 aircraft of the 388th Bomb Group plus 3 spares, took off between 06:45 and 07:02 hours. Its formations were accomplished without difficulty. It was second in the grouping of the 403 Combat Wing. None of the 388th planes aborted, so the three spares returned to base as instructed (the pilots were 2nd Lt, L, Miller, 2nd, Lt. J. Roe and F.O. M.Bowen).

As they headed for their target, they encountered about 30 to 50 enemy aircraft, mostly FW 190's and ME 109s. As usual, they attacked from the late morning sun, pressing home their attacks singly, rolling over and down to attack the low Groups. They attacked from about 500 to 800 yards. But one crew, Lt. Bliss reported later, that some fighters were only 50 to 100 yards away.

Flak, which came from *Antwerpt, Worms,* and *Nurnburg,* was meager and inaccurate. At these places, none of the 388th planes were seriously damaged. The 388th planes were over the target at 1148 hours, and most of the 500 lb. bombs were dropped on the target. Lt. Bliss had one bomb hang up and Lt. Nagorka had two bombs hang up. These three were jettisoned after passing the target. With good visibility, the strike photos show the entire *Messerschmidt* Assembly Plant destroyed.

After bombing the target, the Group proceeded to *Bone*,

Africa as briefed. On the route to Africa, Lt. Parker in a/c 42-3444 "Paddlefoot" ran short of gas and had to ditch in the Mediterranean Sea at 1620 hours. The position was noted by friendly planes, and the crew was rescued the next morning.

But only three of our planes landed at the assigned base. The other 17 had to land at emergency fields because of the shortage of gas. Ten of our aircraft suffered flak damage, and two of our personnel were wounded. Lt. F. Tierney, navigator on Nagorka's crew lost his right hand.

The Paul Swift Crew

The Paul Swift crew came together on Feb. 28, 1943 in Boise, ID, and in April the crew joined the 388th BG, 561st Squadron. at Wendover, UT. The crew was issued its plane, which they named "Virgin on the Verge," in Sioux City, IA, and departed Bangor, ME with their squadron on June 14.

The Swift crew's first mission was to *Amsterdam* on July 17, 1943; it was an easy expedition, but as Paul said, "our real taste of rugged combat" was the July 26 mission to *Hanover*. Two days later, he was credited with the crew's first shoot-down of an enemy plane over *Oschersleben*.

On the August 17 shuttle mission to *Regensburg*, with two engines out from lack of fuel, the crew threw overboard all guns, ammo, and movable armor plate as Swift searched for the nearest landing field. Swift was able to land at a small RAF fighter strip at *Bone* on the African coast and a few days later the crew returned to England around the Spanish coast - the safest route for its weaponless plane.

Because of a last-minute decision to wear his parachute, Paul's life was saved during the September 6 attack on *Stuttgart*. A shell smashed through the nose and hit squarely on the parachute buckle, throwing Paul to the back of the cabin and knocking him out. He quickly revived, but he was almost grounded because it was the Group policy to permanently ground any airman who had been made unconscious during flight. Fortunately, the head medic, who was a friend, allowed him to keep flying. By early October, only five of the original squadron planes remained.

On Oct. 14 Paul's ability to survive was tested again. With "Virgin on the Verge" down for repairs, the Swift crew was assigned to fly "Hardluck," on the *Schweinfurt* mission. As his borrowed B-17 raced down the runway the no. 3 engine suddenly burst into flames. He had no choice but to lift the plane off the ground long enough to retract the landing gear, and then set it back down for a belly landing. "Hardluck" slid uncontrollably down the remainder of the runway, then into the field beyond, toward a grove of trees. Finally she lost speed and stopped. But the excitement was not over yet. A nose count indicated that Otto Bowman, bombardier, was missing. "Swift and another member returned to the rapidly disintegrating plane and pulled him out. Then we watched from a safe distance as "Hard Luck" blew up."

"Virgin on the Verge" was now the last of the original 561st Squadron planes and, on December 5, Swift and his men became the last of its original crews.

Now promoted to the rank of Captain, the options of finishing his military career behind a desk or as a flight instructor did not appeal to him. It took him a year to receive his reassignment to a B-29 bomb group based at Northwest Field on *Guam*. Between April 27, 1945 and the end of the war he flew nine missions averaging 15 hours each. Paul was discharged as a Major in November 1945.

More on Stuttgart

Terrence G. Popravak. Jr., who later became a Lt. Col., offers a second version of this mission, which became known as "Black Monday."

9/24/1943 - HILL AIR FORCE BASE, Utah -- Seventy one years ago, the 388th Bomb Group fought a savage air battle against the German *Luftwaffe* in the wartime skies over Europe during the Eighth Air Force mission to *Stuttgart*, Germany on Sept. 6, 1943. Of the 21 B-17 Flying Fortress heavy bombers the 388th flew that day, 11 did not return to base at *Knettishall* Airfield after this mission. It was the worst single day for the 388th in the unit's

THE 8TH AIR FORCE WON THE WAR IN EUROPE

entire history. So on this 71st anniversary of that fateful mission, we remember Black Monday for National POW/MIA Recognition Day.

In that summer of 1943, enemy fighters strongly opposed 8th Air Force bombing raids going deeper into Germany, and losses mounted alarmingly. The *Stuttgart* mission followed the epic August 17, 1943, "double strike" mission against *Regensburg* and *Schweinfurt* in which 60 Flying Fortresses were lost, 20% of the attacking force - another 100 bombers were written off for battle damage. Fortunately, the 388th only lost one B-17 on this rough mission; 10 other 388th aircraft were damaged by flak and two aircrew were wounded.

On this "Black Monday" the 388th was one of the low groups in the 15-group bomber stream, and with the others flew through marginal weather to get to the target. The group met little opposition en route, with escort fighters brushing off early enemy fighter attacks. But later anti-aircraft fire, beginning at the Initial Point {IP) and into the target area at *Stuttgart*, accounted for at least two of the group's B-17 losses; one fell to flak just short of the target.

Fighters began attacking in earnest around the IP, and mercilessly hammered the bombers after they finally hit the target and turned for home. Most of the group's losses were to enemy fighters; 388th veteran Ed Huntzinger wrote that there were "about 150 enemy aircraft attacking our formation, consisting of FW 190s, ME 109s, ME 110s, and ME 210s with a few JU 88s." Four more 388th aircraft came down in Germany, while five more fell across France.

One aircraft flew to *Dubendorf* in neutral Switzerland rather than hazard a return across deadly, fighter-infested skies. All six aircraft from the group's 563rd Bomb Squadron were lost -- wiped out in its position as the low squadron position in a low group. In return, the 388th was later credited with 15 enemy fighters shot down. The *Stuttgart* mission was costly; of the 45 heavy bombers lost, some 17 percent of the attacking force, 11 were suffered by the 388th Bomb Group.

The day after the painful *Stuttgart* raid, the group received this message from headquarters, VIII Bomber Command:

"The 388th Bombardment Group suffered heavy losses yesterday. The spirit of the Group in bearing these losses and coming back with fighting hearts is a matter of great gratification to me. I wish you would give the Group Commander my commendation to the 388th Bombardment Group for their excellent spirit and confidence in the greatness of the task they are now performing:

The message was signed by Major General Ira C. Eaker, Commander, VIII Bomber Command. It was endorsed by Colonel Curtis E. LeMay, Commander, 4th Combat Wing, who added his own encouragement to the group.

THE 8TH AIR FORCE WON THE WAR IN EUROPE

Part V Some Mission Reports

This one is a dramatic version of one crew on mission #19, bound for *Stuttgart,* Germany on September 6, 1943. It was from the 560th squadron.

"On that date several French families were watching about 200 B-17s pass overhead when suddenly two German "Yellow Noses" took after the last plane. That plane caught fire and suddenly five chutes appeared. This was at *La Chapelle-Champigny*, 60 miles southeast of *Paris*. The first out was the bombardier and the last was the Pilot. The plane crashed with five men inside. Lt. Loveless injured a leg when leaving the plane and was taken in by these French persons. Two of the crew were returned to England by the French underground and the other three were taken by the Germans as POWs. Lt. Loveless was saved by the French family who took him. They wrote to all of the families of the crewmembers in that summer of 1944 and told them of what they had seen.

On September 6, 1947 the people of *La Chapelle-Champigny* held a Memorial Service and Dedication to the downed plane and those killed in combat, due to the efforts of the Mme. Francis Bouchy family a monument was dedicated standing to the right of the place where the fortress laid dead and some trees still black from the fire. At that moment, a French plane made a dive over the ceremony dropping flowers with a French Flag, as homage to the American Heroes.

On September 6, 1973, on the 30th anniversary of the dramatic story of one crew, a ceremony was held with the Air Attache of the U.S. Embassy in attendance[2].

---

[2] This story of one crew was told in the January 1974 issue of the 388th Bomb Group Assn Newsletter.

The Soda Springs, Idaho newspaper, *Deseret,* of May 6, 1943 informed its readers of the first crash of the 388th Bomb Group on May 5, 1943, B-17 42-29562, of the 560th Squadron. Three Army Air Force fliers were in the Soda Springs hospital after a spectacular crash which wrecked the four engine bomber and killed seven of the 10-man crew as Soda Springs residents watched, unable to help the storm-tossed aviators. The pilot was least seriously injured. The plane was on a routine training mission, from Wendover Field to Pocatello.

The civilians nearby attempted to aid the pilots by lining their automobiles along a road out of Soda Springs, but the sleet, wind and snow threw them off their course. Everyone watched the big bomber undershoot on a new landing attempt and crash into the hillside after apparently striking some minor obstruction on the third try. The group which attempted to light a landing strip for the crippled bomber was organized by Sheriff Charles McCracken and his deputy, J. Williams.

The bomber flew over Soda Springs for more than one-half hour and aroused almost the entire town. The first landing attempt probably failed because the pilot was afraid of the many parked cars and he couldn't see well enough. But all parties involved voiced praise for the efforts of the Army Air Corps aviator.

A report of the 388th Bomb Group on July 29, 1943 was of Mission Number 4 to Hanover, Germany on July 26, 1943. The plane involved was the "Impatient Virgin," a B-17F 42-30217.

When we studied the records of courage shown by 8th Air Force Flyers, high on the list was Flight Officer Barlow D. Brown and the crew who brought their battered plane to a safe landing in England after virtually every working part of it had been disabled by German flak and fighters. F/O Brown has been recommended for the Silver Star and the Pilot and Engineer for the Purple Heart.

The Pilot, Lt. Beecham and Engineer, T/Sgt. Delamar were injured by a 20mm shell that exploded in the cockpit and the rudder torn away in a collision with another plane. The B-17 made it back after a two hour battle with German fighters and F/O Brown made an emergency landing in England within 100 miles of their home base.

The fact that he could make a landing is amazing when one

considers some of the damage: the 20mm shell exploded in the right wing, and flak destroyed half of the left aileron; there were two shell holds on the right and one in the left stabilizer; two 20mm shells exploded in the radio compartment, and all oxygen in the front half of the plane was out. The plane was riddled with flak, bullets and shell holes.

After the crew threw out everything – tools, ammunition, guns, clothing and some parachutes to lighten the plane, F/O Brown gave the message to the crew to bail out, but most chutes had been thrown out. The pilot's chute was damaged by a 20mm shell.

Amazingly, while all of this was going on, waist gunner McGee recorded the only confirmed fighter kill – a *Focke-Wulf* 190. When the plane landed, it had no brakes, so it had to overshoot the runway.

A Single Gunner Shoots Down Four German Planes

A July 1987 report tells us that an aerial gunner from Savannah, Georgia shot down 4 Germans in one afternoon. The superiority of the allied gunners was partly the result of the marksmanship of the Eighth Air Force aerial gunners. Staff Sgt. James L. Bragg, 25, of Savannah, was the one who shot down four German fighters during a bombing attack last month. It is clearly a record for enemy planes by a single bomber crewman in a single air battle. The record score was confirmed by Eighth Air Force Intelligence Officers. Sergeant Bragg was the tail gunner on the Flying Fortress "Silver Lady."

He was credited with destroying two single engine *Focke-Wulf* 190s and two twin engine, rocket carrying Messerschmitt 410s. This air battle took place during the bombing attack on synthetic oil plants at *Brus*, on the German-Czech border. The whole crew brought down eight enemy aircraft that day, and the Fortress came back to base without a scratch.

"On the way to the target," Sergeant Bragg described the air battle, "there were about 200 German fighters trying to shoot down stragglers. One plane came within 100 yards of us, so I started shooting. I knocked both the cockpit and the pilot out of the plane. The pilot fell out head over heels. I did not see his chute open. Just seconds later another came in my sights. I did not have to move my gun. I gave him a long burst and four feet of his wing fell off.

The fight for the other two planes occurred on the way back. "We were flying home when 46 ME 410s lined up behind us, and they began lobbing rocket towards us. "They closed in," but we continued aiming in their direction. "As one of them peeled off, I began pouring lead into the plexi-glass cockpit and parts began spilling out. None of the crew got out and finally the plane blew up. The second ME was sitting behind my position, so I poured a burst into his right engine, and it burst into flames. It peeled off and when the right wing fell off, it went into a spin and crashed.

A Knettishall Tale

This was a tricky maneuver by the *Luftwaffe*. On the way back to our air base after one of our missions, we were pretty close to the English Channel. Once we reached the water we were quite safe from enemy retaliation and we could relax a bit.

On one mission, I looked at the 3 o'clock level (at our altitude) when I noticed a B-17 flying in the same direction (west) as ours. Upon more observation I surmised that this airplane was separated from its group and flying close to us to reach the English Channel and safety. I reported my observation to the pilot and crew.

At just about this time our group encountered anti-aircraft fire too close for comfort. The group started evasive action and suffered no casualties. This burst of anti-aircraft fire was quite rare and I was very surprised that it came from this location on the coast.

I looked at the lone B-17 to observe its location. Suddenly it made a 180-degree U-turn and headed east, back to Germany. I then realized what the situation was and knew what the strategy of the lone B-17 was. It was a captured plane that probably had made a forced landing in enemy territory at one time. The Germans checked it out to be able to fly it again.

This lone B-17 with a German crew was able to report our speed and altitude among other information to be used by the other crews on the anti-aircraft battery. This information was then entered into the settings of their guns and therefore would be very accurate.

Fortunately the burst was very short, and we escaped unscathed. Another lesson learned!

AUGUST C. BOLINO

Chapter Eight
A Friendship out of the Blue

Tom Ernsting was born in Holland at *Krommenie*. As a 14-year old he saw an airplane crash near Busch and Dam. The winter of 1944 was very harsh as planes crashed regularly. He saw a man coming down by parachute and he wanted to head towards the crash, but he is stopped.

In 1980, Tom Ernsting came into contact with one survivor, Samuel Gundy, co-pilot of the crashed B-17G, 3rd Bomb Division, 562nd Squadron of the 388th Bomb Group.

During a newspaper report in the *Typhoon* of June 3, 1980 he came into contact with a salvage crew who went to dig up pieces of wreckage in the *Zaam* area and who were trying to trace the exact spot of the crashed plane. The dam must by dug to get them out of the clay.

Tom Ernsting reported everything to his pen friend the war pilot, Gundy. After an extensive correspondence the two friends met in Amsterdam in 1983. Tom was then 53 years old, and Gundy is a biologist at the University of Pennsylvania.

As they talked, Tom reviewed what happened on that day, Thursday, February 10, 1944. From *Knettishall* base the 388th bombers took off in early morning, with a destination of *Braunschweig* (Brunswick) Germany. They are intercepted by German *Focke-Wulfs* at the Belgium coast. The formation lost many planes, and Lt. Feeney's aircraft was hit. The crew members were told to bail out, but three were dead. After Gundy handed a parachute to commander Feeney one part of the wing broke off and the plane went into a spin. The cockpit exploded and co-pilot Gundy was hurled out. In order to come down as fast as possible, Gundy only opened the parachute at 400 meters and as he fell he passed the fuselage, on which

Feeny's cords got entangled. In a rain of falling debris, he landed at the end of Busch and Dam, where the Germans immediately arrived and arrested them. Pilot Feeney was carried on a ladder but died before he could be transported anywhere.

Co-pilot Gundy, with a broken back, was taken to Wilhelmina Hospital in Amsterdam the following day. In the Wilhelmina Hospital matron Tisch looked after Samuel Gundy. As best as she could, she helped American and British pilots, smuggling notes out of the ward and at the risk of her life giving the pilots certain things they asked for. Flyer Gundy recovered eventually and was transferred to a prison camp in Germany.

For Miss Tisch, a Dutch of Austrian origin, who was forced to work in the German ward of the Wilhelmina Hospital, the end was less happy. She was arrested by the Germans and taken to Dachau, but she survived the camp and at the special request of Gundy, Tom Ernsting was able to trace her. It took him a lot of trouble and time. She too met Samuel Gundy in Amsterdam in 1983. A meeting which is deeply engraved in his soul. The meeting was repeated when Tom Ernsting came to America in 1987 to visit his friend. A friend who came falling out of the blue sky before his astonished eyes on a cold February afternoon 42 years ago[3].

Flier Leaps into Hell[4]

Lt. Harry Hobbs of Flossmoor, Illinois, was a navigator of a Flying Fortress, who prepared to resume his combat duties after bailing out of his blazing bomber as it wobbled over the Siegfried line under a hail of small arms fire by the enemy. Hobbs' plane was ridden into a Belgian hillside five miles from the fighting front by its first pilot, J. Gierach of Madison, Wisconsin, who lived several years in Cicero, IL, while

---

[3] This story was reported in the April 1988 newsletter of the 388th Bomb Group Assn.
[4] The Chicago News Service of October 18, 1982 headlined this story "Flyer Tells of Leap into Hell over Nazi Line."

working in Chicago before joining the Air Force.

Both Hobbs and Gierach were on their sixth mission when flak hit the plane after they had dropped bombs on the *Leipzig* area.

"Two of the engines were knocked out," Hobbs said. "We were rapidly losing altitude and fell from formation. We were all alone as we crossed the Rhine, and we were about 3,500 feet when we began crossing a belt of the Siegfried fortifications, and we were still coming down when all hell broke loose. The Germans began firing at us with rifles, machine guns and light anti-aircraft guns. "A 20mm shell burst in the tail, exploding ammunition and starting a fire, but the tailgunner beat it out. Another shell blew off the top turret and another set fire to our two remaining engines."

When the plane burst into flames, Gierach gave the order to abandon ship. Hobbs, first out, was closely followed by six others.

"As I floated down I saw about 70 persons running on the road and we were not sure the Americans had captured this sector."

Gierach and his co-pilot Peter Meed of Margaretville, New York made a belly landing on a hillside. The plane was smashed to smithereens, but the two pilots were unhurt. Hobbs landed on his left shoulder, dislocating it, but it was put back in place without much trouble.

Members of the Belgian White Army took the men to a farmhouse, the first stop on a trip back to England.

A number of Chicagoans are in Hobbs' heavy bombardment group and most of them have been on more than 20 missions. They include Lt. Clifford Hank, 3222 Fulton Blvd.; Lt. Henry Fornell, 1431 Elmdale Ave., who is the group leader and Capt. Daniel Houghton of 3643 Hamilton Ave.

THE 8TH AIR FORCE WON THE WAR IN EUROPE

Chapter Nine
Tailgunner Regains Memoir
By James Johnson, Staff Writer[5]

Tailgunner Tony Rosetano knew he could get in trouble with the Army for keeping a diary, because he violated security regulations by keeping a record on his Vargas Girl pinup calendar of the missions. He flew as a crewman aboard the "Vagabond Lady." The B-17 Flying Fortress bomber carried destruction to the Nazi war machine from the plane's base in Knettishall, England.

Rosetano never got to write the final entry, detailing how the "Vagabond Lady" was shot down with most of its regular crew on November 9, 1944. It occurred at 10 a.m. during a bombing run to Trier on the Mosel River near the German – French border. An anti-aircraft artillery shell blew away the nose of the bomber.

"I'd just heard the bombardier report flak at 12 o'clock," Rosetano recalls. "The plane lurched and suddenly surged downward. I looked up and saw the gunners at the waist start for the hatch, and the right inboard engine was on fire. I knew I had to bail out." But his trouble had just begun. Fumbling his parachute into place, he tried to open his escape hatch. It wouldn't budge.

"Wind pressure was keeping it shut," he said. Rosetano realized that the tail had broken off, and the plane would crash with him still trapped inside.

Rosetano redoubled his efforts to force open the hatch. But nothing worked until the horizontal stabilizer surfaces spreading outward on each side of the vertical fin began to act as wings, breaking the deadly plunge of the breakaway tail section. "The hatch came open and I bailed out, pulling the rip cord almost immediately."

---

[5] This story was published in *The Daily Oklahoman* on December 17, 1990.

When he was on the ground he was captured, he said by an old man in a volksturm (home guard).

The old German stole Rosetano's American cigarettes at gunpoint and then summoned a German army officer. "The officer read to me in English from a paper like a modern Miranda warning card the police read from, to inform me that, for me, the war was over. I was a prisoner of the Third Reich."

That ended Rosetano's 20th bombing mission. He and four fellow crewmen were captured; two others escaped and three were killed.

Held in Pomerania as a prisoner of war, Roseano lost 45 pounds on the thin diet of sauerkraut soup, steamed potatoes and sometimes a piece of cabbage or a tablespoonful of bratwurst.

He said one officer made his group of prisoners, many of them wounded, run three miles from the railway to camp, inflicting non-fatal bayonet wounds on those who couldn't keep up.

Liberated by the British under Gen. B.L. "Monty" Montgomery, Rosetano was in a military hospital when Germany surrendered in May 1945. He remained in the service from 21 years, then worked at the Internal Revenue Service in Oklahoma City until reaching retirement age. He plans to retire from his third career at the State Tax Commission.

Rosetano said he forgot his war diary calendar until May 2016, when the "Vagabond Lady's" former ball turret gunner came calling. "He was sick so he had not flown with us on that last mission. When he heard that we were shot down, he took my calendar and kept it until he found me."

It is no longer a breach of military secrecy, so the calendar is now Rosetano's most treasured memento of aerial combat in World War II.

A Frozen "Relief Tube"

On July 31, 1944 a B-17 was headed on a mission to *Munich*. About an hour before it reached the target, nature called. So one crew member had to use a funnel-shaped device affectionately called the "relief tube," which for the non-commissioned is located in the bomb bay near the Radio

Operator's station. After disconnecting his radio gear and removing his oxygen mask, he proceeded to liquidate his holdings.

Two catastrophes then occurred in short order: the relief tube hose outlet froze and his cup runneth over. Disgusted, he tossed the relief tube to the bottom of the bomb bay and returned to his station. Within one minute after reconnecting his gear, the Ball Turret Gunner queried the Flight Engineer on the intercom, "Is it snowing?" A glance out the window revealed a bright, blue sky. The Flight Engineer retorted with, "No snow here, the sky is clear." The Ball Turret Gunner then emphatically stated, "That's funny, my face is full of ice!" It took the radio man me about one-tenth of a second to realize what he had done.

He had to confess that he never did explain to him how one could encounter snow with a bright, blue sky or I might not have been able to relate this singular instance of a B-17 functional failure. I hope that should the Ball Turret Gunner read this, the snow will have disappeared together with his memory[6].

---

[6] Ray Goldstein, Radio Operator, on B-17 "Star Dust"

AUGUST C. BOLINO

Part VI Victory in Europe
Chapter Ten
The B-17 Flying Fortress

The B-17 was not just an airplane. It was a major part of the winning of Europe in World War II. It was victory and tragedy and part of our folklore. Those of us who flew in them owe our lives to this majestic airplane. Its hundreds of names will forever remind us of the greatness of its accomplishment. We will always remember the "Memphis Belle" and I will always recall the 30 missions I survived in "Wolf Wagon." How could anyone forget what happened in the skies over *Berlin, Munich, Leipzig, Hamburg, Bremen and Brunswick*. How many times did we return with only two engines working? And how many times were we on fire and we had to dive down 20,000 feet to put out the flames.

The Boeing B-17 was not the biggest, the most heavily-armed or the most numerous of the American heavy bombers, but it became a legend and is best remembered for its part in the raids that pounded Nazi Germany into submission. Originally designed in the mid-1930s, 12,731 B-17s were ultimately built. The design of the B-17 saw many alterations through the war, acquiring more armament and other upgrades. The ultimate version was the B-17G, the final production variant.

The Eighth Army Air Corp (the Air Force had not yet been created) was tasked with using daylight precision bombing to remove Germany's capacity to make war. The 388th BG Heavy was part of the Third Air Division of the Eighth Army Air Corp. We flew in daylight to take advantage of the very precise Norden bombsite. The RAF flew at night so it was much more difficult for the fighters and flak to attack them. On the daylight missions a number of measures were taken to make it harder for the fighters and the flak gunners. For example, the

THE 8ᵀᴴ AIR FORCE WON THE WAR IN EUROPE

B-17s would throw out clouds of aluminum foil strips to confuse the radar. They would fly at 20-25,000 feet to make it hard on the fighters. The cabins were not pressurized so the crew members had to wear oxygen masks. The temperature was usually 50-65 degrees below zero. Their flight suits were like electric blankets to try to prevent frostbite. The crew had to check each other in case the hose on their oxygen masks became blocked by ice. There were three types of fighters that attacked the formations: propeller-powered, jet-powered and rocket fighters. On some missions 10 of 36 B-17s were lost or shot down. But the U-boats had the highest casualties in WWII – 7 out of 10.

Not Very Good Odds

Flying on a B-17 crew during WWII might have been one of the most dangerous assignments. A 388ᵗʰ combat crew had a 2 in 5 chance of having their B-17 crash. The crashes were caused primarily by flak, enemy fighters (shooting and in some cases intentional ramming), and mid-air collisions with another B-17, weather, and fuel shortage or engine failure. The crashes took many forms from an instant total explosion, an out of control aircraft spinning to earth, a crash landing in a field or a ditching in the ocean. Each of these had their own life threatening scenarios.

The scenario of a plane disabled over enemy territory had many possible terrible outcomes for a crewman. The second-best outcome was to end up in a POW camp. However, this first required surviving a gauntlet of extremely dangerous challenges.

Assuming that the explosion or attack did not leave the crewman killed, unconscious, or too seriously wounded to bailout, he must be able to make an exit (an onboard fire or a plane in a spin could make an exit impossible). Once he bailed out and didn't collide with any part of the plane, he could try to deploy his parachute (if he still had one). Hopefully by this time he still has enough altitude for a parachute to be effective. Assuming that the parachute had not been damaged, it probably would deploy and let him float to the ground. While floating he was subject to enemy fighters and/or soldiers on the ground shooting at him or fighters diving at the canopy trying to collapse it. Finally the impact with the ground always has its own dangers. Usually evasion was impossible and a quick capture followed. His captors (either soldiers or civilians) were armed, angry and scared which sometimes resulted in a quick death. If not, a series of interrogations and train rides followed which ended up with the crewman at his first POW camp.

Of course the best outcome for a crewman was to survive the crash and evade capture. But evasion itself involved many hardships and extreme dangers.

A plane did not have to crash for a crewman to receive serious injury or even death. Shrapnel from flak or enemy machine gun fire caused many injuries as well as deaths. However, several men died from asphyxiation when their oxygen failed and no one noticed. The extreme cold in the aircraft caused much discomfort as well as frost bite.

All in all a crewman's chances for any given mission were not good. Yet these incredibly brave heroes' flew 25 or 30 or 35 or even in some cases 50 missions. It is absolutely amazing to me.

During World War II, it was believed by many military strategists of air power that major victories could be won by attacking industrial and political infrastructure, rather than purely military targets. Strategic bombing often involved bombing areas inhabited by civilians and some campaigns were deliberately designed to target civilian populations in order to terrorize and disrupt their usual activities. International law at the outset of World War II did not specifically forbid aerial bombardment of cities despite the prior occurrence of such bombing during World War I, the Spanish Civil War, and the Second Sino-Japanese War.

On January 4, 1944, the B-24s and B-17s based in England flew their last mission as a subordinate part of VIII Bomber Command. On February 22, 1944, a massive reorganization of American airpower took place in Europe. VIII Bomber Command and Ninth Air Force were brought under control of a centralized headquarters for command and control of the United States Army Air Forces in Europe, the United States Strategic Air Forces (USSTAF). General Carl Spaatz returned to England to command the USSTAF. Major General Jimmy Doolittle relinquished

THE 8ᵀᴴ AIR FORCE WON THE WAR IN EUROPE

command of the Fifteenth Air Force to Major General Nathan F. Twining and took over command of the Eighth Air Force from Lieutenant General Ira C. Eaker at RAF Daws Hill. Doolittle of course was well known to American airmen as the famous "Tokyo Raider" and former air racer. His directive was simple: 'Win the air war and isolate the battlefield'.

Aircraft and ground crew of Boeing B-17F-25-BO Fortress "Hell's Angels" (AAF Ser. No. *41-24577*) of the 358th Bomb Squadron, 303d Bomb Group, RAF Molesworth. This was the first B-17 to complete 25 combat missions in the 8th Air Force, on May 13, 1943. After completing 48 missions, the aircraft returned to the U.S. on January 20, 1944, for a publicity tour.

During World War II, the offensive air forces of the United States Army Air Forces (USAAF) came to be classified as strategic or tactical. A strategic air force was that with a mission to attack an enemy's war effort beyond his front-line forces, predominantly production and supply facilities, whereas a tactical air force supported ground campaigns, usually with objectives selected through co-operation with the armies.

In Europe, Eighth Air Force was the first USAAF strategic air force, with a mission to support an invasion of continental Europe from the British Isles. Eighth Air Force carried out strategic daytime strategic bombing operations in Western Europe from airfields in eastern England.

Berlin

Less than a week after "Big Week", Eighth Air Force made its first attack on the Reich's capital, Berlin. The RAF had been making night raids on Berlin since 1940, (with heavy raids in 1943) and nuisance Mosquito raids in daylight, but this was the first major daylight bombing raid on the German capital. On March 6, 1944, over 700 heavy bombers along with 800 escort fighters of the Eighth Air Force hit numerous targets within Berlin, dropping the first American bombs on the capital of the Third Reich. On March 8, another raid of 600 bombers and 200 fighters hit the Berlin area again, destroying the VKF ball-bearing plant at Erkner. The following day, on March 9, H2X radar-equipped B-

17s mounted a third attack on the Reich capital through clouds. Altogether, the Eighth Air Force dropped over 4,800 tons of high explosive on Berlin during the first week of March.

On March 22, over 800 bombers, led by H2X radar equipped bombers hit *Berlin* again, bombing targets though a thick rainy overcast causing more destruction to various industries. Because of the thick clouds and rain over the area the Luftwaffe did not attack the American bomber fleet, as the Germans believed that because of the weather the American bombers would be incapable of attacking their targets. However, the "pathfinder" bombers of the RAF Alconbury-based 482d Bomb Group proved very capable of finding the targets and guiding the bombers to them.

Overlord

As a prelude to the invasion of France, American air attacks began in February 1944 against railroad junctions, airfields, ports and bridges in northern France and along the English Channel coastline. Fighters from both Eighth and Ninth Air Forces made wide sweeps over the area, mounting strafing missions at airfields and rail networks. By June 6, Allied fighter pilots had succeeded in damaging or destroying hundreds of locomotives, thousands of motorized vehicles, and many bridges. In addition, German airfields in France and Belgium were attacked.

B-17 Flying Fortresses over Europe during World War II

THE 8TH AIR FORCE WON THE WAR IN EUROPE

On D-Day, over 2,300 sorties were flown by Eighth Air Force heavy bombers in the Normandy and Cherbourg invasion areas, all aimed at neutralizing enemy coastal defenses and front-line troops.

Defeat of the Luftwaffe

The P-51 Mustang was first put into service in Europe by the British in early 1942, but the Allison V-1710 engine did not achieve a success at high altitudes, so the Brits replaced the Allison engine with their two-speed, two-stage supercharged Rolls-Royce-Merlin engine that substantially improved performance. They also replaced the three-bladed propeller with a four-bladed propeller. These changes greatly improved the performance of the P-51. It achieved a level speed of 441 mph at 29,800 feet, over 100 mph faster than the Allison-engine. At all heights, the rate of climb was approximately doubled.

This gave the USAAF an aircraft that could compete on equal terms with the *Focke-Wulf* 190 and the later models of the *Messerschmitt* Bf 109. When the Americans signed a new contract for the Mustangs, the engine utilized was to be the Packard V-1650-3, based on the Merlin 68. In late 1943, the new P-51B Mustang was introduced to the European Theater by the USAAF. It could fly as far on its internal fuel tanks as the P-47 could with drop tanks. They were assigned to three groups in the tactical Ninth Air Force, which created a problem for VIII Bomber Command, which needed a long range escort fighter.

In January 1944, Major General Jimmy Doolittle became the new commander of the Eighth Air Force. He was a major influence on the European air war when he made a critical change in policy that required escorting fighters to remain with the bombers at all times. The American fighter pilots would fly far ahead of the bombers' combat box formations in air supremacy mode, "clearing the skies" of any Luftwaffe fighter opposition heading towards the target. This strategy disabled the twin-engined *Zerstörergeschwader* heavy fighter wings and their replacement, single-engined *Sturmgruppen* of heavily armed Fw 190As. After they cleared these bomber destroyers from Germany's skies, they were then free to strafe German airfields and transport while returning to base, thereby achieving air superiority by Allied air forces over Europe.

The result was that the Luftwaffe was absent over the skies of Europe after D-Day and the Allies were starting to achieve air superiority over the continent. But Luftwaffe did not surrender. They mounted more attacks on the larger formations of Allied heavy bombers. The larger numbers of B-17s and B-24s attacking enemy targets, meant that they simply could not sustain the losses the Eighth Air Force bombers and fighters were inflicting on them.

By mid-1944, Eighth Air Force had reached a total strength of more than 200,000 persons (it is estimated that more than 350,000 Americans served in Eighth Air Force during the war in Europe). At its peak, Eighth Air Force had forty heavy bomber groups, fifteen fighter groups, and four specialized support groups. It could, and often did, dispatch more than 2,000 four-engine bombers and more than 1,000 fighters on a single mission to multiple targets.

In January 1945, the *Luftwaffe* attempted one last major air offensive against the Allied Air Forces. Over 950 fighters had been sent west from the Eastern Front for "Operation." On January 1, the entire German fighter force in the West, comprising combat aircraft from some eleven *Jagdgeschwader* (day fighter wings), took off and attacked 27 Allied airfields in northern France, Belgium and the southern part of the Netherlands in an attempt by the Luftwaffe to cripple Allied air forces in the Low Countries of Europe. It was a last-ditch effort to keep up the momentum of the German forces during the stagnant stage of the Battle of the Bulge (*Unternehmen Wacht am Rhein*). The operation was a pyrrhic success for the *Luftwaffe* as the losses suffered by the German air arm were irreplaceable and over 300 *Luftwaffe* aircraft were shot down, mostly by Allied Anti-Aircraft guns. The losses of the Allied Air Forces were replaced within weeks. The operation failed to achieve air superiority, even temporarily, and the German Army continued to be exposed to air attack.

First seen by Allied airmen during the late summer of 1944, it wasn't until March 1945 that German jet aircraft started to attack Allied bomber formations in earnest. On March 2 when Eighth Air

THE 8ᵀᴴ AIR FORCE WON THE WAR IN EUROPE

Force bombers were dispatched to attack the synthetic oil refineries at *Leipzig*, Messerschmitt Me 262 attacked the formation near Dresden. The next day, the largest formation of German jets ever seen, most likely from the *Luftwaffe's* specialist 7th Fighter Wing, *Jagdgeschwader 7 Nowotny*, made attacks on Eighth Air Force bomber formations over Dresden and the oil targets at Essen, shooting down a total of three bombers.

However, the *Luftwaffe* jets were simply too few and too late to have any serious effect on the Allied air armadas now sweeping over the Reich with near-impunity. A lack of fuel and available pilots for the new jets greatly reduced their effectiveness. I still remember on our 29th mission when an ME 262 attacked our group, and when he flew by in a vertical position I could see his face. He looked to be about 15 years old.

When the 398th Bombardment Group flew on a bombing run to Germany on April 13, 1945, it was one of the last missions. On May 8, Germany surrendered, and Victory in Europe Day was declared.

The Eighth Air Force is one of two active duty numbered air forces in Air Force Global Strike Command. Eighth Air Force, with headquarters at Barksdale AFB, in the Shreveport, Louisiana, metro area, It supports U.S. Strategic Command, and is designated as U.S. Strategic Command's Task Force 204, providing on-alert, combat-ready forces to the president. The mission of "The Mighty Eighth" is to safeguard America's interests through strategic deterrence and global combat power. Eighth Air Force controls long-range nuclear-capable bomber assets throughout the United States and overseas locations. The 8th Air Force motto is "Peace Through Strength."

The Eighth Air Force now consists of more than 16,000 Regular Air Force. This air power includes the heavy bomber force: the B-1 Lancer, B-2 Spirit and the B-52 Stratofortress. These are housed at the 2d Bomb Wing at Barksdale AFB, Louisiana and the 5th Bomb Wing at Minot AFB, North Dakota, and one reserve wing, the 307th Bomb Wing at Barksdale AFB, Louisiana. The B-2 force consists of 20 bombers assigned to the 509th Bomb Wing along with the Missouri Air National Guard's associate 131st Bomb Wing at Whiteman AFB, Missouri. The B-1 force consists of 62 bombers assigned to the 7th Bomb Wing at Dyess AFB, Texas and the 28th Bomb Wing at Ellsworth AFB, South Dakota.

Major General Thomas A. Bussiere was named Commander of 8th Air Force on October 4, 2016 after having served as the Deputy Director for Nuclear, Homeland Defense, and Current Operations on the Joint Staff at the Pentagon, Washington, D.C.

Chapter Eleven
Some Famous B17s

"Little Willie"

The 388th Bomb Group was stationed at Knettishall, England, flying bombing missions over the Netherlands and Germany, when on one of these missions, "Little Willie" earned its place in the wing's history.

In early September 1943, three replacement crews, among others, arrived at the 388th Bomb Group, Knettishall, England. One of these was the crew of Richard Obenschain. He was assigned to the 563rd Squadron. When they went to their assigned barracks they found several empty bunks with luggage and possessions to be shipped to next of kin. It was not a positive sign for them. The crew, after many discussions, settled on "Little Willie" as a good name for our new possession. The name was based upon a wartime military character of that time.

After about 10 days of orientation practice in tight formation flying and area familiarization, they flew their first mission to Rheims, France on Sept. 26, 1943. The mission was at medium altitude and the target was the launching ramps for the V-1 or Buzz Bomb. There was minimal fighter action and anti-aircraft activity. They thought the mission was a "milk-run" but the next two or three more than convinced them that bombing missions, without fighter escort all the way, could be very stressful and deadly.

On March 6, 1944, Flight Officer Bernard Dopko piloted "Little Willie" on its way to *Berlin* to bomb the Robert Bosch Electrical Factory. "Little Willie" joined the formation in the tail end position and headed for the Dutch Coast. As they neared Berlin, fighters attacked the formation and then anti-aircraft gunners took over and flak filled the sky. "Little Willie" lined up on target, but by then the gunners had the range and "Little Willie" took two hits. One engine was knocked out and a second was turned into a runaway, which threatened to rip the wing off.

"Little Willie" dropped its bombs and lost position in the formation. Dopko was forced to dive for the deck and two German fighters followed it looking for an easy kill. "Little Willie" leveled off at 50 feet and the fighters were driven off by the plane's gunners.

Turning for home, "Little Willie's" journey started at an altitude of 50 feet, dodging church steeples and other buildings which had suddenly become obstacles.

Reaching the English Channel, "Little Willie's" altitude dropped to 10 feed off the water. On the horizon loomed the white cliffs of Dover. Luck was riding with "Little Willie" because the engine which was knocked out by flak over Berlin came to life and "Little Willie" climbed over the cliffs to home. This mission, like all the rest, was a mixture of prayer and excitement.

"City of Savannah"

A project of the Mighty 8th Museum was the B-17 named "City of Savannah." This B-17 was acquired from the Smithsonian Museum. While this wasn't one of "our" planes, when completed it would carry the markings of the 388th. The name "City of Savannah" was a patriotic message applied to the 5,000th B-17 to pass through Hunter Army Airfield during WW II. It was flown to England by Lt. Ralph Kittle of the 563rd Squadron. It was damaged by flak on March 5, 1945 and crashed. But it is indistinguishable from the original, and it is the centerpiece of the museum and will be a unique reminder of the 388th Bomb Group. The 388th Bomb Group made a significant contribution of $10,000 to this restoration. But that treasury cannot withstand another donation.

The Mighty 8th Air Force Museum welcomed the B-17 to Savannah on January 15, 2009. It quickly received a new name; "The City of Savannah."
It managed to avoid the scrap yards after the war. It passed through

THE 8ᵀᴴ AIR FORCE WON THE WAR IN EUROPE

a series of civilian owners who used it to perform a variety of functions. It was used for 20 years taking photographs around the world for a mapmaking company in Canada. From1974 to 1984 it was used as a fire-fighting plane in Arizona. In 1984 it was traded to the Smithsonian Institution, where it was stored until it was given to the Mighty 8th Museum.

The restoration of the "City of Savannah" took several years and thousands of hours of volunteer work have gone into the restoration effort and the results are remarkable. The exterior has been thoroughly cleaned and polished to its original, unpainted condition. All fabric-covered control surfaces have been removed, cleaned, re-covered, and reinstalled. Replacements for the gun turrets which had been removed while the plane was in civilian service have been secured. A ball turret shell has been installed. A top turret bubble was acquired. A tail turret was salvaged from a B- 17 that crashed in Alaska over sixty years ago has also been acquired, given a new aluminum skin covering. A fully functional chin turret was acquired along with the cap and fairing required for its installation. The interior of the plane has been thoroughly cleaned and painted.

The radio room was fully restored, and on July 13, 2011 the first transmission was completed to Sister ship "Miss Liberty.' When the exterior was completed, the exterior marking matched that of the plane when it flew in combat—B-17G 42-97542.

The "City of Savannah" 1944

"Sentimental Journey"

This Boeing B-17G 44-83514 was built by Douglas Aircraft in late 1944, and was accepted by the U.S. Army Air Forces on March 13, 1945. It was assigned to the Pacific theater for the duration of the war, and it was later placed in storage in Japan. In 1947, the B-17G was reconfigured as a RB-17B for a new role in photo-mapping and assigned to Clark Field in Manila.

In 1950, the aircraft was transferred to Eglin Field, Florida and converted to a DB-17G for service as an air-sea rescue craft. During the 1950s, it was modified to a DB-17P standard, serving with the 3215th Drone Squadron at Patrick Air Force Base in Florida. One of its important missions was "Operation Greenhouse," the fourth postwar atmospheric nuclear weapon test series conducted by the United States during the spring of 1951. As a mother plane, the RB-17P directed unmanned, radio controlled B-17 drone aircraft to measure blast and thermal effects and to collect radioactive cloud samples. During the test, a drone aircraft would be taken off by ground control. A "mother ship," already airborne, would then come from behind, take control of the drone and fly it to the target area.

On January 27, 1959, the aircraft was transferred to military storage at Davis Monthan Air Force Base in Tucson, Arizona. After a few months of storage, 83514 was acquired by the Aero Union Corporation of Chico, California, receiving civilian aircraft registration: N-9323Z. For 18 years, the converted bomber flew as a forest fire fighter throughout the United States. On January 14, 1978, at a membership banquet for the newly formed Arizona Wing of the Commemorative Air Force, Colonel Mike Clarke announced the donation of the aircraft to the CAF for assignment to the Arizona Wing. A contest was initiated by the local media to name the aircraft, which resulted in more than 800 entries, and the ultimate selection of the name "Sentimental Journey" with nose art featuring World War II pinup Betty Grable, who was the biggest pinup in World War II. Permission was secured from widower Harry James to add Betty Grable in her most tantalizing pose to complete the newly acquired bomber.

THE 8ᵀᴴ AIR FORCE WON THE WAR IN EUROPE

Although it was flyable, "Sentimental Journey" was not an accurate representative of the wartime B-17 bomber and in December 1981, the aircraft underwent an extensive restoration. In four years it added four operational turrets, operational bomb bay doors and navigator and radio operator stations. The addition of the Norden bomb sight and machine guns completed the transformation to its original condition.

Over the years, "Sentimental Journey" performed across North America, as one of the most recognizable "living museums" that educated and inspired the American public, thus helping to keep the legacy of the B-17 alive.

"Memphis Belle"

The "Memphis Belle" was a Boeing-built B-17F serial number 3470, USAAC Serial No. 41-24485, was added to the USAAF inventory on July 15, 1942, and delivered in September 1942 to the 91st Bombardment Group at Dow Field, Bangor, Maine. She was then deployed to Prestwick, Scotland, on September 30, 1942, moving to a temporary base at RAF Kimbolton on October 1, and then to her permanent base at RAF Bassingbourn, England, on October 14. The fuselage bore the unit and aircraft identification markings of a B-17 of the 324th Bomb Squadron letter "A."

The aircraft was named after pilot Robert K Morgan's sweetheart, Margaret Polk, a resident of Memphis, Tennessee. Morgan originally intended to call the aircraft *Little One*, which was his pet name for her, but after Morgan and copilot Jim Verinis saw the movie *Lady for a Night*, in which the leading character owns a riverboat named the *Memphis Belle*, he proposed that name to his crew. Morgan then contacted George Petty at the offices of *Esquire* magazine and asked him for a pinup drawing to go with the name, which Petty supplied from the magazine's April 1941 issue. The 91st's group artist, Corporal Tony Starcer, copied the Petty girl as art on both sides of the forward fuselage, depicting her suit in blue on the aircraft's port side and in red on the starboard. The nose art later included 25 bomb shapes, one for each mission credit, and eight *swastika* designs, one for each German aircraft claimed shot down by the crew. Station and crew names were stenciled below station windows on the aircraft after her tour of duty was completed.

Captain Robert K. Morgan was the chief pilot. The crew flew 29 combat missions with the 324th Bomb Squadron, all but four in the "Memphis Belle." But the crew was not the first to complete 25 missions. The B-17 "Hell's Angels" (41-24577) of the 303rd Bomb Group completed 25 combat missions on 13 May 1943, becoming the first B-17 to complete the feat, one week before Captain Morgan's crew.

The aircraft was then flown back to the United States on June 8, 1943, by a composite crew chosen by the Eighth Air Force from those who had flown combat, led by Capt. Morgan, for a 31-city war bond tour. Morgan's original co-pilot was Capt. James A. Verinis, who himself piloted the "Memphis Belle" for one mission, was promoted to aircraft commander of another B-17 for his final 16 missions and finished his tour on May 13. He rejoined Morgan's crew as co-pilot for the flight back to the United States. During the Second World War, the "Memphis Belle" inspired the making of two motion pictures: a 1944 documentary film, *Memphis Belle: A Story of a Flying Fortress*, and a 1990 Hollywood feature film, *Memphis Belle*.

In his memoirs, Morgan claimed that during his publicity tour he flew the B-17 between the Buncombe County Courthouse and the City Hall of Asheville, North Carolina, his home town. Morgan wrote that after leaving a local airport he decided to buzz the town, telling his copilot, Captain Verinis, "I think we'll just drive up over the city and give them a little goodbye salute." Morgan turned the bomber down Patton Avenue, a main thoroughfare, toward downtown Asheville. When he observed the courthouse and the city hall (two tall buildings that are only about 50 feet apart dead ahead, he lowered his left wing in a 60 degree bank and flew between the structures. He wrote that the city hall housed an AAF weather detachment whose commanding officer allegedly complained immediately to the Pentagon, but was advised by a duty officer that "Major Morgan has been given permission to buzz by General Henry "Hap" Arnold."

THE 8ᵀᴴ AIR FORCE WON THE WAR IN EUROPE

After the war, the "Memphis Belle" was saved from reclamation at Altus Air Force Base, Oklahoma where it had been consigned since August 1, 1945, by the efforts of the Mayor of Memphis, Walter Chandler, and the city bought the B-17 for $350. She was flown to Memphis in July 1946 and stored until the summer of 1949 when she was placed on display at the National Guard armory near the city's fairgrounds. She sat out-of-doors into the 1980s, slowly deteriorating from weather and vandalism. Souvenir hunters removed almost all of the interior components. Eventually no instruments were left in the cockpit, and virtually every removable piece of the aircraft's interior had been scavenged, often severing the aircraft's wiring and control cables in the process.

In the early 1970s, another mayor had donated the historic aircraft back to the Air Force, but they allowed her to remain in Memphis contingent on her being maintained. Efforts by the locally organized Memphis Belle Memorial Association, Inc. (MBMA) saw the aircraft moved to Mud Island in the Mississippi River in 1987 for display in a new pavilion with large tarp cover. She was still open to the elements, however, and prone to weathering. Pigeons would also nest inside the tarp and droppings were constantly needing removal from the B-17. Dissatisfaction with the site led to efforts to create a new museum facility in Shelby County.

In the summer of 2003 the B-17 was disassembled and moved to a restoration facility at the former Naval Air Station Memphis in Millington, Tennessee for work. In September 2004, however, the National Museum of the United States Air Force, apparently tiring of the ups and downs of the city's attempts to preserve the aircraft, indicated that they wanted her back for restoration and eventual display at the museum at Wright-Patterson AFB near Dayton, Ohio. *The Memphis Belle--The Final Chapter in Memphis*, a documentary film by Ken Axmaker, Jr., focused on the history of the plane in Memphis and emphasized the final days and the volunteers who tried to keep one of the most famous aircraft in the world and another Memphis icon from disappearing.

On 30 August 2005, the MBMA announced that a consultant that they hired determined that the MBMA would not be able to raise enough money to restore the plane and otherwise fulfill the Air Force's requirements to keep possession of the aircraft. They announced plans to return the aircraft to the National Museum of the United States Air Force at Wright-Patterson AFB near Dayton, Ohio, after a final exhibition at an airshow in Millington, Tennessee from September 30– October 2, 2005. The "Memphis Belle" arrived safely at the museum in mid-October 2005 and was placed in one of the Museum's restoration hangars, where it was placed at the top of its priorities. In the magazine *Friends Journal* of the museum's foundation, Major General Charles D. Metcalf, USAF (Ret), then the director of the museum, stated that it might take eight to 10 years to fully restore the aircraft. But by the spring of 2009, considerable preparatory work had been accomplished, but the fuselage and wings were still disassembled. After stripping the paint from the aft fuselage of the aircraft, hundreds of names and personal messages were found scratched in the aluminum skin. It turned out that, during the aircraft's war bond tour, people were allowed to leave their mark there.

"My Gal Sal"

This particular B-17 is now suspended from the ceiling in the Boeing Center of the National World War II Museum. It stands now for all the crews who flew over Germany. It was active in 1942, but it had a difficult time reaching England. On June 27, it had to make an emergency landing on an icy part of Greenland, where it stayed for 50 years. It was recovered and restoration began in Cincinnati. When it was completed, it was donated to the World War II Museum.

"Sally B"

Although it never saw combat, the Sally B has an interesting history. The Boeing B-17G now known as *Sally B,* was one of the last to be constructed by the Lockheed-Vega plant at Burbank, California. Accepted by the United States Army Air Force (USAAF) as 44- 85784 on June 19 1945, it was too late to

THE 8TH AIR FORCE WON THE WAR IN EUROPE

see war service, so it was flown to Nashville for modifications. It was then converted for training purposes and was then sent to Wright-Patterson Field in Ohio.

It was next selected for use as a research vehicle and in 1949 allocated to EB-17G status, which meant that the B-17 was used in a variety of research roles, one of the most bizarre being the addition of a man carrying a pod on the starboard wingtip. Also fitted at the time was an infra-red tracking device in place of the Perspex nose. These trials did not yield much, so in 1954 it was returned to its original standard configuration, less armaments, at Hill AFB in Utah.

This B-17 was then purchased by the Institute Geographic National (IGN) in France, which used several B-17s after the war for survey and mapping work. The '784 arrived in November 1954 and was given the French registration FBGSR. Based at Creil, this aircraft carried out work for the French government, and others, faithfully for many years.

As they entered the 1970s it was apparent that the cost of operating the Flying Fortresses was getting prohibitive, also spares were becoming something of a problem. The IGN replaced the B-17s with other aircraft. The aircraft was purchased, restored and flown by Ted White for many years, based here at the Duxford Airfield. The aircraft later was purchased and funded by the B-17 Charitable Trust in 2000, and made the flagship of the American Air Museum in Britain. This aircraft has been used in a number of documentaries and movies, including *The Memphis Belle*.

"The Sally B" had one more official duty. During the Memorial Day celebration at Madingley it makes a flyover, but it may not continue this practice because of new regulations.

"Nine-O-Nine"

This Flying Fortress was widely known for its ability to absorb tremendous punishment and bring its crews back alive. It was one airplane from the 91st Bomb Group, 323rd Squadron. "Nine-O-Nine" #42-31909, flew 140 missions without an abort or loss of crewmen. It was assigned to combat duty on February 25, 1944 and by April 1945 it had mad eighteen trips to Berlin, dropped 562,000 pounds of bombs, flown 1129 hours, had 21 engine changes, 4 wing panel changes, 15 main gas tanks and 18 Tokyo tanks changed aside from considerable flak damage.

When the war was over, "Nine-O-Nine" returned to the United States with 600 holes. Although the war could not stop the historic plane, she was taken to the scrap heap along with thousands of other proud aircraft.

The B-17G that is now restored as "Nine-O-Nine" was built at Long Beach, California by Douglas Aircraft Company and accepted on April 7, 1945. It was too late for combat, but it did serve as part of the Air/Sea Rescue Squadron in the Military Air Transport Service.

In 1965 the Douglas Aircraft was sold to Aircraft Specialties Company which began the restoration of the aircraft. The damaged skin was fabricated and replaced on site; engines and props were stripped, cleaned, repaired and tested. The interior restoration was the major problem. It involved installing 4000 ft. of new control cable and replacing all electrical wiring and instrumentation. As she neared completion, the sounds of the four 1200 HP Wright-Cyclone engines could heard across the desert.

In August 1987, "Nine-O-Nine" crashed while performing at an air show in Western Pennsylvania. It found itself in a severe crosswind just moments after touchdown. The crew was unable to keep it from rolling off the end of the runway. It crashed through a chain link fence and it plummeted down a 10 foot ravine, coming to a stop with extensive damage. The landing gear sheared off, the chin turret was smashed and the Plexiglas nose was shattered. There was extensive damage to the bomb bay doors, the ball turret and the wing. The engines and propellers were shattered, but luckily there were no fatalities to the crew nor passengers although there were injuries. Once again this B-17 was not to be buried. Thousands of citizens from Beaver Falls donated money and time to help to restore the proud heritage of a B-17.

Other Important Airplanes

"Liberator Pride[7]"

Those who flew in the B-24 Liberator had a legitimate complaint, because the newsmen and women who were taken in by the name of "Flying Fortress." Freeman writes that, "When it came to an individual's chance for survival, statistics reveal that there was little to choose between them."

The B-24 was created by Consolidated Corporation in 1938. Its two large tails were ovals which made it more difficult to fly. The very large fuselage gave it the name "flying boxcar" which controlled the oceans. In 1942, they were transferred to Italy in the 15th Air Force. Few people realize that there were more B-24s on D-Day than any other combat units.

The B-24 could fly faster and farther than the B-17, and more B-24s were built – 19,000 compared to just over 12,000 for the B-17. It was a shoulder mounted Davis wing, named after David R. Davis. The Royal Air Force preferred the B-24. Because of its range, it was more suitable for the Pacific. While the B-17s were bombing Berlin, the B-24s were bombing Japan.

There is a restored B-24 in the Duxford Museum.

The WASP Contribution

The WASPs (Women's Auxiliary Flying Squad) were created in 1942 by a famous woman's aviator – Nancy Harkness Love. She was given the authority by General Hap Arnold to put together a squadron of women flyers who would ferry aircraft from factories to Bomb Groups. She was joined by Jackie Cochran, who was authorized by Arnold to train other pilots for the WASPs. This created two separate women's training detachments, which in April 1943 were combined as WASPs in Sweetwater, Texas. They were known as the 318 Flying Training

---

[7] This name was given to the B-24 by Roger Freeman in the September 2017 issue of the *8th AF News*.

Detachment.

Their primary duties were to test and ferry planes to and tow targets for gunnery practice. This seemed like a safe duty, but many recruits were learning to fire anti-aircraft weapons. Once in a while this led to a romantic finish. Deanie Bishop noticed a handsome B-24 pilot, Bill Parrish, while she was towing a target. Parrish told his gunners to shoot the tail off her plane. Nothing romantic came of this ending, but it could be called flirting in the air.

It sounded like an easy program to graduate from, but the statistics make that a lie. Of the 1,879 women who were accepted into the program, only 1,074 graduated. This washout rate broke many hearts, because those who succeeded knew these numbers would determine the future of women in aviation history. Their future, however, was established by the number of males who did not want women in aviation.

The women created a magazine, which they named *The Fifinella Gazette*. In the second issue, Jackie Cochran wrote, "You of the first classes have the real responsibility. By your actions and results the future course will be set." But there was substantial opposition from the male ranks to have women flying. But the women had an important man on their side.

Speaking to the last graduating class, General Hap Arnold told them, "Certainly we have not been able to build an airplane you can't handle. From AT6s to B-29s, you have flown them around like veterans. One of the WASPs has even test flown our new jet plane." He added, "It is on the record that women can fly as well as men."

On December 20, 1944, the WASP was disbanded[8].

---

[8] Some of this information was taken from *The Elks Magazine,* June 2017.

Chapter Twelve
Destroying the German Oil Industry

The Eighth Air Force did not strike at oil industry targets until May 13, 1944 when 749 bombers, escorted by almost 740 fighters, pounded oil targets in the *Leipzig* area and at *Brux* in Czechoslovakia. At the same time, a smaller force hit an FW 190 repair depot at *Zwickau*. Over 300 German fighters attacked the bomber forces, losing almost half its aircraft, with claims of upwards of 47 *Luftwaffe* fighters by American fighter pilots. However, the *Luftwaffe* was successful in shooting down 46 bombers in a very unequal fight.

After D-Day, these attacks on the German oil industry were a top priority which was widely dispersed around the *Reich*. Vast fleets of B-24s and B-17s escorted by P-51Ds and long-range P-38Ls hit refineries in Germany and Czechoslovakia in late 1944 and early 1945. Having almost total air superiority throughout the collapsing German *Reich,* the Eighth Air Force hit targets as far east as Hungary, while the Fifteenth Air Force hit oil industry facilities in Yugoslavia, Romania, and northeastern Italy. On at least eighteen occasions, the *Merseburg* refineries in Leuna, where the majority of Germany's synthetic fuel for jet aircraft was refined, was hit. By the end of 1944, only three out of ninety-one refineries in the *Reich* were still working normally, twenty-nine were partially functional, and the remainder were completely destroyed.

Sid Golden, a photo-gunner who flew with us to *Leipzig,* wrote me a very interesting letter on the details of this mission:

"I had been briefed for this target twice before, and now it caught up with me. It should be a dilly, for once again, Sam Catalano and I were going out on the same raid. When those

Joes in the barrack saw Sam and I both get up, how they groaned. That's not much of a compliment, but it seems that when Sam and I go out on the same raid, all hell breaks loose. It's always a nightmare. Today, however, was the pay-off, we were both flying the same ship – the "Wolf Wagon" – with Danny Houghton and his boys. This crew contains the nuttiest bunch of hotrocks this side of *Potsdamplatz*.

"At first we did not think we would get off the ground as number three engine would not warm up. But dammit it was fixed and off we went to try and catch up with the formation. Houghton caught up with them but how he ever got into that formation to take his position is a mystery that will go down in the annals of combat. One minute we were outside the formation, and the next, zip, we were inside. How those wing men must have cursed him. He flew so tight, that for a while it looked as though our top turret would touch the ball turret of the ship above us. But I felt pretty safe with him. For that boy can fly. He will even tell you if you ask him. But that's the beauty of it, he can prove it.

"Looking out, all I could see was wave after wave of Forts. This was not just a raid, but a planned assault. The entire 8th was out today, and all going in the same direction. About Mid-channel, I started to test fire the gun in the Radio Room, but it was off. All she'd do was brrup, and stop, and brrup and stop. The oil buffer was cockeyed. So, I ripped out the guts, and fixed it. Now it fired like it was intended to. I got into the camera hatch as we crossed the Enemy Coast, and took several pictures, also of the route in. It was a long ride, and our escort was in with us. However, they left us for just a few minutes while we were changing escorts. After all, those little peashooters had to protect their own rears. Some enemy planes came by but they did not bother us.

"In due time, we hit the I.P., and the flak started coming up. It was heavy stuff, and damn accurate. To add to that, we were getting ground rockets thrown up at us, and every time I'd see one of those white trails of smoke, my scalp would crawl. I don't know how anyone else felt about that particular stuff, but it sure scared hell out of this boy. If one of those things blows up in a formation, it's sure fire curtains for somebody. I'd rather see my insurance lapse. Then came 'Bombs Away', and I started to grind away. Our bombs fell into the city, and I got some good shots of it all. But that flak was just thumping the hell out of our bottom, and it felt like it was ripping the ship apart. Then bomb bay doors closed, and "LET'S GET THE HELL OUT OF HERE." But that stuff just tracked us all over the sky, and only when we were out of range did we shake it. Looking back, I could see just a solid wall of black, and how anything got through it was still a mystery. But we paid our price of admission, and left some of our ships behind.

During all that time, the conversation over the intercom was really something to hear. Houghton was telling Gus Bolino (Navigator) all about Penny. She was a pert little blonde, stacked up tighter than a Bomber Formation at a Bandit Call. She was a slick chick. Later on, as we were nearing the Channel, our Navigator turned on the radio to the German broadcast Band, and we heard "Command Performance." Axis Sally came on to spiel about the raid. That babe must have her head up and locked, for according to their figures, we must be a ghost home. Then England and home, after a damn long day."

After D-Day, attacks on the German oil industry assumed top priority which was widely dispersed around the *Reich*. Vast fleets of B-24s and B-17s escorted by P-51Ds and long-range P-38s hit refineries in Germany and Czechoslovakia in late 1944 and early 1945. Having almost total air superiority throughout the collapsing German *Reich*, the Eighth Air Force hit targets as far east as Hungary, while Fifteenth Air Force hit oil industry facilities in Yugoslavia, Romania, and northeastern Italy. On at least eighteen occasions, the Merseburg refineries in Leuna, where the majority of Germany's synthetic fuel for jet aircraft was refined, was hit.

Our fifth mission, on May 12, was a long one to *Brux*, Czechoslovakia – 650 miles from London. We were in the B Group, following the 96th Bomb Group. There was a savage resistance from German fighters, which pounded the 96th. The B Group had excellent results, but the A Group had problems on the bomb run. One of the German fighters, a Messerschmitt 410, banked off Lt. Manuel Head's plane and we believed that it was shot down by our engineer, Bob Vogt. The picture of the plane banking was one of the most famous of World War II, and it engendered a lot of controversy. Our plane-(3395) was in front and to the Right of Head's.

This ME 410 was shot down by our top gunner.
This is one of the best photos of WWII taken by Victor La Bruno.

I received a copy of that photograph from Victor La Bruno, our photo gunner, who signed it "In memories of some rough times." But our engineer, Bob Vogt, told me on June 23, 2001 that Patrick O'Keefe, who was flying photo gunner in our plane, gave him (Vogt) a picture of the ME with O'Keefe's name on it. Bob said that Pat stuck his camera in the window of the radio room to take the picture. Unfortunately, our radioman, Ken Fitz, died in 2000 so we cannot confirm this.

Bob thinks that the picture shows our wing, not Head's. He said that there was a very large hole where the shell just missed the gasoline tank. He claims that if you look carefully at the picture, there appears to be a hole to the left of the letter H. If Manny Head's wing does not have a hole in it, then this must be our wing.

THE 8TH AIR FORCE WON THE WAR IN EUROPE

When the ME 410 banked off our wing, I was shooting at it with my right 50 caliber gun. At an instant after the photo was taken, the German plane was hit. I talked to our co-pilot, Julian "Tex" Carr," also on June 23 and he said that the engine cowl flew off first and then "several pieces came off the plane." He told me that he said to Bob Vogt at that time, "You nailed that one Bob." Vogt confirms that he thought he had shot the ME down, but he did not claim it at briefing.

There are a lot of questions concerning who shot down the ME 410, and a letter from a German historian complicates matters:

Dear Sir,

My name is Gerhard Kaschuba, and I'm a historian working at a high school in Munich, Germany. In addition, I'm very interested in the aerial warfare of World War II. At that time, my uncle was a pilot in the *Luftwaffe*. He was killed on May 12, 1944.

Presently I'm preparing a research project on the May 12 event. This was a day of a great American air strike on German oil plants in the *Leipzig* area and *Brux/Bohemia*. The 388th took part on that mission, bombed *Brux* and was twice attacked by Germans on the way back to England. The Germans belonged to the 2nd Group of the Heavy Fighter Unit 26 and were equipped with 26 aircraft of the type Me-410. My uncle, 2nd Lt. Paul Kaschuba and his radio operator Sgt. Karl Bredemeir, were involved in that attack and died that day.

Their aircraft had the registration number Black 13. There is a photo, taken by Victor LaBruno, radio operator of your aircraft, which shows a German 410. There is a possibility that this is my uncle's plane.

My questions are:

Which bomb squadron did you belong to? What are the names of your crew? The above-cited photograph shows a Me-410 turning to the right. The person who shot down that plane was supposed to be top turret gunner T/Sgt. L.S. Cadena. Is that correct?

I kindly ask if you could write down the memory that you have of this event. I'm especially interested in a description of the attacks of the German twin engine planes in the Saxony area on your way back. How would you judge the attacks of the Germans? How did the Germans attack that day, and from which direction - in climb or descent attack?

Yours Sincerely,
Dr. Gerhard Kaschuba Carl-von-Linde-Str. 7 85716

Lt Manuel Head responded:

Dear Dr. Kaschuba,

I have wondered who might have been flying the German fighters attacking our formations, and after some 50 years your letter arrives. Quite a surprise! I doubt that we can ever identify the crew. The photograph taken by Victor LaBruno was exactly what I saw when I turned my head to see what had disturbed my right wing. I recall saying, "What in the hell is he doing here?" And in a fraction of a second it was all over. The only identification we can make must come from the picture, and I see nothing there that would be unique to your uncle's plane. You will note from the enclosed copy of the 12 May 44, *Brux* mission summary from 'The 388th at War" that we were attacked by a number of Me-410s plus Me-109s and FW- 190s. The tail gunner on our crew (Donald W. Sestak) claimed two Me-109s, and a waist gunner (James F. Coker) claimed a probable Me-109.

Victor LaBruno was assigned to my crew for this mission only. He was stationed in the radio room with Joseph A. DeSantis, the radio operator. During the mission they shared the open hatch above the radio room with one .50 caliber machine gun. When the Me-410 attacked, they were struggling with each other for room to shoot. LaBruno obviously won, and got his photo.

In the copy of the summary of this mission from 'The Mighty Eighth War Diary" you see that we put up 886 heavy bombers (814 effective) aimed primarily at oil production. Our 3rd Bomb Division sent 140 planes to *Brux*. Most of those planes probably came from the three bomb groups (96th. 388th. 452nd) that formed our 45th Bomb Wins. The 96th BG and the 452nd BG formed the lead wing of three aerial groups into *Brux*. The 388th BG and I surmise the 452nd BG, formed the second aerial wing into *Brux*. The 13th Bomb Wing must have formed a third wing to attack *Brux*.

Now note the losses attributed to each bomb group. The 96th BG lost 12 B-17s and the 452nd lost 14; we, the 388th lost one. The other groups had similar, single digit losses. We watched that battle from Frankfurt to *Brux*. The *Luftwaffe* formed ahead and above the B-17 s, dove head-on through the formation, turned clockwise, climbed and then repeated the attack.

They were like a swarm of wasps. Each attack was awesome. Planes collided, explosions occurred; B-17 s drifted back from the formation. Debris floated down and then came the parachutes, forming a staircase of white blossoms.

The radio traffic was minimal, just terse comments, but on one attack a B-17 pulled straight up and hung there while the radio advised a deputy leader to take over. After a few passes the *Luftwaffe's* arm began to thin and stretch out as their losses mounted. Then we were near the IP and the *Luftwaffe* departed. My recollection is that the attack on the 388th BG was all from the rear. I saw nothing of the battle, except for the Me 410 peeling off my wing, and 2nd Lt. Loslo's B-17 with a fire beneath his wing, near one engine's exhaust. That fire flared like an aluminum-magnesium fire as the crew contemplated their options.

Soon the nearby crews got anxious, and radioed him to move away from the formation. The pilot complied, but his neighbors still considered him too close, so he drifted further back. Suddenly the rear fuselage door flew off. A crewman sat in the doorway with his feet dangling. He took several looks down, but made no move to jump; finally someone made up his mind for this first crewman. He shot out of the doorway as if ejected, and the rest of the crew followed like trained 'chutists.

As to your questions:

My squadron is the 562nd Bomb Squadron, 388th Bomb Group, 45th Combat Wing, 3rd Air Division, 8th Air Force.

Over the years I had three crews. The 3rd Head crew had a whole new set of crewmen. I do not have the names of 3rd Head crew.

The name of our plane, *Lady Godiva,* was painted on the nose behind the crew. We named it *Lady Godiva* because it has no camouflage; it was bare, nude. The plane was #42-97184.

T/Sgt. LS. Cadena was the only top turret gunner in a 561st Bomb Squadron plane that claimed a Me-410 destroyed. He was most likely in some other aerial squadron. My summary of the 562nd gunners that encountered Me-410s is: three are destroyed, six probably, one damaged, and one no claim. How you narrow the search from here, I don't know.

I don't recall any attacks on the return trip; so if they occurred they made no impression. In the excerpt from "A History of the 452nd Bombardment Group" in re the *Brux* mission, there is a page from "The First and the Last" by Adolph Galland wherein he writes that a second sortie was successfully mounted by the *Luftwaffe*.

How would I judge the attacks of the Germans that day? Aggressive. Head-on attacks from 12 o'clock high were devastating.

The attack on the first wing demonstrated that. Why did the Me-410s attack from the tail? Perhaps they were less maneuverable, perhaps a tail attack was required because of the mix of airplane types (Me-410s, FW-190s, Me-109s), perhaps the pilots were being introduced to combat against the heavy bombers.

From which direction? From listening to the gunners, the *Luftwaffe* came in level on our heading. Our tail gunner stated that each of the Me-109s bore straight in toward his twin .50 calibers

Signed by Manuel Head

It is obvious that we will never know who shot down the ME 410, because there were more than two planes firing away at it.

To return to our "Wolf Wagon" missions, on our ninth mission to *Liege*, Belgium, on May 25, the lead plane (Colonel Chamberlain) and the deputy lead (Lt. Warren) were both shot down by anti-aircraft fire. All the planes scattered to avoid collisions, so our pilot, Dan Houghton, got on the inter-com and told the group that we were taking over. He called me for a heading to the target, but since I was looking at and shooting at

German fighters, I had to guess at a heading. I used my fingers on my map and I said take a 15 degree turn, which turned out O.K.

The Belgian underground was warned of our coming mission, but we learned at de-briefing that the Germans must have picked up our message. When we got close to the IP we started our bomb run, but we over-shot the IP.

I said to Dan, "Let someone else lead."

Dan yelled, "Hell no. We're taking over."

We bombed the target, and when we returned to base, we were told that we would be given Distinguished Flying Crosses for rallying the group and saving the mission. In some cases, the DFC was given out routinely, but we felt we had earned ours.

On June 4 and June 5, we pounded the Germans in a pre-invasion blitz. The targets were in the *Cape Gris Nez* area. We didn't get any sleep, because pre-briefing was at 23:30 (11:30 p.m) on June 5. The general briefing was particularly tense. We knew it was the big one. General Eisenhower spoke to all of us about what he called our Great Crusade.

Chapter Thirteen
Our Fighter Escorts

Many lines have been written in our newsletters with few lines concerning "Our Insurance Policy" which was furnished by the young and bold fighter pilots who escorted us during our combat missions. They saved a great number of our aircrews from the savage attacks by the *Luftwaffe* fighters which were encountered every day. Many of us owe our lives to the outstanding valor and skill these young men showed every day.

Shortly before his death, Albert Geiger furnished me with a story that I think is worthy to publish. Al was the flight engineer and top turret gunner of the Thurman Esselmeyer crew which was shot down on a mission *to Ludwigshaven* on November 5, 1944. Al finished the war as a POW.

A close friend of Al's was noted WWII Fighter Ace Col. C.E. (Bud) Anderson, who was a member of the 357th Fighter Group, 8th Air Force, based at *Leiston*, England. Bud Anderson had 16.5 confirmed kills in WWII with his P-51 "Old Crow," which I am sure is known by many of you. The 357th Fighter Group was the first to have P-51s and had the most confirmed victories of any Fighter Unit during the War.

In our files is a photo of a P-51 escorting us on a mission. Bud Anderson has identified this aircraft as being flown by 1st Lt. Gerald E. Tyler from the 362nd Fighter Squadron of the 357th Fighter Group. The name of his aircraft was "Little Duckfoot." Gerald Tyler had seven confirmed kills to his credit.

THE 8TH AIR FORCE WON THE WAR IN EUROPE

North American P-51D Mustang "Kimberly Kaye"

It is exciting, after so many years, to find another piece of history that was caught by one of our 388th photographers, and to actually learn the rest of the story.

I know most of you who flew combat were very thankful that these intrepid young American aviators flying the P-51s, P47s. P-38s and those skillful aviators of the Royal Air Force in their Spits and Hurricanes were there to try to insure our safe passage through the enemy skies.

The P-38 Lightning. The Germans called them "fork-tailed devil."

One day we were in the middle of Germany at 25,000 feet when we noted two fighters – a *Focke-Wulf* 190 and P-38 – in a battle about 5,000 feet above our group.

The *Focke-Wulf* 190 got behind the P-38 and destroyed one of its engines. The pilot contacted us, asking if we could help him. Our lead pilot got on the intercom and said, "Open up for our little brother."

All the B-17s scattered and re-grouped with the P-38 in the middle. It was an odd sight as we got to our target.

On the way home, when we got to the English coast, the pilot said "Thank you all" as he dipped his wing, broke away from us, and waved his hat.

We were happy to save one of our little brothers who saved many of our B-17s every day.

Chapter Fourteen
Our Two D-Day Missions

Our most memorable missions were on D-Day, June 6, 1944. The 388th Bomb Group was the first over the target, as we led the 45th Combat Wing. We didn't get much sleep, because pre-briefing was at 23:30 (11:30 p.m) on June 5. The general briefing was particularly tense. We knew it was the big one. General Eisenhower said that we were about to embark on a "Great Crusade[9]," but he hinted that our losses would be heavy.

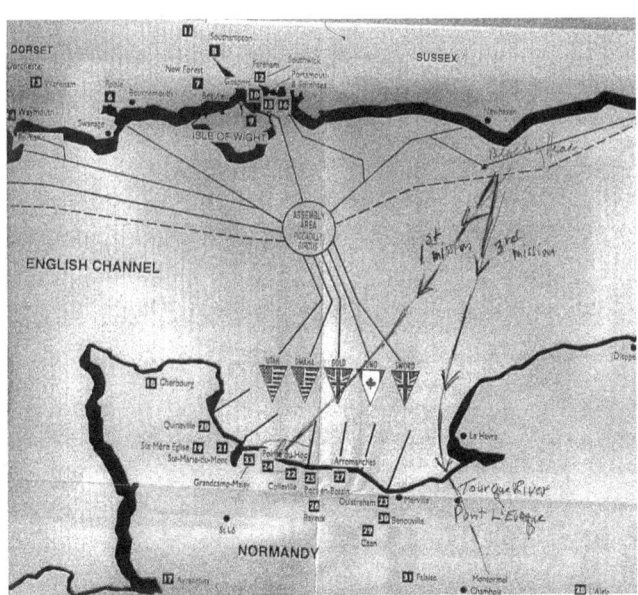

Mission photo provided by A. Bolino

---

[9] When Eisenhower left the military, he became President of Columbia University and during his stay there he wrote a book that he called *The Great Crusade*.

Seventy-two years later, I decided to telephone the surviving member of our crew: Charlie Kemp, our bombardier. When I finished talking to him about D-Day, I remembered a course I took at the University of Michigan in 1947 in psychology. The professor was lecturing on the human brain, and he said that under stress, the brain deteriorates. Apparently there was a lot brain deterioration among our crew, because we didn't agree on much, so I did what Al Smith said to do when he ran for President, "Let's look at the record."

Our crew flew the first and third missions on D-Day. In reviewing this history, I referred to four sources: my fortieth anniversary audio cassette, which I dictated on June 6, 1984; Ed Huntzinger's *388th At War*; the mission statements of the National Archives and the June 18, 1944 *Yank* magazine, in which Saul Leavitt, a Yank reporter, flew on the first mission with Jim Gabler's crew[10].

Stephen Ambrose in his book on D-Day offered a few bits of information about D-Day. He states that the allies flew 1400 sorties that day. Before we bombed on the morning mission of June 6, the British landed 130 men near Pointe du Hoc, who used a homing device called Eureka to get to their target, which was our target also. On that famous day, 2,876,000 Allied troops were involved, and there were 10,500 planes and 5,000 ships crossing the English Channel. By the time we took off for our second mission, there were already over 100,000 troops on the French beach. The U. S. Army Air Corps put in the air the largest air force ever committed to battle in a single day.

D-Day was the continuation of an unusual three-day episode. June 4 was a Sunday and there was some kind of celebration going on at the base so we got little sleep for that mission to Wissant, France. On June 5, we were supposed to go on the invasion, but it was postponed, so we bombed Cape Gris Nez,

---

[10] For those who are interested in doing research on our missions at the national archives, as President of the 388th Bomb Group Association I gave information on getting mission statements by mail. Write to the National Archives, College Park Branch, and ask for Record Group 18, stack Area 190, Row 58, Boxes 1200-1300.

THE 8TH AIR FORCE WON THE WAR IN EUROPE

France as a diversionary target. Again, little sleep. On D-Day, during the navigators pre-briefing, I received all the maps and general instructions concerning flak batteries, and I was told that our target was a 16 inch gun on the coast at Point du Hoc that was encased in tons of concrete on a hillside.

H hour was scheduled for 06:30 a.m., when the Higgins boats, with just two feet of draft, were to land. After we bombed, the 2nd Ranger's Battalion was scheduled to use steel hooks to scale the 100 foot cliff to get to the 150 millimeter gun if we failed to take it out.

When the landing crafts approached the beach, the leaders of the boats decided that they could not reverse the boats to leave the shore, so they ordered all GIs to jump into the water and make it to the beach. They must not have remembered that those GIs were carrying 65-70 pounds on their backs. When they jumped into the water, they sank and never came up. The estimates are that 4,000 of the GIs drowned. This was about 44% of all the dead on D-Day, when 9,200 died.

At briefing, the Colonel told us that there was no place to ditch, so all pilots were to make sure that they could make it to France and back before heading over the Channel. Ordinarily, if you had trouble getting back to the base you could ditch in the Channel, usually nose up, and air-sea rescue would pick you from your last position, after you gave a "mayday mayday" signal.

During navigation training, we practiced ditching, and we were supposed to evacuate the B-17 in 30 seconds, the average time it would float. We were also told during briefing that "Guns will be manned but not test fired. Gunners will not fire at any planes unless attacked." Also, "No secondary runs will be made on any primary target."

After briefing, we took the jitney to our plane. For the first mission, the 388th supplied two groups. Our group was headed by Lt. Colonel Cox, with Lt Col. Henggeler as deputy leader. You might be interested in knowing how Leavitt described Col. Cox. He wrote, "Lt. Chester C. Cox, of Superior, Wisconsin, strolled around operations with his hands in his pockets. This morning flying in the lead ship of the earliest formation of American heavy bombers to cross the enemy coast on D-Day, had given him the honor of being the first U. S. bombardment pilot to drop bombs in direct support of the landings in France."

It was a very epic occasion but a very routine mission. We took off at 02:19 and we assembled over Buncher 10 to 20,000 feet. Our pilots, Dan Houghton, and co-pilot, Julian "Tex" Carr took us up in aircraft 666, which, I believe was an old plane named "Quarterback." We were part of the A Group of 16 aircraft and 2 PFF planes. Our objective was a German battery, which could fire as much as 13 miles off shore.

The takeoff was over four or five trees that were at the end of the runway, which is another story. When we took off with bomb loads about one-third heavier than normal, we needed the whole runway to just make it over those trees, and we often hit the leaves. Our Commander Colonel Goodman had gone earlier to the local constabulary to ask if we could cut them down. He said that when we are gone, the trees would be there still. He was correct, when we returned to Knettishall in 2003 for the 60th anniversary tour that I sponsored, those trees were still there.

At 03:58, we headed for the English coast at Beachy Head, which is a triangular piece of land about 15 miles east of Brighton Beach in Southern England. We made it to the target on a heading of 238 degrees. The flight was a milk run, and because it was 10/10ths undercover, the targets were attacked by PFF methods, Bombs were away at 06:56 hours from 15,050 feet. After bombs away, according to the official mission statement, "An excellent pattern of release was noted." We encountered no flak or enemy aircraft, although there were 25 ground rockets fired at us near the target. All aircraft returned over Beachy Head for letdown and landing." We landed at 10:00 a.m.

According to Stephen Ambrose, in the two months before D-Day, the Allied Air Forces lost 12,000 men and 2,000 planes. Nevertheless, we were able to put 1,200 Flying Fortresses in the air for the D-Day landing. I remember well standing at the astrodome and looking in all directions and seeing nothing but contrails. What an impressive sight. On that one day, The 8th Air Force dropped more tonnage in two hours than all the bombs dropped on Hamburg in 1943—the most heavily bombed city of Europe in World War II.

THE 8ᵀᴴ AIR FORCE WON THE WAR IN EUROPE

After we returned to our base, we had a very quick debriefing and we all hit the sack totally exhausted. Very soon after, our sleep was interrupted by a sergeant with a flashlight who yelled "Mission." I can't tell you the exact words we shouted at him, but it meant "go away." We thought he was joking, because we had never flown two missions in one day before.

He said, "You have to go back out again because 'the mission is in jeopardy.'" At the second briefing, the major told us that "the Germans are pushing us into the sea." He said that ordinarily we flew strategic missions with designated targets, but this second mission it would be a tactical mission to support our troops.

Then he explained the difference. When the Germans invaded Poland on September 3, 1939, the Brits sent 300 spies into Germany. All of which spoke perfect German. Their primary job was to keep track of the anti-aircraft guns. Each day at midnight they sent the results to London using their short-wave radios. When London got the message, the flight planners chose a target for the next morning. This is a strategic mission. A tactical mission has no such plan. Each plane chooses its own target and altitude, but he concluded by saying you must hit a target that is heading south to kill Americans.

For me, this was a more difficult mission. As you know, the B-17 has a nose hatch that is above your head. When I first saw a Flying Fortress, I learned why we had to do all those chin ups in navigation school. Well, on the second mission of June 6, I couldn't make it up wearing my flying suit, Mae West jacket, flak suit and carrying a parachute. I only had about four hours sleep in two days. You might remember that Gregory Peck had the same problem in "Twelve O' Clock High." I got to the nose by the rear door, crawling through the bomb bay.

Colonel David led our second mission, which took off at 17:37 p.m., and we assembled over buncher 10 at 12,000 feet. The instrument assembly was achieved at 24,000 feet over Knettishall. We flew next to buncher 12 and we circled waiting for the 452ⁿᵈ A Group that was 5 minutes late. Lt Kneemeyer was lead pilot in aircraft 627, and we were just behind him flying in 666 again. There were 17 aircraft and only 1 PFF airplane that started out.

We left the English coast at 15,000 feet at 19:55 hours, and we reached the IP (the initial point of the bomb run) at 20:15 at 20,000 feet. We had no primary target, but I suggested that we go back to the Normandy beach and turn left up the coast of France.

After several turns, we headed north and I saw two black lines on the horizon. I was baffled, so decided that I would check each two minutes. I saw nothing I knew at two, four and six minutes. On the eight minute I saw horizontal objects across the blacklines and I knew what it was. I phoned our pilot Dan and I informed him that here was a railroad depot ahead, and we agreed to make it our target.

I called our bombardier who was sitting behind me. I pointed to the object ahead, and I asked if he would prefer the Norden bomb site or his eye sight. He chose the Norden, and he set the instrument for 12 minutes. At the time of the setting, when the rear white line touched the stationery white line, the bomb bay doors opened and the bombs headed down to totally destroy the depot. This "target of opportunity" was a "railroad choke point in the southern part of Flers."

The mission report tells us that we bombed at 22,000 at 20:58. It was a visual bomb run at Pont L'Eveque on a heading of 160 degrees. The target was on the Touques River, about 20-25 miles east of Caen. Bomb Kerns, our ball turret gunner, said that on the second bomb run, he turned his guns straight down and he could see the structure of the bridge that we bombed. He said he heard the "clack-clack," those were his words, of the anti-aircraft guns that were firing at us. He also mentioned all the gliders that were on the ground in various positions, some crashed into trees. I can confirm that we could see gliders.

The June 18 *Yank* magazine wrote that on our second mission "There were broken clouds below us and through them we saw the first real glimpse of the invasion. You could see the miles-long columns of ships moving the herds across the waters." This is confirmed by the book *388th at War*, which states that "on our second mission there was a $5/10^{th}$ to $7/10^{th}$ cloud cover." so we were able to see the ground.

The mission statement also tells us that there were only 12 planes that reached the IP at 20,000 feet on a mag heading of 148 degrees, and the strike photos showed that we did not hit the MPI, (maximum point of impact) but we did hit a choke point and a road intersection.

We returned to Knettishall at 23:40, which was over 25 hours later than when we first started out on June 5. Six of our aircraft landed at other fields, probably because of bad weather. When I talked to our bombardier, Charles Kemp, about the second mission he said that using a B-17 for tactical missions is a mistake, because of the great danger of hitting your own troops and pattern bombing is too wide for close engagement. This is confirmed by Stephen Ambrose, who wrote that the B-17 raids were a bust "because of the weather and the airmen not wanting to hit their own troops ... most blockbusters came down in Norman meadows."

The crew of "Wolf Wagon" after bombing mission, 1944.
L-R: Charles Kemp, Bombardier; John Hollister, Waist Gunner; Robert Vogt, Engineer; Daniel Houghton, Pilot; Julian Carr, Co-Pilot; Robert Kern, Ball Turret; Ken Fitz, Radio. Photo provided by A. Bolino.

When we finally returned to our barracks, we were allowed to sleep all day on June 7, but we had a mission on June 8 to Tours, France. It was designed to give cover to the troops that were invading. The B-17s and the B-24s bombarded bridges, railroad depots and nearby air fields. On June 11 about 2,000 American warplanes, including 1,000 Flying Fortresses destroyed Nazi supply and communication lines. June 14 was our nineteenth mission—this time to St. Trand, Belgium. It continued the tactical missions of the previous days, but this time losses were heavier. The 8th Air Force lost 131 bombers.

On the next day 1,300 bombers blasted Germans at Beauver, France. They hit an air field at Bordeaux, railroad bridges and an aircraft assembly plant. All of these post D-Day missions were designed to holdoff the Germans from attacking American soldiers.

There is one more story about D-Day that I cannot omit. I asked my wife several times if we could go back to Normandy so I could see where we bombed and why we did not take that gun out of operation. She always said no, until one day in May in 2014 she called me to the kitchen to ask me why we have not gone back to Normandy. I told her, I will make all of the plans.

A week later we flew to Paris, got on a bus to Point du Hoc, and I walked down into the very large gun. The walls and ceilings were three foot thick of concrete, so I knew we could not destroy it with 500 pound bombs.

I turned around and headed up to the street when I saw three soldiers marching toward me with guns on their shoulders. When they got to me they saluted and thanked me for my service. As I turned around I saw nothing but white crosses facing me.

I asked the superintendent, "How many graves are there?"

He answered, "9,200."

I could not believe the number, so I asked, "Were they all killed on D-Day?"

He answered, "Yes."

I left the three of them speechless. When we returned home, I went my computer to ask Google if the 9,200 is the largest number of soldiers killed in a single day. The answer surprised me. The largest number killed on a single day occurred in World War I, when a British Colonel ordered his troops to leave the trench and attack the German trench that was only 150 yards away. The Germans had mounted several machine guns on top of their trench. When the order was completed, 13,700 British were dead, making the 9,200 second highest.

THE 8TH AIR FORCE WON THE WAR IN EUROPE

Another Photographer

Sid Golden and Patrick O'Keefe shared their duties as photo man on the "Wolf Wagon." When T/Sgt. Patrick O'Keefe was stationed at Knettishall, he saw action in 27 heavy bombardment missions over enemy occupied Europe between March, 16, 1944 and July, 17, 1944 flying in B17s. He too was assigned with the 562nd Bomb Squadron.

During that time, they were usually the 11th man in the B17 as the aerial photographer. They also qualified as flight engineers and turret gunners. Many of their missions were in the "Wolf Wagon" with Lt. Daniel G. Houghton, pilot. O'Keefe, who was awarded the Distinguished Flying Cross, was discharged in September 1945, and he died on September 29, 2010.

On June 29, our 23rd mission, we returned to *Leipzig* to bomb the German synthetic oil plant and other targets deep in the heart of Germany. Our 24th mission was very unusual. The code word for the mission was "No Ball." It was aimed at the V-2 rocket launches at the Pas de Calais area. Prime Minister Winston Churchill told his people that this mission destroyed 100 ramps for the robot installations.

The July 8 mission was a harrowing experience, because the Germans were stung by the damage done to their rockets on the previous day. They sought revenge with more planes in the air and more rockets from the ground. As we flew over Mantes, France a burst of flak hit our left wing, and we were on fire. The two pilots told us to hold on as they made a severe dive. We went from 25,000 feet to about 700 hundred, which put out the fire. When we levelled off Dan Houghton told us to check our parachutes. He wasn't sure we could make it all the way back. The oxygen test was my job, so I called out "oxygen test." Each person had a number, which they responded by. They all answered from one to ten.

We flew towards our base with one engine feathered. In the commotion, the right waist gunner called me on the intercom to tell me that Staff Sargent John Hollister's eyeball was hanging out, and he asked me, "What shall I do with it?"

I told him, "Push it back in and tape it."

When we landed the ambulance was waiting for us, and it took him quickly to a flight to Walter Reed Hospital in Washington, D. C. They could not save the eye, but when I met him several years later, I learned that he was given a glass eye and he was granted a dispensation that allowed him to stay in the Air Force so that he could fly until he reached twenty years of service.

THE 8TH AIR FORCE WON THE WAR IN EUROPE

Chapter Fifteen
Our Monthly Leaves

Once a month we were given a two-or three-day pass in London, and this was an interesting episode because London, of course, was blacked out and was constantly being bombed. On my first leave, I briefly sat alone in a pub and a British soldier asked if he could join me. Of course, I welcomed him. After we introduced ourselves he began to talk about surviving the blitz with a stiff upper lip, and he joked about sheltering an army of tens of thousands of American soldiers, who were making do without complaint on a minimum of food. "It's a myth," he said. And he emphasized the difference between myth and reality.

I hesitated to ask him what I wanted to know. "Is it true that crime in London is up?" I asked.

He was not sure how to respond. "Crime in wartime London is really at a minimum. There is some looting, but few Londoners behaved badly." Before I could say anything, he spoke up, "The people of London endured the blitz with dignity and courage and they retained their good humor."

I felt the need to bolster him. "You English do not fully appreciate the great discipline of your people. The blitz was the high time of your resistance to Hitler, so you should be proud of what you have accomplished after nearly six years of being bombed. As you would say, you have had a stiff upper lip from the blackout to rationing to homelessness to unexploded bombs. And the Germans were sending over their buzz bombs which had just enough fuel to go so far and then would head down and then become a flying bomb. They were, in fact, called flying bombs."

"Thanks, Yank. You've bucked me up a bit," he told me as I was about to leave.

A few odd things happened in my trips to London. The first one was on me. I was to meet our crew in a restaurant, so when I got off the train I caught a taxi and gave him the address. He said, 'Righto Yank," and drove off. It seemed like a long way. When he stopped he said, 'That's a pound, Yank." So I paid him what was equal to the exchange rate of 4 dollars and 3 cents. When he drove off I could see the restaurant and it was close to where I got on the taxi. I was cheated.

The second thing one had to learn was the blackout. There was not a light anywhere. No one could even light a cigarette outdoors. It took several days to learn how to navigate the streets in total darkness. One evening I was walking very slowly down a street when I felt a cold hand on my face.

"How about it, Yank. Five pounds and breakfast in bed."

I was temporarily shocked by the price and the offer.

"No thank you," I answered.

She swore at me with an F word, so when I entered a Pub I asked a Brit why there were so many prostitutes in England. His response was serious and well done. "We have been in this war for five years and many women lost their husbands. They really are destitute and they are hungry. There are very few farmers now. Most have gone into battle, so we really depend on the USA for sustenance."

I thought his answer was first rate, and from that time I felt sorry for all the women who were street walkers.

The third interesting development I encountered was the restaurants. They simply had no food to offer you. They always offered an omelet that was made with powdered eggs. I learned from my fellow officers that the only source of good food was at the Covent Gardens, where you could get high tea for a few pounds and you could dance with one of the many hostesses. The many sandwiches that were served were small but elegant. It seemed true that the rich are never hungry. In 2003, when I took a group to Knettishall we visited Covent Gardens, and our guide did not believe me when I told her of this story. Later, she came back and apologized for her error.

On one leave we were in a hotel when a wing of the

THE 8TH AIR FORCE WON THE WAR IN EUROPE

hotel was hit by a flying bomb. It scared the hell out of us. And, in fact, after that I decided I would rather go to Cambridge. First, because it was a university town and didn't involve a long train ride, and also because I didn't see any sense in going to London and risking being bombed.

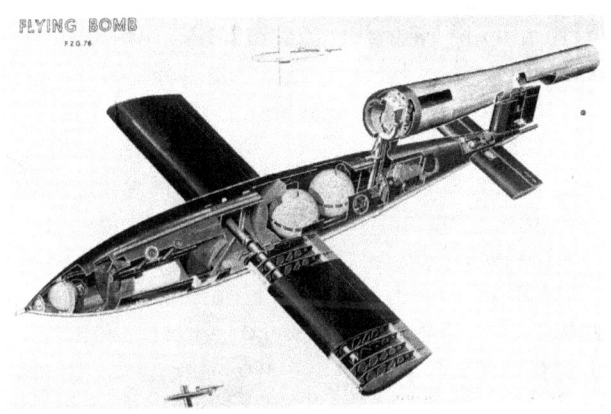

Cutaway drawing of a German V-1 flying bomb

We did get to see Piccadilly and a bunch of other sites of London although I must admit I wasn't in London looking for sightseeing. We would look for bars and good food and we would have tea at the Ritz where we could dance. It was just getting away from the bombing and from planes going down and that kind of stuff. We had enough of unusual missions.

For the rest of my tour, I went to Cambridge to enjoy my leaves. I first walked all through the area of the famous university, then I learned about its history. The medieval university was patterned after some of the old Italian universities. Trinity College was founded by Henry VIII, and he forbade the study of scholastic philosophy. After him, each monarch was primarily interested in providing the leaders of the church and the country.

My next objective was to find a dance hall. After making an enquiry, I learned about Dorothy's Place. It was upstairs and usually full of dancers. My first surprise was how well they could dance, and most of the music was American. But there was one hitch: Americans danced in the middle of the

123

ballroom, while the Brits danced in a circle counter clockwise. I learned this early when I stopped and a man behind me said, "Come along Yank."

When the war was over and we returned to Cambridge we visited the American Cemetery, where we learned that there were nearly nine thousand missing and dead there—all of them not returning to base during a bombing mission.

Returning to our base, I saw that our 26th mission was aimed at destroying the city of Munich. It was bombed for five straight days. Our first one was on July 11. On that day 1,100 bombers left England for that purpose. There were rumors that Prime Minister Churchill wanted a German city to be destroyed because the *Luftwaffe* had really battered London.

As we approached Munich, I turned on Axis Sally on Berlin radio. We always enjoyed Glenn Miller, Benny Goodman and Artie Shaw. When we were close to the target she announced that "Today the 8th Air Force attacked Munich." When we got close to the target she made her usual spiel:

"Hello my American friends. Wouldn't you rather be home now? Do you know that your 4-F neighbor is dating your girlfriend? You know you can fly to Sweden now and end the war for you. Have you looked at the casualty numbers lately? Your chances of going home are pretty small. Do you not know that the Eighth Air Force has the highest number of dead of any group in this War? Don't say I did not warn you. Good bye you flyers from the Squadron with the Pale H."

When we got to the target we ignored her suggestions. When we looked down we saw the entire city burning. We had dropped thousands of one pound fire bombs, whose flames could not be put out. On the next day we returned to Munich.

There is one more story that goes with this mission. Because we usually traveled between 20,000 and 25,000 thousand feet, we wore winter flying suits, which were bulky and heavy. They were lined with fir – they felt like lamb. More than once, the gloves were not useful. When the German fighters attacked us I usually turned to the right gun to respond. The glove went from fingers to elbow, so they were cumbersome. The glove had one finger that was supposed to bend when you went for the trigger of the gun. But usually it would not bend because it was 65 degrees below zero. As the German fighters approached me I had no choice—I ripped off my glove and grabbed trigger. What happened next is guaranteed to happen—the skin peeled off your finger. This is a no-win condition for the manufacturer. If he makes the glove lighter, the finger could freeze.

AUGUST C. BOLINO

Chapter Sixteen
Some Lucky Missions

I remember that P-38 that joined us on a mission. We usually had escorts of P-51s or P-38s. On one mission there was a dogfight going on above us and one P-38 was crippled, so it couldn't hit its maximum speed. The P-38 was an unusual airplane because it was really a fighter-bomber. It had a twin fuselage and the cockpit was suspended between them.

Apparently the pilot of the P-38 contacted our colonel and told him of his predicament. The colonel said, "Come on in, little brother." (We were big brothers). We opened up our formation and stuck this little airplane right in the middle of the bombers. It only had to fly at 150 miles per hour airspeed. It was strange to see this little fighter in our midst. When we arrived at the English Coast, it peeled off, dipped its wings and the pilot waved goodbye to us. We all felt good about it, because it would have been shot down if we hadn't come to the rescue.

Another interesting tale was that a pilot of a B-17 of the 388th Bomb Group rode its plane for twenty minutes while it was on fire before bailing out. As flames moved inside the right wing dangerously close at a gasoline tank, Lt. Glenn K. Thompson, of Ashland, Kentucky, piloted the burning Fortress and waited before his crew could bail out over friendly territory.

When they got over the German lines in Belgium, the Fort was temporarily knocked out of control by a burst of flak that damaged the controls, shot out an engine and set the wing on fire. When he regained control of the plane, Thompson went on a 15,000-foot dive in an effort to extinguish the flame.

Because this failed, the crew sweated out a 20-minute

flight to the other side of the Meuse River where the entire crew bailed out, the last man jumping only a minute before the bomber exploded. They all landed behind American lines, not far from a small piece of German land, where they had to convince a bunch of American doughboys that they weren't disguised Nazi paratroopers.

The other members of the crew were: Lt. Clifford H. Bewig Jr., co-pilot from Baltimore; Charles D. Price, navigator from Duncan., Oklahoma; Donald E. Jackson, bombardier from Altoona, PA; T/S. Joseph W. Turley, engineer from New Albany, IN.; Thomas E. Linzee, radio operator from Boston; Sgt. Emmanuel J. Guzzo, radio operator from Alexandria. LA.; Guy N. Craig, Jr., ball turret gunner from Dallas, TX; Robert D. Lint, waist gunner from Johnstown, PA.; and Chester C. McFarland, tail gunner from Cincinnati, OH.

AUGUST C. BOLINO

Chapter Seventeen
The 388th's Most Disastrous Mission

It was Mission no. 19 to *Stuttgart* on September 6, 1943. On this mission, 24 aircraft took-off by 05:47 Greenwich Mean Time not knowing that this would be the most disastrous mission in losses for the 388th bombardment group of all the 306 missions flown. Eleven of our aircraft failed to return this day.

One of our aircraft aborted early due to low fuel pressure on no.1 engine, two remaining aircraft aborted as they were not needed to fill the formation. Twenty-one aircraft proceeded to the target. Lt. Wick in aircraft 42-3389 "Wolf Pack," was hit on the bomb run and the plane caught fire. Five chutes were seen. Then several targets of opportunity appeared, but as we were flying the low group to the 96th bombardment group lead, our lead bombardier dropped on their assigned target.

Fighter opposition was the strongest encountered to date with about 150 enemy aircraft attacking our formation, consisting of approximately 40 FW 190's, 35 ME109's, 10 ME 110s, 10 ME 210's, With a few JU 88's and JU 87's helping out. Some of the FW 190's had belly tanks which is the only deviation from the usual characteristics of the enemy aircraft. A few spasmodic attacks were made on the formations on the route to *Stuttgart*, but the large concentration was first met in the vicinity of the IP the attacks were very intense from this point to the target, decreased over *Stuttgart*, but regained intensity until the formations reached Bernay on the route out.

The attacks centered on the low groups and as a result of this, one entire (563rd) low squadron was missing. 45 of our P-47's escorted the 2nd task force on the route to LeChatelet and 112 Spitfires rendezvoused with the formations south of Bernay on the route out. The low squadron was hit by flak after the IP, then as the

THE 8ᵀᴴ AIR FORCE WON THE WAR IN EUROPE

planes would drop out of formation, they would be hit by fighters.

The head of the 388th bombardment group wrote the following:

"We suffered heavy losses, but the spirit of the group in bearing these losses and coming back was a matter of great gratification to all the members of our Bomb Group. I wish that you would give the group commander my commendation to the 388th bombardment group for their excellent spirit and their confidence in the greatness of the task they are now performing."

Signed by Gen. Eaker[11]

---

[11] This a true story from the book: *"The 388th at War"* by Edward Huntzinger. Because there is no pagination, one can find this story in the section called 'Miscellaneous Mission Reports'.

AUGUST C. BOLINO

Chapter Eighteen
A German Prison Camp

Briefing was at 0300, on September 28th, 1944. Our target was *Merseburg*, Germany. We were told to aim at the oil refineries, although *Merseburg* was also the headquarters for the Hitler Youth and the Gestapo strong arm elite. The Major at briefing informed us that there would be 1,100 antiaircraft guns aimed at us.

It was a beautiful day as we flew over *Brussels* and *Holland*. Everything looked so peaceful and settled. It was hard to imagine that down below was devastation from war. At 12:15 p.m. we were about 10 minutes from the target. In the distance we could see a black cloud in the sky. This told us that the flak from anti-aircraft gunfire was going to be intense. All men on board our B-17 had their flak suits on. They were all very tense. Each second brought us closer to that frightening wall of black smoke.

When we got to the target we were at 26,500 feet on the bombing run. We were prepared to drop our 6000 lbs. of death. In just a few seconds we dropped our load, and we could see that the bombs were falling towards the target. It is a pretty picture!

Suddenly, the scene changes, as our ship lurches. It was hit in the right wing. The number four engine was burning and the wing tip was gone. Another burst shattered the nose, scattering all navigation equipment, breaking the radar system, bomb sight, oxygen bottles and the interphone system. Again, a burst hits the number two engine. Still another burst sends shards of Plexiglas blinding the top-turret gunner and cutting the pilots face. (I thought of the Air Corp song playing in the faint distance – "We live in fame or go down in flames.")

Our ship lost altitude and airspeed. We fell out of the formation and we were far behind. The airspeed hovered at 130 mph, and soon formation can no longer be seen in the sun, as it heads for England. We were alone in the middle of Germany!

After first aid is rendered to the wounded, it was decided that we should head towards American occupied France. The magnetic compass read 265 degrees. We could see flak ahead coming through the layer of clouds. Slowly, we flew around the "flak," but we lost valuable time and gasoline. Can we get to France?

One hour later we are still fighting our way towards safe ground. Again, flak was fired at us point blank. We suffer another direct hit. At an altitude of 5500 ft., our ship is a "sure kill" for the Germans! The order to "bail out" is given and all the crew parachuted out towards the enemy.

Just twelve hours ago, we were free men in England. Now, we will fight our war from a German prison camp[12].

A More Detailed Story

This story was presented by Joseph Garber of the 96th Bomb Group. It happened on July 21, 1944. They were on their way to *Regensberg* when their B-17 was hit by heavy flak and they all bailed just east of *Schwaebisch,* Germany in an area of the *Heubach* Forest.

They were all captured, and even though Garber had broken his ankle, the German soldiers spent several days interrogating them instead caring for their wounds. Finally, a doctor set his broken bones, and the entire crew were jammed into railway cars for the journey to *Stalag Luft* IV. They found out immediately that it was a very poor POW camp. Fortunately, they had a potbellied stove, most of the other huts did not have. Their mattresses were paper bags filled with straw or sawdust. No one knew what medical care meant, because, too often guys would be removed from the camp for 'medical care' and would never return.

Because they were located less than 40 miles from the North Sea, winter came early and it was bitter cold. Garber who was from Wilkes-Barre, Pennsylvania, was accustomed to snow

---

[12] This story was presented by Navigator F. H. Stachyra.

and ice and cold, but not in uniforms they were issued without gloves.

By Christmas time, Garber was a 'guest' of the Germans for over five months. By this time, the prisoners were exhausted and starving. The guards taunted them, saying that the Germans were winning the war and bombing the major cities of the United States. But the Americans knew it was all a lie, because they had sneaked a small radio into the camp.

They were allowed one post card and one letter per month. They looked forward to the Red Cross packages when they came, which they had to share one box per two prisoners. But the meager items didn't go very far. They spent all the time of that season remembering all their past Christmases. Their real Christmas came in May of 1945 when they looked out into the yard and saw no guards. Soon Russians came into the camp and they offered Farber what he thought was water, but it was 120 proof Russian Vodka. It did not matter. They were free.

When Joe Garber was captured he was 154 pounds. Ten months later he was 89 pounds. He recovered quickly, and he is now the President of the 96th Bomb Group Association[13].

In the bitter winter of 1944-1945, the war in Europe seemed over as the Allied forces were on the edge of the German frontiers. But months of brutal combat were ahead, despite the fact that the Allied planners had been preparing for the surrender of German forces since the D-Day landing in June 1944. The chief questions were how would the *Wehrmacht* surrender its weapons and how would prisoners of war held then by Germans be returned to Allied control.

This issue of POWs was at the top of the priority, because there were hundreds of thousands of them – the majority being Russians but also 300,000 British and American prisoners sickened in camps that were scattered across Germany. The Western planners assumed that the POWs would simply wait for their liberators. But the chaos of the last months of the war in Europe could not be imagined. The roads were blocked by a tidal wave of German refugees, surging away from the Advancing Red

---

[13] His story may be found in the December 2013 *8th AF News*.

THE 8TH AIR FORCE WON THE WAR IN EUROPE

Army. All roads were already jammed with disorganized *Wehrmacht* units, as the SS began emptying the death camps in Poland, sending hundreds of thousands of Jews and slave laborers to their deaths in frozen boxcars.

The "untold story" of what happened to the Allied prisoners of war is the subject of a book by John Nichol and Tony Rennell. They tell a powerful and compelling story, using interviews and firsthand accounts of the British and American prisoners. But the title--*The Last Escape*--is a bit misleading, because the majority of POWs did not break out. Instead, the world of the Kriegies, as they called themselves (short for *Kriegsgefangenen*-prisoners of war), was one of deprivation, loneliness, anxiety and fear. Some prisoners, mostly British, had spent three, four or even five years behind German barbed wire.

The Germans began early to move prisoners. In July 1944 as the Russians got near, the first evacuations began. The inmates of *Stalag Luft VI* in East Prussia were sent by ships across the Baltic Sea to a camp at *Gross Tychow* in Pomerania. Then in February 1945 they began an epic march of 86 days on a circuitous course that covered 500 miles. Starving, the men ate dogs and rats. When they were liberated in April, many were not more than skeletons, appearing to look like inmates of the liberated concentration camps at *Bergen-Belsen, Buchenwald and Dachau*.

This cruelty was a common ordeal. The 10,000 British and U.S. fliers at *Stalag Luft III* in Silesia were evacuated in the middle of the night during a howling blizzard and forced on a torturous march in sub-zero temperatures for eight days and nights, before making a grim journey in cattle cars to other camps.

In the south, the prisoners waited for Patton's 3rd Army, in the north for Montgomery and in the east for the Russians. They feared that they might be murdered before Allied troops could reach them. "Friendly fire" was also a threat. In the spring of 1945, prisoners of *Stalag XIII D* stood watching the vast rail yards at Nuremberg with a mixture of pride and terror as heavy bombers pounded the city. Then the Germans emptied the camps again.

Prisoners filled the roads as Allied planes strafed the columns. Because the POWs were on the move, the Western

Allies could not determine where they were. Even the International Red Cross, which had food form them, could not locate the columns. The food parcels, which came by ship to *Lubeck* and by train to *Munich*, were stockpiled for distribution. But whenever the parcels appeared, they were the only source of food for the starving POWs.

Nichol and Rennell are at their best in presenting the stark human drama of the thousands of men who suffered the traumas of captivity, especially in the last frenzied months of the war in Europe[14].

---

[14] The Nichol and Rennell book, *The Last Escape*, was reviewed in the *Washington Post* on October 29, 2003.

Chapter Nineteen
A Mission to Russia

A least successful mission took place after an agreement was reached between the United States and the Soviet Union, whereby American bombers could bomb East Germany and fly on to a Russian airfield in a shuttle mission. We knew that this mission was in the planning stage, so when our leave time came, we had to decide whether or not to give up the leave and be a part of this historic mission. We gambled by going to London (I went to Cambridge). While we were away, in the second week of June 19, the 388th was briefed for a mission to Germany and was told to go on to Poltava to land.

We missed all the fun, and when we got back to Knettishall, the base was empty. 1 got all of the details later from my friends who returned. As soon as they landed, very large Russian women began to service the planes and the Russian colonel asked if any of our men wanted women. They told us that after seeing the women, they all refused and they headed for food and plenty of drinks.

Earlier that day, while we were bombing Germany, a Heinkel photo plane followed our bombers as they headed eastward. The Americans and Russians, who were celebrating this unusual event, were not aware of this activity, so while they celebrated German bombers plastered the planes, most of which caught fire. They sat like sitting ducks on the concrete runways. We lost 43 B-17s and 14 P-51s. The Germans did on the ground what they couldn't do in the air. They exacted a very heavy toll of bombers, and it was a total disaster. There was no plane that could be flown back to England, so the crews had to make their way by whatever means. Some crews returned by way of Morocco and some made it from Sweden, which was a neutral country.

Some of the flyers milked the situation totally. They wrote checks on the United States and lived royally. A fellow navigator, Sandy Arnoff, told me he was in no hurry to return to combat what with all the booze and broads that were available. Our Colonel, when he learned of this high living, sent telegrams to all the flyers that if they did not return to base immediately they would be considered AWOL.

In this connection I can relate another story. Several planes that were crippled and could not make it back to Knettishall or the English coast simply headed north to Sweden to live out the war there. I was told of one crew that took their B-4 bags and all their personnel belongings on a mission and went to Sweden, as planned. Those who fled to Sweden were considered deserters and could have been subject to a firing squad.

I remember our last mission on July 17, 1944. One more and we were going home. Of course we were nervous. Nobody wanted to get shot down on a last mission. At briefing the colonel told us that the code word for the mission was "No ball," and that we would hitting the Pas de Calais area. We were aiming at the flying bomb supply dumps.

It was really a milk run, because we saw no enemy aircraft and we landed without any fanfare. Several of us kissed the ground after embarking. We went to the debriefing area and then celebrated with a drink or two.

One last item about Knettishall. One evening, Curtis Le May, who was the commander of the Eighth Air Force, came to our base at Knettishall for one of our dances. I believe one our 2nd lieutenants cut his tie in half, which was the price of admission for anyone not a member of the 388th Bomb Group. The Colonel was pretty angry, but he did not show it.

Chapter Twenty
Death Bombers

This is one of the great secrets of World War II. It was disclosed by Franklin Banker, an Associated Press correspondent, and it is one of the most dramatic chapters of war – how dozens of daring American airmen flirted constantly with death as they worked in the greatest secrecy to develop a "death bomber" as an answer to the Germans' rockets and buzz-bombs. It was authorized by the Army Air Forces.

The "death bomber" was described as a forerunner of the atomic bomb, because it was designed to destroy enemy personnel and war installations over a wide area at a single blow. It was born at a U.S. bomber base in England.

It made use of worn out Flying Fortresses which provided a destructive blow at the enemy. They were good for no other purpose because heavy duties of a tour of bombing missions made it unsafe for further formation flying.

These pilotless B-17s were originally worth $250,000. In their final flight, they were sent crashing down on a target by means of radio communication in a small control plane flying nearby.

The project was a product of Lt. Gen. Jimmy Doolittle's Eighth Air Force. It was developed in the Eighth's Third Bomber Division, commanded by Maj. Gen. Earle E. Partridge and earlier by Maj. Gen. Curtis E. LeMay, who commanded the B-29 bombers in Japan.

The experiment began at the crack Flying Fortress group of Col. William David of Calhoun, GA, who was a star football player at the University of Georgia. Most of the engineering work was done at his base.

The war-weary Forts were stripped of guns and any movable equipment which allowed a maximum of space for explosives. Its capacity of explosives were many times more powerful than TNT. If one of these bombers should crash on take-off it might have killed everyone at the base. Once it was safely in the air, the two-man crew of a pilot and co-pilot bailed out and the bomber was guided over the English Channel by radio control.

These Fortresses were salvaged after the 1944 invasion of France. Any old bombers were saved for this project. But because the Air Force would never use any weapon whose accuracy was in question these "death bombers" were never employed in any great numbers. A few were used to destroy the launching pads of buzz bombs in the Pas de Calais area.

This use of "death bombers," which was known as Operation Aphrodite, was responsible for the death of Lt. Joseph Kennedy, the oldest brother of John F. Kennedy, who was elected president in 1960. Joseph Kennedy, Jr. finished a tour of missions and was ordered to return to the United States, but he volunteered to pilot one of the "death bombers."

When they took off, everything seemed in good order until they reached the target. We will never know why the bomber detonated before they could bail out. If Joseph Kennedy, Jr. had survived this mission his father, Joseph Kennedy, would have run him for President instead of John. It would have changed the political course of American history.

Peter Wittenberg wrote that "History took a little-known but momentous twist exactly 40 years ago when the oldest of the Kennedy brothers died over wartime Europe, leaving ascendancy to the family crown open to the next in line."

Few men can speak with greater knowledge of Joseph P. Kennedy Jr.'s fate than the commander of the top-secret project in which he served -- Roy W. Forrest of Houston. Forrest, 71, lived in retirement, with his memories of the company. But on Aug. 12, 1944, he was a Lieutenant Colonel in the Army Air Corps, Commanding Project Aphrodite at Fersfield, England.

"We were acquaintances," Forrest said of Kennedy, one of a staff of a dozen Naval Officers attached to the project.

THE 8TH AIR FORCE WON THE WAR IN EUROPE

"Naturally, I'd drop in and have a drink with them. He was just one of the fellows." The pair shared a spirit of derring-do. Kennedy had a certain flamboyant generosity about him, while Forrest loved the kind of conventional nose-tweaking he could give the Germans through special weapons warfare.

That attraction to special missions was to cost Kennedy his life and was to leave East Texan Forrest with pangs of guilt over what he perceived as his failure to warn of the project's flaw. Aphrodite, as history books now relate, was the codename of an American bombing project in which a "mother" aircraft electronically maneuvered a "baby," or drone, aircraft laden with explosives into an enemy target.

The most dangerous work was that of the crew members -- no more than two -- who took off in the drone, activated the explosives for impact, then parachuted out as the aircraft began its glide across the English Channel.

Forrest said he suspected that once the device was activated, it became grounded to the plane's un-insulated bulkhead and created a potential hazard --"so in cocking the device, they actually sent an electric impulse to the electronic detonators." Whatever went wrong, the result was that the Navy PB4Y (B-24) drone from which Kennedy and a Fort Worth Airman were to have parachuted exploded in the air, leaving no trace of it's occupants.

It is still a mystery. "I'm not sure what happened," said Forrest, who was flying some distance ahead in a P-38 fighter plane. "Joe and his partner might have been cocking the thing, let skip it for all I know."

Forrest disagreed with the charge the mission was useless but supported the story of a cover-up effort.

"This was as much psychological warfare as anything else, like their buzz bombs," he said. "It wasn't a total failure because we sure had those bastards staying up late at night. We were shooting at everything. We did hit one refinery."

Of the hush-hush campaign, Forrest said: "How he died was covered up pretty well. I guess. I was told to keep my mouth shut, period."

The reason for that order goes back to Forrest's qualms

about the flawed electrical system.

"I called it the 'Guillotine,'" he said. "I was doing a lot of kicking myself in the ass about how I should have scrubbed the damned Guillotine, and the Deputy Commander of the 3rd Air Force said to keep my damn mouth shut.

I didn't understand the sensitivity of it, until I got home and found out what a powerhouse the old boy (Ambassador Joseph P Kennedy Sr.) was. FDR was still alive, and he and old Joe were good buddies.

Yet he has memories of Kennedy which don't disappear. "He was a hell of a nice boy," Forrest said. "I had orders restricting everyone to base, but he'd slip out in a jeep and go to London 80 miles away and come back with a case of a hell of a good scotch, when we were drinking green stuff I'd help him drink it. I'd pay for it, of course."

Kennedy's family sent him boxes of cigars which he passed around generously, Forrest said.

The kind of man drawn to the kind of command which Forrest gained could appreciate the Kennedy clan. Forrest admitted having a flair for practical joking going back to his flaming youth.

Typically, at the time Aphrodite ended, Forrest was planning to stick his tongue out at Hitler, so to speak, by rigging a drone to go over Berlin, sending off messages before hitting a target below, he said.

A World War II encyclopedia says Aphrodite, which lasted three months, was shut down after a "mother" plane momentarily lost contact with its drone near an English coastal city. Forrest disagrees[15].

---

[15] HOUSTON VETERAN REMEMBERS FORGOTTEN KENNEDY: JOE JR DOOMED By Pete Wittenberg *Houston Post Reporter*, The Houston Post/Sun., Aug. 12, 1984.

Chapter Twenty-One
Bombing Peenemunde

While the United States was just beginning to build an atomic bomb, the German research center at *Peenemunde* was producing very damaging rockets and bombs. It was founded in 1937 on the Baltic island of *Usedom*, which location was suggested by the mother of Werner von Braun. Its early emphasis was on rockets, which produced the V-1 and the V-2 bombs. This research lead naturally into atomic bombs.

The British began bombing *Peenemunde* in 1943 under a code of operation Hydra, and on July 18, 1944 the 8th Air Force sent 377 B-17s to bomb the rocket center. In August it sent out two more groups of Forts for the same purpose.

The invention of an atomic bomb would have meant that a single aircraft could carry a weapon sufficiently powerful to devastate entire cities. This indicates the importance of the German nuclear energy project, including talk of an atomic weapon. That project failed for one primary reason: German Antisemitism. Half of continental theoretical physicists including (Einstein, Bohr, Enrico Fermi, and Oppenheimer) who did much of their early study and research in Germany, were either Jewish or, in the case of Enrico Fermi, married to a Jew. When they left Germany, the only leading nuclear physicist left in Germany was Heisenberg, who apparently dragged his feet on the project, or at best lacked the high morale that characterized the Los Alamos work.

He made some faulty calculations causing him to suggest that the Germans would need significantly more heavy water than was necessary. Otto Hahn, the physical chemist who was a central figure in the original research on fission was never given enough resources to complete the project. The project was doomed due to insufficient resources.

This story begins in 1937 at *Peenemunde, Mecklenburg*, in Northern Germany, where scientists developed A3 and A4 Rockets (that later came to be called V1 and V2 buzz bombs), but their main goal was to produce atomic bombs. Hitler ordered 5,200 of these rockets.

The RAF was the first to bomb *Peenemunde* in August 1943. During 1944 the 8th Air Force kept sending Groups of B-17 Flying Fortresses to bomb *Peenemunde*. On July 18, 1944 377 B-17s bombed *Peenemunde* with 3 lost. On August 4, 1944 221B-17s bombed with 3 losses, and on August 25 376 bombed with 5 losses. On one of these missions a group bombed a submarine factory on the Northern Coast, and on its way back the 388th Bomb Group saw a very small house in the middle of a large farm. We learned later that this house contained 200 German scientists who were working on producing atomic bombs.

Wernher von Braun was one of these scientists. He graduated from the *Technische Hochscule in Berlin*, and in 1934 he received a doctorate in physics for his study of "The Problem of Liquid Propellants." He developed the V1 and V2 rockets (which we called buzz bombs) that burned the eastern part of London and killed thousands of British. Von Braun was able to do this because of an oddity in the Treaty of Versaille, which prohibited all forms of weaponry, but it did not include rocketry.

When World War II ended on May 8, 1945 von Braun was moved to the United States, with 1,600 other German Scientists. He was appointed Director of the Marshall Space Center, which developed the Saturn V launch vehicle that took Americans to the moon. In an odd historical occasion, during the World War II von Braun worked with Robert Goddard who wrote a paper on "A Method of Reaching Extreme Altitudes."

The road to atomic energy led from a basic principle of physics: matter can neither be created nor destroyed but can only be changed in form. From this came Albert Einstein's idea that matter could be converted into energy, so that an increase in matter can be converted into more energy.

Albert Einstein won a Nobel Prize in Physics for his work on photoelectric effects. But he was best known for his known

THE 8TH AIR FORCE WON THE WAR IN EUROPE

E=MC2. In 1933, while visiting the United States, he decided to stay here because he was a Jew. He became an American citizen in 1940.

When World War II began several foreign physicists began to talk about the possible military use of atomic energy. These include Leo Szilard, Edward Teller, Enrico Fermi and Max Dresden. Szilard had met Einstein during a visit to Berlin. It was there that he learned of the possibility of splitting atoms from Hans Bethe. Szilard hoped to duplicate the German process.

In 1938 Szilard came to the United States carrying the idea of a bomb with him. He and Fermi decided that FDR had to be warned of this German possibility. They contacted Alexander Sachs, a Jewish refugee, who was one of FDR's advisers. Sachs recommended that they write a letter to the President and that Einstein should sign it.

On July 12, 1939 Fermi and Szilard went to Long Island to talk to Einstein. they thought Sachs said Patchogue but he had said Peconic. When they found him, he was not interested in the plan. But after much negotiating, he agreed to sign the letter. But they were not sure whether to write a short one or a long one, so they wrote two letters.

On August 2 Szilard and Teller returned to Peconic, and Einstein dictated the letter in German. When it was translated into English Sachs delivered it to FDR on October 10, reading it aloud. Roosevelt seemed uninterested until Sachs reminded him of the time when Robert Fulton took his design of a steamship to Napoleon because the USA was not interested. The President was convinced. He called General Edwin Watson and he told him this required immediate action. A Committee was established with a $6,000 grant.

In 1945, when World War II was over, Von Braun and 100 other scientists began work on a rocket at Bliss, Texas. During the 1950s he tried to obtain funds for an American space program, but his efforts failed until the Soviets launched Sputnik. The United States put a Redstone Rocket into orbit from Huntsville, Alabama on January 31, 1958. The first moon landing occurred on July 20, 1969, when Neil Armstrong and Buzz Aldrin landed on Apollo 11.

Von Braun had popularized the idea of a manned expedition to the moon, so when John F. Kennedy was elected President, he told Americans that we would put a man on the moon before that decade was concluded. He was looking for a project that would capture the public's imagination. He asked Wernher Von Braun to help him beat the Soviets to the moon. It required a rocket (the Saturn V) that Von Braun provided. When the moon landings were concluded the United States had 24 astronauts that made it to the moon, and 12 walked on the surface.

When I was at *Knettishall* in August 1944, I was told that the 8th Air Force had just destroyed over 200 German scientists who were working on an atomic bomb. The strategic importance of the bomb did not become fully apparent until the United States lost its monopoly on the weapon in the post-war era. The Soviet Union developed and tested its first nuclear weapon in 1949, based partially on information obtained from Soviet espionage in the United States. Nuclear competition between the two superpowers were a large part in the development of the Cold War.

Later, I learned that Fermi had an element named after him – element 100, which was radioactive with a symbol of Fm. It is an actinide. It is on the element chart.

The road to atomic energy led from a basic principle of physics: matter neither can be created nor destroyed but only changed in form. From this came Newton and Einstein's idea that matter could be converted into energy, and that increase in mass led to an increase in energy. In the 1930s, research in physics concentrated on tying nuclear forces to quantum mechanics. Experiments over the world aimed at penetrating the nuclei of atoms to release radioactive isotopes. It was found that an atom of lithium could produce a million kilowatt hours of electricity.

In keeping with his racist policies, Adolf Hitler separated general physics (meaning non-Aryan) and German physics. After the Austrian *Anschluss*, its physicists were classified as Germans. One of those Austrian physicists, Lise Meitner, was a leading analyst at the *Berlin Kaiser Wilhelm Institut*. She was working with Otto Hahn and Fritz Strassmann on nuclear fission, but when it was learned that she was a Jew, she was locked up in her laboratory. Colleagues went to Hitler to stress that the Germans

THE 8TH AIR FORCE WON THE WAR IN EUROPE

had achieved many more Nobel prizes than any other nation, and they told him that there was no such thing as German physics, but he angrily charged that she was a "white Jew" and ordered her arrest.

She stole across the Dutch border disguised as a tourist and went to a Swedish seaside town of *Kungaly*, near *Goteborg*, where she would be near other noted physicists, Niels Bohr in *Copenhagen* and Otto Hahn, who fled to *Stockholm*. They were pursuing research that was suggested by Einstein's theory of relativity: a body in motion has a greater mass than one at rest. The German physicists were splitting atom nuclei, making new elements and creating large amounts of energy in the process.

One German physicist was important for both Germany and the United States. After obtaining his doctorate, Werner von Braun was fascinated with rockets. He created the V-1 rocket, which was uncontrollable. It was able to fly in one direction until it was out of fuel. At that point it headed straight down to the ground. This rocket was used to burn one-half of London. His next project was the V-2 rocket, which was controllable electronically.

The Germans used this rocket to try to down Flying Fortresses. When I learned of this ability, I told our tail gunner to be on the alert for rockets coming from behind us. On one of our last missions the tail gunner screamed at our pilot, "Rocket in rear heading for our plane. Our pilot raised the plane about 50 feet and the rocket went flying by us.

When Adolph Hitler decided that he did not want any Jews to remain in Germany, he gave them a few days to leave. Five of the top German scientists, including von Braun, headed for the United States. These Germans led them to expect that the element uranium may be turned into a new and important source of energy in the immediate future. This new phenomenon would also lead to the construction of bombs. It is conceivable that extremely powerful bombs of a new type may thus be constructed.

On December 22, 1938, Otto Hahn published a paper on these results in the *Naturwissenschaften,* but he did not believe his own work. As he said, "The manuscript had been mailed, the whole thing once more seems improbable to me that I wished I could get the document back out of the mailbox." At least half of

145

the world's physicists were dismayed and they confused the possibilities. Hahn said it would be "contrary to God's will."

During the late 1930s, most of the leading physicists left Europe for the United States, many of whom were Jews. Fermi had married a Jew, so they escaped over the Swiss border. Many of them gathered in Washington D.C., where they hoped President Roosevelt would finance their research on nuclear weapons.

Einstein and Szilard wrote the letter in German, and they had one of Roosevelt's assistants translate it into English. They handed it to Roosevelt and he read it aloud on October 10. But the President was bored.

To F. D. Roosevelt
President of the United
States White House
Washington, D. C.

Sir:

Some recent work by E. Fermi and L. Szilard, which has been communicated to me in manuscript, leads me to expect that the element uranium may be turned into a new and important source of energy in the immediate future. Certain aspects of the situation which has arisen seem to call for watchfulness and, if necessary, quick action on the part of the Administration. I believe that it is my duty to bring to your attention the following facts and recommendation.

This new phenomenon would also lead to the construction of bombs, and it is conceivable – though much less certain – that extremely powerful bombs of a new type may thus be constructed. A single bomb of this type, carried by boat and exploded in a port, might very well destroy the whole port together with the surrounding territory. However, such bombs might very well prove to be too heavy for transportation by air.

In view of this situation you may think it desirable to have some permanent contact maintained between the Administration and the group of physicists working on chain reactions in

THE 8TH AIR FORCE WON THE WAR IN EUROPE

America. One possible way of achieving this might be for you to entrust with this task a person who has your confidence and who could perhaps serve in an unofficial capacity.

Roosevelt said any action at that time was premature, but Sachs persisted, asking if he could meet again on the topic. The President assented. They met at breakfast, where Sachs reminded Roosevelt that many leaders had rejected new ideas as impractical only to find that another country eagerly embraced the invention. He used the example of Robert Fulton, who took his designs of a steamship to Napoleon because the United States was not interested.

Roosevelt was convinced. He called General Edwin Watson and told him that this letter required immediate action. Not long after, Roosevelt appointed a Committee, led by Lyman J. Briggs, Director of the National Bureau of Standards, to study the possibilities.

Following the conclusion of the European Theater in May 1945, two atomic bombs were then employed against the Empire of Japan in August during the Pacific Theater, effectively terminating the war, which averted the need for invading mainland of Japan.

When World War II was over, we learned that The Empire of Japan was also developing an atomic bomb, however, it suffered from a lack of resources.

AUGUST C. BOLINO

PART VII The Success of Strategic Bombing

The first requirement of a combat tour of duty consisted of 25 combat sorties. Later in the war, the number was increased to 30 and then finally to 35. This would typically take one month of practice and five months of combat (if they were able to finish their tour – the lucky bastards).

A combat sortie was any combat mission that actually flew over enemy held territory (even if no bombs were dropped). So an abort over the English Channel on the way to the target did not qualify. The dreaded *Berlin* (Big B) mission counted the same as a milk run to France.

It was better if the original crew flew all of their combat missions together, because replacements might not work well. But crew members often were replaced because of injuries or sickness.

If a crew had a vacancy, it was common for another man from the same squadron to be assigned to that crew. It was rare if a crew flew all of its missions without a replacement. When the tour was completed the crew was sent back home. Some persons chose to take a 30 day R&R in the states and then return for a second tour. This happened to our pilot, Dan Houghton, who was shot down on the sixth mission of his second tour.

Strategic bombing during World War II began on September 1, 1939 when Germany invaded Poland and the *Luftwaffe* (German Air Force) began bombing cities and the civilian population in Poland in an indiscriminate aerial bombardment campaign. As the war continued to expand, bombing by both the Axis and the Allies increased significantly. In September 1940, the *Luftwaffe* began targeting British cities in "The Blitz". From 1942 onward, the British bombing campaign against Germany was increasingly targeted towards industrial sites and eventually, civilian areas. When the United States began flying bombing missions against Germany, it reinforced these efforts and controversial fire bombings were carried out against *Hamburg*

THE 8TH AIR FORCE WON THE WAR IN EUROPE

(1943), *Munich* (1944) and *Dresden* (1945), and other German cities.

The Nazi's air bombing raids early in the war shocked President Franklin Roosevelt. As the death tolls rose, President Roosevelt strongly condemned Germany's deliberate bombing attacks on civilians.

As he said, "The ruthless bombing from the air of civilians in unfortified centers of population has sickened the hearts of every civilized man and woman, and has profoundly shocked the conscience of humanity ... I am therefore addressing this urgent appeal to every Government which may be engaged in hostilities publicly to affirm its determination that its armed forces shall in no event, and under no circumstances, undertake the bombardment from the air of civilian populations."

Hitler disregarded Roosevelt's condemnation, however, and by the time the United States entered the war in December 1941 the Allies had rejected Roosevelt's plea as well. Hitler's barbarity terrified Allied citizens and leaders alike. Worried that the Axis powers might prevail, American and British military strategists developed more accurate and more deadly bombing tactics, seeking to cripple both war industries and urban centers, forcing the Nazis to concentrate on defending their homeland.

In February 1942, the British Bomber Command gained approval from Churchill to target Germany's industrial cities and their civilian populations. The policy of dropping bombs on large, typically heavily populated areas rather than narrowly defined targets became known as "strategic bombing." The practice expanded and was utilized by both sides as the war years went on.

While Churchill publicly referred to the policy of "de-housing" German workers, neither he nor Roosevelt told their people about the extent of the Allied bombing of German population centers. The war objective remained, as President Roosevelt stated, "a policy of fighting hard on all fronts and ending the war as quickly as we can on the uncompromising terms of unconditional surrender."

By early 1945, Adolf Hitler's ambitions had been smashed. Allied forces were marching into Germany from the west while the Soviet army was pushing back the Nazis in the east. Nonetheless, to ensure Germany's unconditional surrender and to assist the Soviet advance in the east, the Allies staged one of the largest raids of the war against the German city of Dresden, involving nearly 2,800 aircraft. The firestorm that resulted was visible for two hundred miles. Approximately one hundred thousand Germans, mostly civilians, were killed--the largest loss of life in a single day up to that point of the 20th century. Three months later, on May 7, 1945, Germany surrendered unconditionally after U.S. and Soviet forces met in central Germany. Because this surrender was not told to newspaper columnists on the 7th, this is now celebrated on May 8th.

In January 1944, the B-24s and B-17s based in England flew their last mission as a subordinate part of VIII Bomber Command. On February 22, 1944, a massive reorganization of American airpower took place in Europe. VIII Bomber Command and Ninth Air Force were brought under control of a centralized headquarters for command and control of the United States, code-named Operation 'Argument' and supported by RAF night bombing, on the German aircraft industry at the earliest possible date.

Evaluating Strategic Bombing

When the war was over in Europe, there was considerable argument as to whether the bombing raids were a success or a failure. The entry of the American Eighth Air Force in Europe was slow, and the American force had no desire to join the night raids with the British. Instead, minor attacks were carried out against precision targets (usually railways, factories, oil refineries and submarine pens in France, Belgium, and the Netherlands.

With their Norden bombsights, the American bombardiers were anxious to brandish their daylight precision bombing technique, which they had practiced daily at the American bombing ranges. The North African campaign detoured any bombers from the western European theater. But during the Casablanca conference in January 1943, the Eighth was authorized to return to Britain ready to bomb "around-the-clock" with the

THE 8ᵀᴴ AIR FORCE WON THE WAR IN EUROPE

RAF raiding Hamburg at night, and the American daylight raids followed on July 25-26, 1943.

The haughty Americans refused to learn from the earlier British trials and errors; the American bomber leaders said simply, 'We will learn for ourselves,' which meant they were duplicating the same RAF mistakes, which had been earned three years before. There were other problems. One was the cloudy weather and the haze that was found down the industrial *Ruhr* Valley. This haze greatly reduced the Norden sight's accuracy.

There was another problem: the American bomb run required a long straight approach to guarantee accuracy, which meant that the bombers were more vulnerable to anti-aircraft fire (flak). Because fighter escorts in 1943 had a small range the B-17 and B-24 bombers in formations were like fish in a barrel. On August 17, 1943, 315 B-17s made an attack on ball-bearing plants at *Schweinfurt* in which sixty Flying Fortresses were shot down. This 19 % loss was not acceptable. Yet the bombers were sent to another raid on *Schweinfurt* on October 14. On this raid the bombers had no fighter escort, and 62 planes out of 228 were destroyed. This one-in-four loss ratio caused the Eighth Air Force, for the time, to give up any more raids of this type.

The invasion of Normandy switched the bombing priority: the rail lines of western France were to be cut in order to hinder German reinforcements being sent to the area before D-day. But these targets were very close to urban populations, which resulted in unnecessary loss of lives of the French citizens. In April 1944, British and American bombs killed 250 persons at Juvisy, 200 at Toulon, 500 at Lille, 850 at Rouen, and 650 at Paris. With the OVERLORD landing and COBRA breakout, the Eighth Air Force returned to its bombing missions over Germany proper.

But the return brought new techniques. It changed in a two-step process. The first phase was a result primarily of General Eisenhower's changing position. Eisenhower stated, "While I have always insisted that U.S. Strategic Air Forces be directed against precision targets, I am always prepared to take part in anything that gives real promise to ending the war quickly." President Roosevelt himself summarized in August 1944 a common belief among military circles:

151

"We have got to be tough with Germany, and I mean the German people not just the Nazis. It is of the utmost importance that every person in Germany should realize that this time Germany is a defeated nation. The German people as a whole must have it driven home to them that the whole nation has been engaged in a lawless conspiracy against the decencies of modern civilization."

The first new approach was Operation CLARION. This plan was drafted in December 1944 and was intended to break civilian morale. The targets were transportation, but the real objective was the psychological collapse of the German populace at large. It was a deliberate strategy of telling the German citizens that the Allied air forces would continue to pummel them without end.

The second phase was Operation THUNDERCLAP. It was a plan enacted in January 1945 which made *Berlin, Leipzig, and Dresden* acceptable targets. The objective was to add to the "existing pandemonium," which would hasten the collapse and surrender of Germany and, the Soviets would see for themselves the destructive power of the Anglo-American bomber forces. When *Berlin* was attacked on February 3 by 900 B-17s, some military objectives were hit, but 25,000 civilians were estimated to have perished. Ten days later, historic *Dresden* was walloped by a two-day combined British and American raid which killed at least 30,000 civilians. The American bombing policy over Germany would have continued had the European war not ended. The ruthless attacks that summer on were noted by numerous Japanese cities.

By this time, American strategic air forces had developed into a gigantic operational group. At its maximum in August 1944, the U.S. Army Air Forces had over 619,000 combat personnel. These men dropped 1,461,864 tons of bombs on Germany. Together with RAF Bomber Command's substantial efforts, 3,600,000 German dwelling units (20% of the total) were destroyed or heavily damaged. The homeless totaled between seven and eight million. Estimates suggest that 780,000 were wounded in bombing attacks and that 305,000 civilians were killed. These are minimum figures, though. It has been estimated that more than 600,000 people in Germany were killed by "terror bombing."

We are left with one simple conclusion: after correcting some early errors, the 8th Air Force was a major factor in winning the War in Europe[16].

Did Georgia Win the War?

The Tattnall Journal of Reidsville, Georgia seems to suggest this as a possibility. Here is some of what it published on November 11, 1993.

Our nation is now commemorating the 50th anniversary of World War II which was supposed to be the war to end all wars. Therefore, I would like to give some views of the outstanding accomplishments of several Georgians in the aerial warfare against Nazi Germany. This is where the war was won or lost and the fate of millions of lives was at stake. Our victory is a taken for granted thing and no one considers if we had lost or the consequences.

There were many, many unsung heroes in the war and also in the area of technology. We were sent off to fight with equipment, and the know how to use it, that were hastily thought up and sometimes not very workable.

I (Tommy Durrance) became 18 in November of 1942 and was inducted two months later in January of 1943 at Fort McPhearson in Atlanta, Georgia. The processing in Miami, aircraft armament training at the Oldsmobile factory in Michigan and final assignment to the 388th Bombardment Group (H) of B-17 Bombers.

This article deals with the turning around and winning the air war with Germany. Our 388th Bombardment Group went to Britain in June of 1943. We were to join an existing U.S. B-17 Bomber Force which had been in operation one year. However,

---

[16] If any reader wants more information about our bombing missions, I sent all of our mission summaries to the Library of Congress when they asked World War II veterans to send their military histories to them. Go to www. Library of Congress/ World War II/ August C. Bolino.

they had been unsuccessful in daylight bombing and suffered heavy casualties. Our B-17 Group and all others were given engine exhaust covers and told that we would fly with the British RAF and do sporadic night bombing.

The B-17 Eighth Air Force Commanders appealed to leaders Roosevelt and Churchill for one more try. It was believed that ours and the B-17 Groups that went over with us to form a new Air Division were better trained with new tactics that would be successful.

The 388th was commanded by Col. William B. David from Calhoun, GA, and also had several other area Georgia boys as Jack L. Rogers of Reidsville; James Bragg of Brooklet; John V. Kicklighter and myself of Glennville. John Victor was a pilot in my squadron and flew 15 rough missions before grounding with a bad, bad, sinus problem. John then returned to the U. S. and did an excellent job in training B-17 air crews that would join us later.

Col. David also revised the Bomber formation tactics and strategy. We could now prepare and take off quickly and outwit the German intelligence and bomb targets with great success and less damage and losses to our planes.

The next big help to our Air War was the success in shooting down enemy fighter planes. Thanks to gunners like Sgt. Jack. L. Rogers of Reidsville and Sgt. James Bragg of Brooklet. Our aerial gunners were taught by Jack and other instructors the gunnery techniques to hit the enemy fighters in their attack angles. The enemy knew they needed to destroy the 388th to blunt the Eighth Air Force spearhead. They did a massive fighter attack on our Group and had about 200 of their fighters shot down or damaged. The 388th lost no planes and suffered only minor damage. Sgt. Bragg shot down a number of planes and as far as I know, was the only aerial gunnery Ace of the war. The enemy Air Force never tried us again.

To all those in our Group Col. David was the No. 1 hero of the war. He led our Group on mission after mission into the teeth of the enemy Air and Anti-Air Craft defense at the worst times. His contributions to the overall Air Force Tactics and strategy for our heavy bombers, the P-51 and P-47 fighters and attack bombers was great. However, one thing after the war made me sick. Col.

THE 8ᵀᴴ AIR FORCE WON THE WAR IN EUROPE

David was in the last class of engineers to graduate from the University of Georgia. He also had a degree in Electrical Engineering and also was a star athlete in several sports including football. I called the University of Georgia football office and suggested that Col. David be honored at a football half-time ceremony. They tried to tell me no such person existed in their files. I faxed them some information and they finally admitted there had been a football player and athlete named Bill David but no big deal. I have just never known of another man of his caliber.

I know there were a lot of unsung heroes in the war who had the nail for the horse shoe so to speak. However, the 388th Bomb Group of the Eighth Air Force did a remarkable job. We were mostly a bunch of small town kids and farm boys. A few of us like myself had built model airplanes as a high school hobby and every little bit of knowledge helped.

To sum it up, the war was against our principal enemies Japan and Germany which tried to bring about our defeat. They had planned for the allied forces to be defeated in the invasion but the Germans had been bombed into oblivion. From the easy way the Germans collected intelligence information it was believed that a lot of people liked them The Germans are very intelligent but methodic. They do things by the book. They could have won or ended the war in a stalemate by using their Jet Fighters fully in Air Defense. Due to all the pressure we had kept on them they had not done their technical evaluation of the plane. It was really a close war.

As word passed among the officers and enlisted men of the 388th Group that their commander had received assignment to duties elsewhere, they felt a moments chagrin, almost alarmed by their loss. Colonel William B. David had won their high esteem by the comforts he had secured for station personnel; he had their admiration for his prowess as a combat airman, and for his leadership which had spearheaded the many military successes of the 388th. They were sorry to have Colonel David leave their organization.

Indication of Colonel David's outstanding participation in the war against Germany are the awards that he has received. He holds the Air Medal with three Oak Leaf Clusters, the Distinguished Flying Cross with two Oak Leaf Clusters, the Purple Heart with one Oak Leaf Cluster, and the Silver Star.

    A leading daily newspaper from Georgia ran an article that stated that Georgia had won the war because Georgians had more medals and more rank than any other state. The Georgia School of Technology opened its doors in October 1888, and this was the beginning of the transfiguration from being an agrarian state to being a part of the national industrial economy. Over the years, it changed itself several times. It grew from a trade school to a technological university. It admitted women students in 1952, and in 1961 it was the first southern university to admit African-American students without a court order.

    "The Ramblin' Wreck Fight Song" was inspired by an old folk ballad, "The Sons of the Gamboliers." But a Gambolier is a Venetian boatman who propels a gondola. The Ramblin' Wreck was adopted from a 1908 old drinking song. The lyrics are:

I'm a Ramblin' Wreck from Georgia Tech, and a hell of an engineer –
A helluva, helluva, helluva, helluva, hell of an engineer.
Like all the jolly good fellows, I drink my whiskey clear.
I'm a Ramblin' Wreck from Georgia Tech and a hell of an engineer.
Oh! If I had a daughter, sir, I'd dress her in White and Gold,
And put her on the campus to cheer the brave and bold.
But if I had a son, sir, I'll tell you what he'd do –
He would yell, 'To hell with Georgia!' like his daddy used to do.
Oh, I wish I had a barrel of rum and sugar three thousand pounds,
A college bell to put it in and a clapper to stir it round.
I'd drink to all the good fellows who come from far and near.
I'm a ramblin', gamblin', hell of an engineer!

    The cheerleaders are six women, who wear a uniform of a white skirt and a white and gold cropped top with the word "Tech" on the front. They ride onto the football field on the running boards and rear seat of a white-and-gold-painted antique car.

THE 8ᵀᴴ AIR FORCE WON THE WAR IN EUROPE

The Ramblin' Wreck tune has had some notable moments in its history. It was the first school song to have been played in space. And Gregory Peck sang the song while strumming a ukulele in the movie *The Man in the Gray Flannel Suit*. John Wayne whistled it in *The High and the Mighty*. Tim Holt's character sings a few bars of it in the movie *His Kind of Woman*.

There are numerous claims that many GIs in Higgins boats crossing the English Channel on the morning of D-Day sang the song to calm their nerves. It is difficult to relate this history to the winning of the war in Europe. The Asian war was finished by a couple of atomic bombs.

David Backhouse Comments on the War

Dear 388th:

Coney Weston Hall is the nearest residence to Knettishall Airfield. Most days I pass the Memorial which stands where the entrance to the base was and at 76 I still manage to fly a light aeroplane from the base – but only on a really nice day when a pleasant breeze blows almost exactly down the grass strip we use as a runway! And this strip happens to be over and along part of what was your main E-W runway. You may be sure that the exploits of the 388th are often in my mind.

I have another reason for feeling an affinity with Americans. Obviously, we could not have won the war but for you, and it fell to my lot to deliver aircraft – mostly American – across the North and later the South Atlantic to their selected base. To this end I flew Hudsons, Baltimores, Marauders and the most excellent Dakota. Often our routes would take in U.S. air bases such as Belem or Natal in Brazil where we would be welcomed and stay the night before proceeding on the next leg.

Coney Weston Hall, as some of you know, was run as a Country House Hotel by my son, Stephen for a few years. But Stephen has gone on to do other things and we are now again a private residence. As I said, it is the nearest building to the airfield and the real purpose of this letter is to say that any member of the 388th, be he Cook or Captain and would still like to make a trip to visit the old base, they would be more than welcome to stay here as my guests, with of course wives or relatives. Best regards to you all and as Wilbur James would say, "Keep 'em flying."

As David wrote, "We could not have won the war but for you (Americans)."

THE 8TH AIR FORCE WON THE WAR IN EUROPE

Chapter Twenty Two
The End of War in Europe

When I was at a meeting in 2016 in Wisconsin with General Robin Rand, who is in charge of all the airfields and airplanes in the U. S. Air Force, he wanted to know about my 30 missions over Germany in 1944, including two on D-Day. He was also very interested in my Distinguished Flying Cross. When I finished telling him about all my Air Force experiences, he said, "The 8th Air Force won the war in Europe. Don't you agree?"

I had to think a few minutes, then I responded. "We did it methodically. First, we destroyed the largest submarine pen in Germany, which was on the North Sea. Then we went for German oil. We destroyed all the refineries around *Leipzig* and as far as east as *Brux* in Czechoslovakia. When the war ended, only 3 of 91 oil refineries were functioning. Next, we went for the factories in the Ruhr Valley along the *Rhine River*, which were producing airplane parts, bullets, rockets and other necessities of war. This is the largest industrial area of Germany. We obliterated all railroad depots, so that they could not supply things of war to their troops. And lastly we bombed all the trains carrying troops as replacements, so that by the end of 1944 Germany had no means of continuing what Hitler called his 1000-year war. On May 7, 1945 General Jodl walked into the American base to surrender."

General Rand was elated over my summary of the war's end. "I told you," he said forcefully. He pointed a finger at me and said, "You guys won the war."

I didn't respond to him because I knew that our losses were very high.

Defeated Germans surrender, June 19, 1945. Photo provided by A. Bolino.

Chapter Twenty Three
The War in Asia

After pondering my discussion with General Rand, I checked the exact figures. I was amazed to learn that the 8th Air Force had 47,000 casualties in WWII, and I was more astounded to read that 26,000 of them died in battle. As I thought about these statistics, I had to compare them to the losses in the Southwest Pacific.

On April 26, 1942, General MacArthur chose the islands he would attack. From then until 1945, Naval troops battled their way to Japan.

In 1943, 1,000 died attacking *Tarawa*. In 1944, they invaded *Peleliu, New Guinea,* and *Guam.* At these places many Japanese banzai charged.

When the European war ended, the US Navy lost 12,540 in the Southwest Pacific. This was less than one-half of those killed in combat over Europe. Compared to the 8th Air Force losses, these statistics tell us that the war in Europe was more deadly.

AUGUST C. BOLINO

Chapter Twenty Four
Merciful Missions

While I was preparing to leave the Air Army Air Corp, the Air Force in England was planning some merciful missions for people who were starving. Joseph Bornstein was one of them. He first arrived at *Knettishall* airfield in 1945. As he said, "By then, things were winding down, and there weren't enough bombing missions to go around. Since they had enough planes, we weren't included," he added.

Despite the situation, few of the airmen who participated in the operation understood its severity until they began their low-level runs over the Netherlands. That certainly was the case for Bob Cooperman of Syosset, NY. Cooperman belonged to the same bombardment group as Bornstein.

"We had never been so close to the ground, you understand," Cooperman said, "but we were about as close as a plane could get to a food drop."

Operations Chowhound and Manna gave the Netherlands an intimate view of the planes carrying needed nourishment. Using U.S. flight plans developed for the possibility of having to deliver food to prisoner of war camps deserted by the German army, B-17 Flying Fortresses flew barely 200 feet above the ground with wheels and flaps lowered to slow the aircraft to just about a stall speed of 110 mph. The four-propeller planes roared past church steeples and just above rooftops -- necessary for the parachute-less sacks of powdered eggs, canisters of meat and other supplies to survive their trip down to designated drop sites at air strips and race tracks.

"You could have been shot down with a stone," Cooperman said, and some planes returned with holes from being shot at by rifles. Cooperman, unlike Bornstein, had flown 25 bombing missions above Germany as a radio operator and gunner. He hoped

THE 8ᵀᴴ AIR FORCE WON THE WAR IN EUROPE

his plane's payload would strike at least a few "Hitler types" on the ground as it targeted factories and transportation corridors.

He briefly thought of what it must have been like to live through six-and seven-hour marathon bombings of *Berlin* – "But now." Cooperman said. "There were enemy aircraft, but never individuals."

Now, coming in low and slow on their first mission over the Dutch countryside, American flyers saw people in the streets and on the tops of buildings. Bornstein saw immense tracts of land that were flooded when the Nazis broke the dikes. People waved colored cloths at the planes and shouted even though there was no hope of the air crews hearing them over the engines.

The merciful missions left two very different impressions on Bornstein who would never make a bombing mission and Cooperman who had made his fair share of them.

"I can't recall thinking about it," Bornstein said of the effects of Operation Chowhound on Dutch citizens. "We tried to do what we were assigned to do. I just kind of took things from day to day."

Yet Cooperman struggles even today to find the right words to describe how quickly and deeply he realized the importance of the five missions he eventually flew over the Netherlands.

"When we first started going over, it was a chore," he said. "We didn't know that these people were literally starving."

"The following days seeing these people, it just kept building and building. When we finally stopped dropping food it was like a letdown. We wanted it to continue."

What lasted from April 29 to May 8, 1945, as one of the greatest humanitarian endeavors of the 20th Century, ended quickly, and it was ignored in the annals of World War II. It was called "Chowhound" by the Americans and "Manna" by the British, but it mattered not what it was called. It saved the lives of thousands of Dutch who were literally starving to death. The Americans were not given combat credit for dropping food to the hungry, but they received the undying gratitude of the Dutch people for generations to come.

The allied air drop of supplies over Holland during Operation Chowhound. Image is from the public domain via www.warbirdinformationexchange.org.

The early history of hatred for Germans began when Holland was occupied by the Germans in May 1940, The Netherlands and its peoples had been a constant thorn in the side of Nazi Germany. When Queen Wilhelmina escaped to England, the Nazis tried to impose their own regime under *Reichskommissar* Arthur Seyss-Inquart.

But the Dutch never volunteered to become a part of the *"Herrenvolk"* (the master race); instead they listened to the broadcasts from the BBC, and they even declared a nationwide workers' strike in February 1941.

When the first groups of Jews were deported, the Dutch began to hide Jews, risking their lives. The Nazis tightened the screws by *"Arbeitseinsatz"* (drafting of civilians for forced labor). All men between ages 18 and 45 were forced to work in German factories, but hundreds chose to hide instead.

But again the screws were tightened: this time by rationing food. The Nazis gave each adult a ration card, and those who refused to work for any reason would forfeit their weekly food ration. Again, the Dutch refused to comply. They created resistance groups and they killed German officials. Which led to swift reprisals.

Everything changed after D-Day. Field Marshal Bernard

THE 8ᵀᴴ AIR FORCE WON THE WAR IN EUROPE

Montgomery developed a plan to advance from Holland into Germany. To support this operation, Queen Wilhelmina's government called for a railroad strike. Within a single day, all Dutch railroad personnel disappeared underground, but the Germans began a six-week embargo of all food shipments to Western Holland. Queen Wilhelmina appealed directly to President Franklin Roosevelt for help. The President replied that everything would be done to help *after* liberation.

The Germans retaliated again by cutting off all electricity to civilians, and then they cut off gas supplies to *Amsterdam*.

In October, the Supreme Headquarters Allied Expeditionary Force (SHAEF), for strategic planning purposes, had divided the country into three sections. Area "A," south of the River Waal, was soon to be liberated. Areas "B" and "C," to the north. Where only dykes stood between the reclaimed land and the sea, the Allies saw the area of most dire need, so the 21st Army Group was ordered to begin stockpiling food to feed 3,600,000 people on a daily basis. But there was no way to get the food into the hands of the people, until allied planes began the first of more than 5,300 flights and dropped 12,000 tons of food during the 10-day effort along the western edge of the Netherlands.

When the Germans surrendered on May 7, 1945, the Netherlands went to work repairing its wounded country and nursing its residents back to life. Cooperman readied himself for an air war over Japan that was ultimately grounded when the United States dropped atomic bombs on Hiroshima and Nagasaki.

The Dutch government invited two airmen from each bomb group back for a reunion in 1980 and have held a similar event at the end of April and beginning of May every five years since. Cooperman and Bornstein have attended these events, at which airmen are presented to mayors and paraded through towns that benefited from the drops. People of all ages approach the men and express seemingly endless gratitude.

"They'd say, 'I wouldn't be here if it wasn't for you.'" Cooperman said. "And I'd tell them, 'You're too young. This is 40 years ago."

What Cooperman ultimately realized was that the younger

generations were thanking the fliers for saving the lives of their parents and grandparents.

The Dutch food drop transcended military orders and governments, and it was superseded later by the better-known, Berlin Air Lift. But it was not political; it was truly humanitarian," Cooperman said. "In this instance, they knew that they were eventually going to win.

"It was just that there were starving people down there.[17]"

---

[17] This article appeared in the September 24, 2000 issue of the *Burlington, VT Free Press*. It involved an interview with two members of the 388th Bomb Group.

THE 8ᵀᴴ AIR FORCE WON THE WAR IN EUROPE

Part VIII Flying Home

What a joyous time. When we completed our last mission, we took a train to *Prestwick*, Scotland for three or four days. Immediately, we noticed the difference between the British and the Scots. They were much more outgoing and friendly. And whereas the British offered the same, boring breakfast, the Scots had a more varied set of options. It was a different culture and a different language.

We left Scotland in a C-47 (the old DC-3) and headed for home. There were no seats, just two long benches on each side of the waist. No one complained because we were going home. At about the half-way point of the journey, we all took out a one dollar bill and noted the date on it — on mine was August 23, 1944. It was our "Short Snorter." It was supposed to accompany a drink, but none was available.

The first stop was Iceland. As we tried to land, we had trouble finding the small island because we hit high winds. The pilot said we would be socked in for a while, so we went to barracks and hit the sack for three hours. Not long after, we were awakened and told that we were ready for takeoff.

To continue our story, we left the *Keflavik* airport in perfect sunlight. We made one more stop in Greenland and headed towards New York City, where I took the train to Boston. Now, I never told anyone in Boston that I was coming home because I might have been shot down. So no one knew when I got off the train in South Station. I took the subway and streetcar to Day Square, East Boston. We lived in a three-story building at Prescott Street.

My mother worked in a textile mill near Maverick Square, and she usually walked down Bremen Street, along the railroad tracks, to Prescott and across the square to our house.

I remember the post-combat shakes. I flew 30 combat missions, and when I got home to Boston with a leave, my hands shook. I remember one night at dinner when my mother handed me a cup of coffee, and as I held the cup I spilled some all over the table. My mother screamed in Italian, "What have they done to my boy?" I told everyone that it was nothing and that it was temporary. Of course, that was true, because as I got further away from combat, 1 became what you might call "my old self."

During that leave, I was never more alone. I spent all my time in local night clubs which were frequented by women and 4-F males. I really did not want either, so I just sat alone, drank and listened to the music. I did meet two friends. Joe Bonito was home after serving on *Saipan*. He was discharged because he contracted gonorrhea, and he was receiving treatment at the Veteran's hospital. I also renewed my friendship with Pat Sozio. He was back from *Guadalcanal*, and he was a wreck. He had worse shakes than I did. He described how the Marines captured the island using flame throwers. As he said, "The Japs came screaming out of their caves covered with flames." He said the Marines had a single rule: take no prisoners.

R&R (Rest and Rehabilitation)
Chapter Twenty Five
Atlantic City to Hollywood

When my leave expired, I was ordered to report to Atlantic City, which I got to easily by train. I met our bombardier, Max Kemp, and we enjoyed the R & R at a hotel on the boardwalk. I guess the rest of the crew were sent to different R & R sites. Max and I were enjoying beach beauties, but our stay was cut short when a hurricane hit. It flipped the boardwalk over, damaging several hotels, including ours. It was my second hurricane, because I experienced the 1938 hurricane that hit Boston. That one came up from Providence unannounced and did considerable damage.

Max invited me to his home in California, so we took the train to Nashville, where Max lost his baggage. From there we hitchhiked on an ATC (Air Transport Command) plane to Memphis, Love Field (Dallas) and on to Long Beach, California, where we picked up Max's 1940 Plymouth convertible. We stayed in his mother's house at 1244 Gower in North Hollywood. I was very impressed with the fact that he lived next door to Artie Shaw. It was great to be in a private home again after all those Army barracks. I found one aspect of Max's house very fascinating. I was sleeping in an upstairs bedroom, when he came in and told me to go out on the balcony. We stepped outside and he reached up and pulled an orange from the tree adjoining the bedroom. As a Massachusetts native, I was very astonished.

Max asked me if I wanted to do some sightseeing, and, of course, I did. He first took me to Paramount Studios. We walked onto a set where Allan Ladd was making a movie. He was a runt (he wore five or six inch heels), but he was friendly. He asked about our war experiences. We left him and went to *see* a movie being made. It was a pirate adventure featuring Maureen O'Hara, who was a gorgeous redhead, and Paul Henreid. It was called *The Spanish Main*. They were on the ship in a storm, and when the ship was on rockers acting commenced, the ship pitched and yawed and a large hose was turned on and fan sprayed them with water. It was all so fake, and it shattered my image of Hollywood reality. It was a real comedown.

The next day Max asked me if I wanted to see the Walt Disney Studio. He knew someone there and could get me a tour of the place. Of course, I accepted. We drove to the place, and we entered a long building, where there were hundreds of persons drawing Mickey Mouse, etc. Walt Disney was there with his brother. They showed us around the building. At that time, most of Hollywood was happy to serve as guides for war heroes around the studios. I guess they were sorry for having missed all the fun.

I remember one more thing. Max told me we were going to Hollywood High School. I asked him "Why?"

He responded, "You'll see."

When school was finished, I saw the most amazing group of young teens leave the building and some walked to our car. Max said they were all starlets hoping to make it big in movies.

I asked one where she was from, and she said, "Kansas." And she added, "I was the Beauty Queen of Topeka."

"Well then," I enquired, "how are you doing?"

A slight mist came in her eyes as she leaned towards me and whispered, "You can't get a contract unless you lie down with the directors. I will never do that, because I am due to be married with my high-school sweetheart soon."

I hugged her and told her she will be much happier living that kind of life, and she gave me a quick kiss on the side of my face.

The next day we received orders to report to Denver in ten days. We drove to Arizona and New Mexico, a trip of about 100 miles to Albuquerque. We stayed overnight in Santa Fe, where we replenished our cash. Since we were close to Las Vegas, we decided to see the Hoover Dam, because we knew it was a colossal structure. As we drove on top of the structure, we got a flat tire and immediately several armed soldiers confronted us. They asked our names and "What are you doing up here and what is your destination." We showed them our IDs, and they he helped us to fix the flat.

Chapter Twenty Six
Denver, CO

We drove to our new R & R site at Ft. Collins, just north of Denver. It was an old Civil War fort. I chose to be rehabilitated in the woodworking and machine shop because I had been a machinist before enlisting. I made a cigarette lighter out of a fifty-caliber shell, and I carved a B-17 out of wood. In the evenings I would go downtown to listen to a good trio performing at one club, so I dropped in. It turned out to be the King Cole Trio. At that time, Nat Cole played a cool, jazz piano and he did no singing. He later became a famous balladeer.

I met other celebrities in Denver. One evening, at another bar, I sat next to a man and he asked if he could buy me a drink. It was Edmund O'Brien. He was with Joe Bushkin, who played piano for Tommy Dorsey. Later, we were joined by another person, and O'Brien introduced me to Harry Goodman, who was Benny's brother. They asked about my bombing missions, and they bought me drinks. They were in town with one of the patriotic shows. I think it was "Winged Victory."

As the evening progressed, we became more friendly, and they invited me to a hotel room where they said I could meet Benny Goodman. To this day, I still cannot understand how I refused to meet my boyhood idol.

THE 8TH AIR FORCE WON THE WAR IN EUROPE

Chapter Twenty Seven
Leaving Santa Ana, CA

I remember that after a few days, we received orders. I was told to report to Santa Ana, California, and Max was sent to Albuquerque. Since Santa Ana was a classification and reassignment center. I really didn't know what I would do there, and in fact, in all the assignments I received after returning from combat I had no real function. I sat around the Officer's Club not knowing what I would do. On December 31, 1944, a sergeant came in and yelled, "Anyone want to go to the Rose Bowl?" I was always a big sports fan, so I ran up and answered, "Yea."

The next day we took a bus to Pasadena for the game between Southern California and Tennessee. The halftime entertainment was better than the game. The temperature was 75 degrees and very sunny, and I was amazed to think that here were people in shirt sleeves and many persons stripped to the waist, while the temperature in Boston was probably below zero. Incidentally, Southern California won the game by a score of 26 to 0.

One morning I was sitting with nothing to do, and a Colonel came into the Officer's Club and he spoke loudly, "Is there a navigator in this room?"

I did not speak, but everyone pointed at me. The Colonel came up to me and said. "We are taking off in a half hour. Prepare for a trip to Columbia, South Carolina."

I said, "I'll be ready." I got some maps of the southeast and I wrote the best course I could find. It was about a three-hour flight in a B-29. I could not believe the difference between the B-29 and the B-17. The B-29 had a pressurized cabin, so the crew could walk around in their t-shirts. It had four computer-controlled turrets, and it excelled in low-altitude bombing missions. It carried the bombs that destroyed *Hiroshima* and *Nagasaki*.

I did not realize that the Colonel was staying overnight, so I was not prepared for an overnight stay. He told me to be ready for a morning flight back to Santa Ana. I learned that he graduated from the University of South Carolina, and he was heading for a house of one of his collegiate buddies. So I was on my own.

I checked in to a downtown hotel, and I asked the clerk what I could see that was of interest. He mentioned the South Carolina Relic Room and Military Museum. I thought about the Massachusetts 54th Regiment that tried to capture Fort Wagner where most of the regiment were wounded or died, and I decided that I would skip the museum and instead I entered a local restaurant for lunch. The waitress said, "Have a seat, sweetheart. I'll be right with you."

When I ordered lunch, she asked, 'Do you'all want grits?" She pronounced it as gree-its. When she brought the fried chicken, it was floating in some liquid. I picked at it, paid the bill and ventured into a local bar. As soon as a couple of gents learned that I was from the North, they were anxious to discuss the "War of Northern Aggression," which we call the Civil War. I really did not want to argue, so I accepted his statement that the South had won that war.

I said my goodbyes and headed back to my hotel. On the way I came upon a statue of Andrew Jackson. It was impressive as he was mounted on his steed and waving a hand of victory. The trip back to Santa Ana was uneventful.

I decided to go back to Los Angeles. Santa Ana was connected to Los Angeles by way of an electric train, so I did visit the city regularly. The problem was that Los Angeles was over 50 miles across, and it was difficult to get to any of the other suburbs. But if you stuck out your thumb, you could usually get a ride, because the citizens were very sympathetic about the welfare of service men.

One evening as I was walking downtown and I saw a sign at Symphony Hall that said "Jazz at the Philharmonic Tonight." I bought a balcony seat and sat back to enjoy a fantastic jam session by all the jazz greats, including Les Paul, Illinois Jacquet, Charlie

THE 8TH AIR FORCE WON THE WAR IN EUROPE

Parker and Buck Clayton and other sidemen of the Ellington and Basie bands. Later when the phonograph record was available of this concert, I bought one. I had it at the University of Michigan, and it was a favorite of my roommate, Allan Neef.

Chapter Twenty Eight
Gunnery at Las Vegas, NV

While I was having fun at Santa Ana, the Air Corps made a discovery: I was called into the office of a major, who had his head down reading my personnel file. He said, "Lt. Bolino, I notice that you have never been to gunnery school." I thought he was joking, so I said, "I just came back from 30 combat missions, and I even shot down a ME 109." I told him I could take a 50-caliber gun apart blindfolded, but he was not impressed.

He looked at me and said, "It's regulations."

I reported to Las Vegas Gunnery School to take a gunnery course I should have had before going into combat. It was good training but a bit late. We started with an interesting part of gunnery training--firing from a moving target. We took off in a small plane and headed for another one that was towing a cylindrical target. I was able to hit the target most of the times because I had learned how in combat.

Next, we turned to shooting at a moving target from an open truck, which was driven around a paved half-mile track at about 25 to 30 miles per hour. I stood in the truck inside a metal retainer that was mounted to the floor of the truck with a 12-guage shotgun. Then came the fun. As we proceeded down the track, we came to a number of skeet towers which fired disk-shaped clay pigeons in all directions. I had just enough time to shoot and reload. Each tower had a different configuration, so the shooter could not memorize when the pigeon would be ejected. We did this several times during our training, and by third or fourth week I got pretty good at destroying the targets. Of course, having already been to combat. I was really doing it for fun. The good news was that when we fired no one fired back at us. I received my certificate, but the training was all wasted, because I was never

THE 8ᵀᴴ AIR FORCE WON THE WAR IN EUROPE

going to fire a gun again.

Las Vegas had a seedy side. Downtown was a circus. There were more call girls and more money than I had ever seen. At that time there were only three casinos in Vegas. One of them featured the very popular Mildred Bailey, who sang a variety of Bawdy songs. One of them was "It Takes Two to Tango."

While in Las Vegas, I met two persons at the base that I became friendly with – Hugh Andrews from Denver and Jim Byrnes, who claimed to be related to the Former Governor of South Carolina who was in Roosevelt's cabinet. Each payday we converted paychecks into silver dollars and headed to the gambling tables at the Pioneer Club where we lost all of our money.

One evening when I was in the Pioneer Club, I heard a shot. A man had blown his head off while eating a sandwich (presumably after losing a lot of money). The sheriff came over, looked at the situation and said, "I wish these god---- people from Los Angeles would kill themselves in California." Everyone else went on eating their sandwiches.

After about six months of this, I said enough, so I took a young lady to the movie, and for some reason I still remember her name – Carlie Conger. Jim and Hugh went off to the crap table. When I returned from my date, I went to the barracks and found them counting their money. Jim had won $7,000 and Hugh $4,000. It was the costliest date I ever skipped, and I don't believe I have gambled since. I knew that with that kind of money, I could have bought three or more Ford automobiles, if they produced any. Or I could have bought a small two-bedroom house in most towns. Or if I had invested the money at 10 percent I would now have $1.2 million. It was certainly the most expensive date I went on.

After this, gambling ceased to interest me. In fact when my wife TJ and I went to Atlantic City (by bus years later) on a deal where they gave you $15 dollars to gamble with, we brought our rolls of quarters home with us.

Chapter Twenty Nine
Parachutes at Shreveport, LA

When I completed my gunnery course, I said goodbye to Las Vegas and I reported to my last duty station in Shreveport, Louisiana. It was my second stint in that state, since I had been a flying cadet in Monroe.

I was very puzzled as to my assignment because I was placed in charge of parachutes. I guess they expected me to count them each day. What a colossal waste of my time and talent. I went to the parachute building, and found the sergeant in charge, and I said "Sergeant, you seem to know what you are doing."

He said, "Yes, Sir." So I told him to keep track of chutes and call me if he needed any help. I spent most of my time either by the swimming pool or downtown. As we recreated by the swimming pool, we were served by German POWs, who seemed like an arrogant bunch of SOBs, so we would often taunt them by calling them *schwein* or *schwartz* (pig or black or both).

I was sitting by the swimming pool on April 12, 1945, when I got the word that FDR had died. We never knew that the President was so handicapped. We were aware that he had contracted polio and that he went to Warm Springs, Georgia each year for treatment, but the extent of his debilitating illness was kept from us by reporters. We saw in the newsreels that Roosevelt was aging, but his death was a shock to us and the entire nation. We knew nothing about his Vice President, named Truman, but he did turn out to be a pretty good president.

When the European war ended, we were all waiting to get out of the Air Force. The system the military devised was called points. A person received so many points for each month of service and so many for each month of combat, and 60 points were needed to qualify. I easily qualified for early discharge.

A year earlier, the Congress had passed the GI Bill, so I knew I would be able to attend college full-time in daytime, so I wrote to six universities. Since I had been an engineering student at Northeastern University, I chose leading technical schools, such as Georgia Tech, Cal Tech, Purdue, Northwestern and Michigan. I told the admission officers that I had completed three years of evening college and had graduated from navigation school, and I asked them how much advanced credit they would give me. I told them that in my three years of evening school that my grades were poor, but I explained that I was working long hours in the defense industry and that I was certain that I could improve my performance if I was a full-time student.

Most replied with a form letter, but the Dean of the University of Michigan sent me a friendly letter telling me that Michigan wanted war veterans and that they were appreciative of what we had done. He said he would give me the highest class standing that was possible. He said I would receive one semester credit for my Air Force work and a maximum credit for the rest. When I met him, he said I would be admitted as a junior, but I would be on probation. If I did not keep a B average, I would be dismissed. I never got a grade below B from 1945 to 1957 when I completed my MBA and Ph.D degrees.

My choice of Michigan was a very good one as it turned out.

Chapter Thirty
Leaving Fort Smith, AR

I sat around for months waiting to be discharged. When the Air Force dropped atomic bombs in August, 1945 on *Hiroshima* and *Nagasaki*, the war ended. Now there were 15 million service people who were anxious to get out quickly. Since I had points above the requirement, I was told to report to Camp Chafee at Fort Smith, Arkansas. When I got there, the place was bulging with people. It was a madhouse. I went through processing, got a going out physical examination and was waiting for my discharge. At this point, I was told that those who joined the Air Force Reserves were released first, so instead of getting a discharge paper, I was sworn in as a Reserve Officer and was given orders to report to my home in East Boston.

THE 8TH AIR FORCE WON THE WAR IN EUROPE

Part IX Casualties, Honors, and Awards

All of the achievements in war carried a high price. Half of the U.S. Army Air Force's casualties in World War II were suffered by the Eighth Air Force (more than 47,000 casualties, with more than 26,000 dead). Seventeen Medals of Honor went to Eighth Air Force personnel during the war. By war's end, they had been awarded a number of other medals to include 220 Distinguished Flying Crosses, and 442,000 Air Medals. Many more awards were made to Eighth Air Force veterans after the war that remain uncounted. There were 261 fighter aces in the Eighth Air Force during World War II. Thirty-one of these aces had 15 or more aircraft kills. Another 305 enlisted gunners were also recognized as aces.

One in ten of all persons killed in World War II were members of the Eighth Air Force. If you added all those who died on *Guadalcanal, Saipan, Iwo Jima* and all the other Islands of the Southwest Pacific it would not equal the number of dead of the Eighth Air Force. By war's end, there were 261 fighter aces in the Eighth Air Force during World War II. Thirty-one of these aces each had 15 or more aircraft kills. Another 305 enlisted gunners were also recognized as aces.

The First Silver Star

The Fall 2010 Newsletter of the 388th Bomb Group Association relates how Flight officer Barlow Brown was given the first Silver Star by General Curtis LeMay On September 5, 1943. Brown was the 388th Bomb Group's first recipient for his actions on July 26 during the Hanover, Germany mission. The following description is the official public relations release.

When the records of courage and tenacity are written high on the list the name of Flight Officer Barlow Dean Brown of 817

East 88th Street, Seattle, Wash. and the crew of the Flying Fortress "Impatient Virgin," who brought their battered ship to safe landing in England after virtually every working part of it had been shot out of commission by German flak and fighters. Flight Officer Brown was recommended for the Silver Star and two injured crewmen were recommended for the Purple Heart.

With the pilot injured by a 20 mm shell explosion in the cockpit and the vertical stabilizer torn away in collision with another Flying Fortress, the "Impatient Virgin" was brought home safely by a Flight Officer after a two-hour battle with German fighters that extended far out to sea.

The crew described what happened to their plane when they made an emergency landing in England within 100 miles of their home base:

"A 20 mm shell had exploded in the right wing behind the no. 3 engine."

"Flak destroyed half of the left aileron."

"A shell tore off most of the trim tabs."

"Another shell entered the left window of the pilot's compartment and ------exploded there."

"Two shells tore huge holes in the right horizontal stabilizer and another tore a hole in the left stabilizer. The vertical stabilizer bent into an inverted "J" in a collision with another Fortress, had finally been blown free of the plane."

"Some of the instruments, including fuel gauges, were out. All the oxygen supply in the front half of the ship was out, and eight of the plane's guns would not fire."

"The electric system, the brakes and the hydraulic system were also out."

The plane had completed its bombing run over Hanover, Germany and was heading home with 2nd Lt. William P. Beecham of Omaha, Nebraska as pilot. He and Flight Officer Brown had alternated in piloting the plane.

"We were in formation and had just left the target," said Brown. "I'm not sure whether Beecham had been hit then or not. I saw a plane going on top of us. I shoved the stick down and threw the ship into a dive. I didn't feel anything myself, but crew members said the vertical fin was knocked into a sort of upside

THE 8TH AIR FORCE WON THE WAR IN EUROPE

down J. It was a B-17 that skidded across us and his horizontal stabilizer clipped our vertical."

It was shortly afterward that German fighters began their attacks on the plane with renewed fury and continued them as they saw the big plane was in distress. The plane was flying at 22,500 feet when the 20 mm shell entered the cockpit and exploded behind the seat. Lt. Beecham suffered wounds from the fragments in his back, shoulder, neck, head, and left arm, and all the forward oxygen system went out of commission. Soon half the ship's controls were out and it was losing altitude rapidly. It started into a spin, but Brown managed to pull it out.

"The wing started to go down," said Brown, "and I couldn't get it up. I used up all the trim tab and it started going down. I told the guys to prepare for a water landing.

"We were going from one Fortress formation to another all the way back, for protection. The crew threw out everything that could be moved, even their chutes.

"Half an hour later the vertical fin fell off which again threw the ship off flying level. I sent the word back for the crew to bail out, but some of them had thrown away their chutes.

"We started into a dive again and I switched from AFC to manual control. I used the throttle and trim tabs. You could hardly move the rudder.

"I would speed up the engines on one side to turn right or left and also could use the aileron a little on manual."

The Nazi fighters followed the stricken Fortress more than 50 miles out to sea, 6 or 8 of them diving at us continually. "I picked out the first field we saw in England, circled once, got the wheels down and came in," Brown said.

"She seemed to float; she was so light I couldn't set her down. I couldn't get the flaps down either. She landed about midway on the runway. The brakes held for a moment, enough to straighten the ship out, and then they gave way. I reached for the emergency and that wasn't working.

"We went off the end of the runway and on to the grass, but the ship didn't turn over. It wasn't damaged anymore."

The Lucky Bastard Club

When the 388th Bomb Group was formed, it was nearly impossible to complete twenty-five missions, so the higher ups developed an award to be given to anyone who reached that goal. The first crew to quality was the "Memphis Belle." They actually flew 29 missions, all in 1943.

Captain Robert Morgan named his plane after his girlfriend, Margaret Polk, who lived in Memphis, and he called her Pretty Girl. When he was back in the United States he was given permission by Henry "Hap" Arnold to buzz the downtown of Asheville, North Carolina.

By 1944 it was much easier to complete 25 missions, so that when a crew reached that goal the officers qualified for the Award. I qualified on July 17. My award reads:

"On this 17 day July 1944, the fickle finger of fate has traced on the rolls of the Lucky Bastard Club the name of Gus Bolino, Navigator, "Wolf Wagon" who on this date achieved the remarkable record of having sallied forth, and returned, no fewer than twenty-five times, bearing tons and tons of high explosive Goodwill to the Fuehrer and would-be Fuehrers, through the courtesy of the Eighth Bomber Command , who sponsors these programs in the interest of Government of the people, by the people and for the people."

Signed: Gilbert Goodman, Major Air Corps

THE 8TH AIR FORCE WON THE WAR IN EUROPE

Completes 30 Missions

LT. GUS BOLINO

2nd Lt. Constantino (Gus) Bolino, 21, son of Mr. and Mrs. Nicholas Bolino, 72 Prescott street, who was recently awarded the Air Medal for his participation in "rallying a formation of Flying Fortresses and making a successful bombing run," somewhere in England, has also received two oak leaf clusters for more missions over continental Europe.

Lt. Bolino, a navigator, enlisted in the air corps on Feb. 27, 1943. At Selman Field, La., he became one of 'the little tin guys' (men that never make a mistake)—our navigators. He received his wings on graduation day, Oct. 16, 1943. For being active in sports he received a medal for his pole vaulting championship. He received his commission in January, 1944, and went overseas in April.

The lieutenant has completed 30 missions over enemy territory. He has sent home as a souvenir, a piece of the metal tail of his "Wolf Wagon" flying fortress which was hit in a raid. As a good luck token, he wears on all his missions an old woolen scarf that belongs to his father.

Lt. Bolino is a graduate of Mechanic Arts High School and was attending Northeastern University prior to his enlistment.

Photos provided by A. Bolino

The OshKosh Award

In August 2016, the 388th Bomb Group Association met in Oshkosh, Wisconsin. Only nine veterans of World War II attended. General Robin Rand, who was in charge of all Air Force groups, gave a brief biography of each veteran and gave each an Award, on which he wrote, "Thank you for winning." Here is what it says:

OFFICE OF THE COMMANDER, AIR FORCE GLOBAL STRIKE COMMAND, 245 Davis Avenue East, Suite 200 Barksdale Air Force Base, Louisiana 71110

I am honored and humbled to have the opportunity to express my gratitude for your service. You and nearly sixteen million other Airmen, Soldiers, Sailors and Marines selflessly responded to our Nation's call to help turn back the seemingly overwhelming forces of our adversaries. Regardless of where, or in what capacity you served, the blood, sweat and tears of you and your fellow Airmen allowed America and its allies to prevail and helped usher in the most peaceful period in world history.

Even though many people would have been content to return home and enjoy this hard-won peace, you and your peers merely redoubled your efforts. In a few short years you turned a nation geared to churn out the instruments of war into its greatest economy, bringing about one of the most prosperous periods for our Nation.

Your efforts laid the groundwork for our continued military and economic predominance. As both a citizen and military officer, I am proud to follow in your footsteps. On behalf of myself as well as the men and women of Air Force Global Strike Command, thank you for your service, thank you for your sacrifice and thank you for your selflessness.

Signed ROBIN RAND General, USAF.

THE 8ᵀᴴ AIR FORCE WON THE WAR IN EUROPE

Lt E
Bolino

HEADQUARTERS
THREE EIGHTY EIGHTH BOMBARDMENT GROUP (H)

July 23,

SUBJECT: Combat Missions.

TO : Whom it May Concern.

Date	Ind. Missions	Target	Time
4-30-44	1	Lyons, France	9:00
5-8-44	2	Berlin, Germany	7:00
5-9-44	3	Juvincourt, France	5:20
5-11-44	4	Liege, Belgium	5:30
5-12-44	5	Brux, Czechoslovakia	9:20
5-20-44	6	Brussels, Belgium	6:00
5-22-44	7	Kiel, Germany	7:10
5-23-44	8	Carpiuquet, Belgium	7:50
5-25-44	9	Liege, Belgium	5:40
5-29-44	10	Leipzig, Germany	8:20
5-30-44	11	Troyes-Reims, France	6:50
5-31-44	12	Soest, Germany	6:50
6-4-44	13	Wissant, France	4:30
6-5-44	14	Cape Grisneg, France	5:40
6-6-44	15	Cherbourg, France	8:00
6-6-44	16	Pont-L'Eveque, France	6:30
6-8-44	17	Tours, France	7:00
6-11-44	18	Pontaubault, France	6:30
6-14-44	19	St. Trand, Belgium	6:20
6-15-44	20	Beauvior, France	4:30
6-18-44	21	Bremen, Germany	6:00
6-24-44	22	Bremen, Germany	6:30
6-29-44	23	Leipzig, Germany	8:20
7-6-44	24	Noball - A	6:05
7-8-44	25	Mantes, France	4:30
7-11-44	26	Munich, Germany	9:30
7-12-44	27	Munich, Germany	9:20
7-16-44	28	Stuttgart, Germany	8:30
7-17-44	29	Noball	4:30
			197:15

Photo provided by A. Bolino

AUGUST C. BOLINO

Chapter Thirty One
Caring for the Wounded

The 8th Air Force lost over 26,000 men killed in World War II. In addition, over 7,000 flying personnel were wounded in aerial combat.

Thousands of other flying air crewmen and non-flying personnel were injured in crashes and accidents or suffered severe illnesses. Perhaps not all remember that during World War II the U.S. Air Force was the Army Air Force (AAF) and not the separate branch of the U. S. Armed Forces that it is today. Thus, all Air Force casualties were cared for by the U. S. Army hospitals located throughout East Anglia. However, because many of the special medical problems that were associated with flight the Air Force did have its own limited medical division. In addition to aero physiologists, this division had specially trained flight surgeons who acted as general physicians at each Air Force base, responsible for the health and medical problems of the air crews as well as the base ground force personnel. The flight surgeons operated small dispensaries of up to 25 beds where patients could be treated with minor illnesses or injuries that required only short-term care. The head of the Air Force Medical Division was Air Surgeon Major General David N.W. Grant. His subordinate and Chief Surgeon of the 8th Air Force was the feisty, aggressive and innovative Brigadier General Malcolm C. Grow.

When the Air Force began operations on August 17, 1942, no U. S. Army hospitals were then ready in East Anglia, and the first 8th Air Force casualties were cared for by British EMS (Emergency Medical Service) hospitals. In spite of the high priority given by the British Ministry of Works to the construction of hospital plants in East Anglia, their completion fell far behind schedule due to the shortage of skilled workers and materials. The first U. S. hospital site in East Anglia was at Diddington in Huntingdonshire. It was opened for patients on December 26, 1942. In the late spring of 1943 another East Anglian hospital was completed at White Court, Braintree, Essex. Finally by the fall of 1943 all the hospitals scheduled for East Anglia were completed.

During World War II the 65th General Hospital was located on the grounds of Redgrave Park. It was a reserve unit of Duke University, which is located at Durham, North Carolina. It was a crude construction of Nissen Huts, which was supplemented by tents. It had 1,456 beds and served the wounded from February 10, 1944 to August 29, 1945. It treated thousands of wounded who were brought to England from the Continent.

Mr. George Stebbings helped establish a replica of a 65th General Hospital room at the Second World War airfield al Rougham, near Bury St Edmunds. A few years ago he and his wife attended a reunion of hospital stall and patients in the United States but, through ill-health, he was unable to attend this year's final reunion. Now he is to receive a special citation from the Duke University Health System for his efforts in East Anglia to preserve the memory of the hospital, and the staff which helped to evacuate those wounded in the D-Day landings.

The hospital was an elite unit. It was there for American casualties but they also took some British casualties. The standard of care was well in advance of what was found in this country at the time," said Mr. Stebbings. He said the hospital flag could still be seen in Rickinghall Church where staff and patients had attended services. Ralph Snyderman, president and chief executive officer of the Duke University Health System, said the wartime staff at Redgrave were "steadfast and highly skilled" under the most difficult conditions."

AUGUST C. BOLINO

Chapter Thirty Two
We Lost a Long-Time Friend

Surrounded by his family, George Stebbings passed away peacefully at his home on Dec. 9, 2004. Considered by many to be the foremost English Historian of the 388th Bombardment Group (H), he was 75.

George was born July 5, 1929 in Rickinghall on the Suffolk/ Norfolk border and lived there all his life. Always interested in aircraft, he would have liked to have served in the Royal Air Force but, unfortunately, was found to be color-blind. At age 14 he lied about his age to join the Air Training Corps (ATC), minimum age for enrollment being 16.

George's life-long relationship with the 388th BG began when, at Col. William B. David's direction, his ATC squadron was "adopted" by the Group. His first visit to Knettishall for a conducted tour of the Base, finishing at the No. I Hangar for a close-up look at a B-17 Flying Fortress, was chronicled in *388th Anthology Vol. I.* Although his first flight in a B-17 was with the 385th BG at nearby Great Ashfield, after his ATC squadron's adoption by the 388th a great many of George's Sundays were spent at Knettishall adding to his flying hours.

Lt. Eugene Yarger piloted George's first flight from Knettishall to a nearby RAF Base at Shepherds Grove. Among the many pilots who also allowed George to accompany them on routine local flights were Major B.C. Reed and Lieutenants Casey Sulkowski, Paul Patten, Billy K. Faurot, Arthur Gordon, Garth Hill, Alvin Boyd and James Comer.

After leaving school, George went to work on a local farm and, after a while, met Margaret, who lived in the nearby town of Diss. They married on Dec. 20, 1947. Later George found work in the construction industry, where he remained for the rest of his

THE 8^(TH) AIR FORCE WON THE WAR IN EUROPE

working life. He and Margaret built their home "Little Patches" on a small plot of land on which, as a village school boy many years earlier, George had tended his own garden. Margaret and George have one daughter, Gloria, and two grandchildren, Abigail and Nick. Nick is in the British Army, in the Parachute Regiment.

After the war George joined the Royal Observer Corps, a part-time voluntary organization, and remained a part of this until it was disbanded in the 1990s.

George remained in contact with many members of the 388th and also with members of the 65th General Hospital which was based at Redgrave Park, just outside the village where he lived. In 2002 he received a Citation from the Duke University Health System in North Carolina, thanking him for all he had done with regard to the 65th General Hospital.

Around 1984 George suggested to Ed Huntzinger and other members of the 388th BG (H) Assn Board of Directors that a Memorial should be erected in memory of all those members of the 388th Bombardment Group who gave their lives between 1943 and 1945. The Memorial was designed by John J. "Pat" Ryan, and a committee was formed in England to welcome back veterans and families. On May 17, 1986, this beautiful Memorial was unveiled at the entrance to the Group Headquarters of Station 136, George being one of the Trustees.

Over a period of years George received many photographs relating to the 388th and, at his own expense, had transparencies produced which could be projected onto a screen for the entertainment and enjoyment of many people in towns and villages over a wide area. He and Margaret frequently guided visitors around the old Base area and brought them to see The 388th Collection at Hillside Farm in neighboring Market Weston. For many years he laid a wreath on behalf of the 388th BG (H) Assn. during the Memorial Day Service at the American Military Cemetery at Madingley, Cambridge.

Although his main interests were the 388th BG and the 65th General Hospital, both units of which he was recognized as being the English Historian, he was an authority on anything connected with the 8th Air Force.

George was first diagnosed with cancer seven years ago

and, over this period, had many operations and sessions of treatment. Although this extended his life, this scourge of our time succeeded in the end and George passed on to glory. At his funeral the sum of £650.00 was donated to the Addenbrookes Oncology Cancer Unit in Cambridge. I, with my wife Mary, and Dave and Deborah Sarson of The 388th Collection, had the privilege of representing the 388th BG (H) Assn. at this solemn yet uplifting event during which many tributes were presented.

Any further donations from his many friends in the 388th Bombardment Group (H) Assn. will, with Margaret's blessing, go toward the upkeep of the 388th Memorial in Coney Weston.

Written by David Calcutt

Chapter Thirty Three
The "Greatest Generation" Honored

The National World War II Memorial was an overdue tribute to the Americans who helped win World War II, which was the largest war in human history. The dedication of the World War II Memorial in 2004 was part of a 100-day celebration commemorating the exploits of the "Greatest Generation." It honors the four million veterans who were still alive and the 12 million others who served in all the military services.

The idea for the Memorial came at a fish fry in a small Ohio town that was sponsored by Congresswoman Marcy Kaptur. She was asked by veteran Roger Durbin why there was no memorial to World War II for all the persons who fought in the greatest war in history. On returning to Washington D.C. she made inquiries and was surprised to learn that he was correct. She proposed legislation that was signed by President Clinton on May 25, 1993. In that Same year, the American Battle Monuments Commission, an independent agency of the Executive Branch of the Federal Government, was authorized by the 103rd Congress to establish a memorial to honor those who served their country during World War II, and to commemorate our participation in a war that lasted for almost four years.

It wrote that on the hallowed ground in the shadows of Presidents Washington and Lincoln, we will dedicate this World War II Memorial to our nation's sons and daughters who took up the struggle to preserve our inalienable rights to life, liberty and the pursuit of justice.

The Commission acknowledged with praises the many and significant contributions of our predecessors. Under the leadership of General Fred Woerner, U.S. Army (Retired), former Chairman of the Commission, and Mr. Pete Wheeler, Chairman of the

Memorial Advisory Board, they nurtured the Memorial through many of its formative years. They were also thankful to the many people who joined together in help create this magnificent testimonial.

None of this would have been possible without the dedicated leadership of former Senator Bob Dole, Chairman of the Memorial fund-raising campaign, and FedEx Chairman Fred Smith or Tom Hanks, who also volunteered his time to be our national spokesman.

On Memorial Day 1995, President Clinton dedicated the site by placing a bronze plaque there. The location chosen was on the east end of the Reflecting Pool between the Washington and the Lincoln Memorials. The layout of the Memorial is rationally planned. On the east is the Washington Monument signifying the victory of the Revolutionary War in the eighteenth century, on the west is the Lincoln Memorial telling us that he saved the union in the nineteenth century and in between is the World War II Memorial, which in the twentieth century saved mankind from fanatic despots and preserved our liberties.

Because of several court challenges by revisionist historians and lawyers, construction was delayed for seven years. There were two arguments for moving the World War II Memorial: It would block the view along the mall and it would endanger the foundation of the Washington Monument. The revised design handled these complaints by lowering the site eight feet, including the reflecting pond, and by eliminating the museum that had been planned beneath the Memorial. One fear was that excavating for the museum would have caused the Washington Monument to lean (so, I guess we would then have a leaning tower of Washington).

The Monument as it now stands is a structure of bronze and 17,000 pieces of granite. Within two 43-foot granite pavilions, labeled Pacific and Atlantic, at the north and south entrances, there are bronze eagles holding laurels signifying victory. The 56 granite pillars making up a circle denote the 48 states and territories and Washington D.C. Each has a laurel wreath, and they are bound by a sculptured bronze rope. There is a freedom wall with 4,000 gold stars, each commemorating 100 dead.

THE 8TH AIR FORCE WON THE WAR IN EUROPE

There are a number of bronze bas reliefs on the walkway as you enter the monument. Of particular interest to us in the 388th Bomb Group is the one depicting the crew of a Flying Fortress. There are also quotations etched in stone on each side of the Memorial. These are the ones on the Atlantic half:

On the Home Front

They have given their sons to the military services. They have stoked the furnaces and hurried the wheels. They have made the planes and welded the tanks, riveted the ships and rolled the shells.
... Franklin D. Roosevelt on D-Day

You are about to embark on the Great Crusade towards which we have striven these many months. The eyes of the world are upon you. I have full confidence in your courage, devotion to duty and skill in battle.
... Dwight D. Eisenhower

The official reunion began on May 27 on the Mall, where tents were constructed for meeting buddies and for discussion groups. I went to the reunion tent hoping to find any 388th veterans. There was one name posted; it said he was a prisoner of war. I did not take his name, because I left my name, squadron and phone number; but he never called me.

It was an amazing coming together on the mall. Children everywhere were running up to veterans, especially those in wheel chairs, asking for autographs. Many asked if they could be photographed with veterans. One woman sat on a bench weeping. She had no tickets, but she said she had to come to Washington to honor her dad, who was a Seabee. She said, "I just wanted to see the vets, really."

For me, the highlight of the 27th was the session in which Senators Bob Dole and George McGovern told their war stories. Each of them had a harrowing experience in World War II. Dole lost the use of his arm and McGovern had his B-24 crew bail out and then brought his plane in on two engines. They became good friends, because each was from a farm state, and each pushed for legislation that their constituents desired. McGovern endeared himself to the world by establishing the "Food for Peace" program, by which the United States fed many millions of starving people all over the world.

McGovern told one story that I'll pass one to you. He said, "My parents were life-long Republicans, and I know that they are now looking down on me from above saying, 'Look he's sitting with Bob Dole. This is his finest hour.'" Dole's best comment was, "We both ran for President and we both lost."

The afternoon show on May 28, for those who had tickets, was held at the MCI Center, where the Washington Wizards play professional basketball. It was a three-hour extravaganza, in which one family's life was followed throughout World War II. The mother and daughter worked in a defense plant and the two sons joined different military services. We were able to see reenactments of the bombing of Pearl Harbor, the invasion of D-Day, the taking of a Pacific Island and war's end. Shots were fired, cannons were exploded using dummy shells and horses ran across the stage.

After a brief intermission, the swing band played a number of our songs (Miller, Shaw, Goodman), and then each service band marched in full dress playing its song. I think the Air Force song got the most applause.

On May 30, we left home to take the Metro (subway) to the Smithsonian stop, and we walked around the Washington Monument to our seats in Section 1 just off 17th Street. We got there at noon and were surprised to see the first one hundred rows already taken. We were told people had shown up at 6:30 a.m. There was a two-hour show before the official dedication, mostly speeches and some music.

At exactly 2 p.m. with Presidents Bush I, Bush II and Clinton present, the Memorial was turned over to the nation and those involved in this enterprise gave fairly brief remarks. Here are my comments about who said what.

Bob Dole:
As he began to speak, he looked over the mass of humanity

THE 8TH AIR FORCE WON THE WAR IN EUROPE

and said, "I never got a crowd like this when I was campaigning." Then he got serious. He said, "During World War II, everyone sacrificed. Today nobody is sacrificing except the troops. The average stay of World War II vets was 16 months, considerably longer than the terms set by the generals in Iraq." Dole called our war "the defining event of the Twentieth Century."

Tom Brokaw:
"Some people have criticized me for calling you the 'Greatest Generation.'?' he said, "but I am sticking with it, because I believe you are the greatest."

Tom Hanks:
"Many of you know that true human morality can only be demonstrated. I thank you personally, because you saved the world from tyranny. We enjoyed freedom for 60 years, we do remember D-Day. It was the beginning of the end for Hitler's fortress."

George W. Bush:
He choked back tears when he looked at his father and said, "He helped save our country, and thereby saved the liberty of mankind." He added, "These were the modest sons of a peaceful country, and millions of us are very proud to call them Dad."
He ended, "Every man and woman who saw and lived World War II ~ every member of that generation ~ please rise as you are able and receive the thanks of our grateful nation."

Newspapers have always underestimated the size of crowds at the Fourth of July firework celebrations, so I was not surprised to read that the estimated crowd at the dedication to be 140,000. This is clearly wrong, because the Memorial commission gave out 118,000 tickets for Sections 1 and 2, and there were five other sections along the mall from Seventh Street to Fourteenth Street that did not require tickets. Folding seats were provided and very large TV screens. There were probably 300,000 to 400,000 persons in those seats and this does not count all the persons who stood or sat on benches along the way.

There is much criticism even today of the Memorial as

being too bland, not telling a good story about the battles carved in stone, and one critic went so far as to say that the bronze wreaths were a Nazi symbol.

It is true that the designer is an Austrian, but these comments are unfair, because the story was to be told in the museum that was cancelled, as I mentioned earlier. It is up to the teachers and the National Park Service guides to answer questions about what is written in stone.

One disappointing aspect of the celebration: on July 4 the Memorial was closed, because there was fear that the sparks from the fireworks would damage the granite making up most of the structure. It was first suggested that the fireworks be moved westward over the Potomac River, but that would have necessitated covering the entire Lincoln Memorial ~ an impossible task. Instead, the World War II Memorial was covered with a fire-resistant fabric.

This means that the half-million persons who attend the July 4 celebrations each year will not be able to visit our new Memorial[18].

The World War II Memorial honors the 16 million who served in the armed forces of the U.S., the more than 400,000 who died, and all who supported the war effort from home. Symbolic of the defining event of the 20th Century, the memorial is a monument to the spirit, sacrifice, and commitment of the American people. The Second World War is the only 20th Century event commemorated on the National Mall's central axis.

Visiting the Memorial

The memorial opened to the public on April 29, 2004 and was dedicated one month later on May 29. It is located on 17th Street, between Constitution and Independence Avenues, and is flanked by the Washington Monument to the east and the Lincoln Memorial to the west. The memorial is operated by the National

---

[18] The above article was written by August C. Bolino for the Fall 2004 Newsletter of the 388th Bombardment Group Association

THE 8TH AIR FORCE WON THE WAR IN EUROPE

Park Service and is open to visitors 24 hours a day, seven days a week. For more information about visiting the memorial, accessibility, parking, directions, special events and other details, please visit the National Park Service Web site at www.nps.gov/nwwm or call the Park Service at 202-208-3818.

The World War II Memorial in Washington, D.C.

The Person of the Century

While it is quite proper to celebrate the "Greatest Generation," we must not forget that in 1999 *Time* magazine prepared a list of the 10 most influential persons of the twentieth century, and when they tabulated the votes they chose "The American GI."

Sailors and Marines wanted to be known as Sailors and Marines. Airmen, notwithstanding their origins as a rib of the Army, wished to be called simply Airmen. Collectively, they were blandly referred to as "Service Members." I persisted in using G.I.s and found I was in good company.

Newspapers and television shows used it all the time. The most famous and successful government education program was known as the G.I. Bill, and it still uses that title for a newer generation of Veterans. When you added one of the most common boy's names to it, you got G.I. Joe, and the name of the most popular boys toy ever, the G. I. Joe action figure. And let's not forget G.I. Jane. G.I. is a World War II term that two generations later continues to conjure up the warmest and proudest memories of a noble war that pitted pure good against pure evil and good triumphed.

The victors in that war were the American G.Is, the Willies and Joes, the farmer from Iowa and the steelworker from Pittsburgh who stepped off a landing craft into the hell of Omaha Beach. The G.I. was the wisecracking kid Marine from Brooklyn who clawed his way up a deadly hill on a Pacific island. He was a black fighter pilot escorting white bomber pilots over Italy and Germany, proving that skin color had nothing to do with skill or courage. He was a native Japanese-American infantryman released from his own country's concentration camp to join the fight. She was a nurse relieving the agony of a dying teenager. He was a petty officer standing on the edge of a heaving aircraft carrier with two signal paddles in his hands, helping guide a dive bomber pilot back onto the deck. They were all Americans.

They reflected our diverse origins. They were the embodiment of the American spirit of courage and dedication. They were truly a "people's army," going forth on a crusade to save democracy and freedom, to defeat tyrants, to save oppressed peoples and to make their families proud of them.

They were the Private Ryans, and they stood firm in the thin red line. For most of the G.I.s, World War II was the adventure of their lifetime. Nothing they would ever do in the future would match their experiences as the warriors of democracy, saving the world from its own insanity. You can still see them in every Fourth of July color guard, their gait faltering but ever proud[19].

---

[19] This speech was prepared by Colin Powell, the Chairman of the Joint Chiefs of Staff

Chapter Thirty Four
Honoring Our Dead

When Janet Pack and I brought 47 members of our Bomb Group Association to Knettishall in May 2003, there was much talk of honoring the persons who died in battle. The idea of adding wings to the original Memorial faced a number of legal problems. John Wallace was the legal owner of the site. If he sold the land this would put the Memorial in jeopardy. Originally, George Stebbings suggested that Wallace deed the land to him but Wallace preferred to retain title.

The size of the monument area would be about 1-1/2 to 2 acres. This would cost about 3,000 pounds or $5,000 per acre. If the land is not used for farming, the price could be higher. A primary problem is that Wallace has little interest in the Memorial, despite the fact that he is a trustee. The persons who have been active in obtaining the wings for the Memorial are:

David and Deborah Sarson, owners of the 388th Museum at Hillside Farm
David Calcutt, George Stebbings, 388th historian in Great Britain
John Wallace, owner of the farm land which is the site of the old airfield. Wallace also owns the land where the 388th Memorial is located.

David Calcutt believed that John Wallace should be invited to all meetings of the Board of Trustees, and David Sarsons favored a very long-term lease such as the 100th Bomb Group has. It has a 999 year lease. There has been some talk of an American group purchasing the required land, but there appears to be little chance of this happening, because it is a Crown possession.

Janet Pack, who served as the liaison to the above trustees of the 388th Memorial, made a presentation on "Project Ultimate Sacrifice" at the 2010 Association Reunion on the 623 men who died in service. She related that the two wings of the Memorial would cost $16,500 and would have to be funded by private donations.

At the 2010 annual meeting of the 388th Bomb Group, a proposal was approved to honor all 388th BG men who died during World War II. The project, proposed by the 388th Memorial Trustees, would add two granite wings to the Memorial site. The stones, set at a 30-degree angle and spaced 24 inches from the center piece, would bear the inscription "In Freedom They Lived ... For Freedom They Died" along with depictions of the group's Square H. Names of all 388th BG war dead would be featured alphabetically and be separated by American military stars.

The project researchers counted 620 388th BG deaths, beginning with the crew killed in the Soda Springs, ID training flight on May 5, 1943, and ending with the crash of a sight-seeing flight on May 3, 1945. The numbers also include men from ground crews and fliers who died as POWs.

To verify the total numbers, researchers have poured through the 388th BG Unit Histories, Missing Air Crew Reports, National Archives databases, and even genealogy services. A third and final verification was completed in November.

It was the goal of the Trustees to collect a substantial portion of the funds so that the stones could be put in place before Jan. 1, 2011, when the British VAT (value-added tax) would increase from 17.5 to 20 percent. The work wound be done by H.L. Perfitt Ltd. Stonemasons, who created the original Memorial.

On the afternoon of May 9, 2011 a truck from H.L. Perfitt Ltd. Stonemasons arrived at the site of the 388th BG Memorial with its precious cargo - two granite stones, bearing the names of 623 men of our organization who lost their lives in service to their country and in the cause of freedom.

Within four hours the installation was completed, bringing

THE 8TH AIR FORCE WON THE WAR IN EUROPE

to an end a year and a half of intensive research, planning and development. Project Ultimate Sacrifice, approved unanimously at last year's reunion in October 2009 during conversations between the Association's historian, U.K. Liaison and Memorial Trustees Chair about how to increase awareness of the 388th Bomb Group in the Knettishall area.

The initial idea of creating a second Memorial at a separate location was first explored, then discarded in favor of adding wing stones at the site of the original Memorial, which was dedicated in 1986.

Project responsibilities were divided equally between Jan Pack Singer in the U.S. and Tony Goff in the U.K., with Janet Pack Singer undertaking the names research and Goff pursuing costing, permitting, contracting, and other project aspects which included securing permission from the landowner and arranging for the importation of two black granite slabs, identical to the original, from India.

The multiple-phase research concluded with a list 621 confirmed dead, to which the names of the bomb group's two known MIAs were then added.

The first 388th veteran to see the completed work was Al Sao, former 563rd Squadron navigator, who was visiting the area with his family. The locals agreed that the additions blend so seamlessly that is difficult to believe that 25 years actually separate the two installations.

With the installation completed, focus now turns entirely toward repaying the loan that has made Project Ultimate Sacrifice possible. As of this writing eight years have passed since this installation was completed.

A colleague told me that the Dylan Thomas poem of the "good night" would be appropriate for remembering those who died in battle.

Do not go gentle into that good night,
Old age should burn and rave at close of day;
Rage, rage against the dying of the light.

Though wise men at their end know dark is right,

Because their words had forked no lightning they
Do not go gentle into that good night.

Good men, the last wave by, crying how bright
Their frail deeds might have danced in a green bay,
Rage, rage against the dying of the light.

Wild men who caught and sang the sun in flight,
And learn, too late, they grieved it on its way,
Do not go gentle into that good night.

Grave men, near death, who see with blinding sight
Blind eyes could blaze like meteors and be gay,
Rage, rage against the dying of the light.

And you, my father, there on that sad height,
Curse, bless, me now with your fierce tears, I pray.
Do not go gentle into that good night.
Rage, rage against the dying of the light.

Madingley Without the Sally B?

Each year on Memorial Day there is a service at the American Cemetery at *Madingley*, Cambridge, England. For many years George Stebbings carried the 388th Bomb Group wreath with the wreath carriers. Rain or shine the service proceeded in its usual well-rehearsed manner.

The presentation of the floral tributes is always very moving and impressive. The 388th BG Association contribution was presented by Margaret Stebbings in memory of her late husband George, who had done the honors for many years.

A formation of four F-15 Eagles from RAF Lakenheath flew over in the "Missing Man" Formation, followed by two P-51 Mustangs. Both flyovers were equally as impressive. Usually the P-51 was accompanied the B-17 "Sally B," but due to new regulations made by our "friends" in the EU in 2005 the "Sally B" could not fly because of a new ruling which categorized it as an

THE 8ᵀᴴ AIR FORCE WON THE WAR IN EUROPE

aircraft in the Boeing 737 class, which requires insurance of about £1,000 per flying hour!

This means that the "Sally B.," Britain's last airworthy B-17, was in danger of being grounded indefinitely unless there can be a negotiation with the European Union regarding the insurance regulation purposes. By putting the bomber in the same category as a commercial airliner, the new annual operating expense would increase to £25.000.

Sir Richard Branson, the owner of Virgin Atlantic, later purchased 90 days' worth of insurance coverage, which allowed the "Sally B" to fly over Buckingham Palace (to mark the 60th anniversary of the end of WWII in Europe).

Meanwhile all participants in this annual dedication are seeking a resolution of this commercial quandary[20].

The Shrinking Zuiderzee

The Zuiderzee started out as an inland sea but in 1932 the Dutch built a dike 25 miles long across the inlet to make it an inland lake. The salt water was replaced by fresh river water. This lake was 12% of the area of the nation. The Friesian Islands off the coast and The Netherlands land area were hazards for bomber crewmen who were still gaining altitude on our way to Germany so we were quite vulnerable to ground antiaircraft fire.

The Dutch pumped the water from various sections of the Zuiderzee. Upon pumping a section dry, they often discovered the remains of aircraft (British, German and American) that crashed into the water during World War II. In some instances they found the remains of men missing-in-action for decades, remains which were subsequently identified and given religious burials in marked graves.

It is hard to believe that over 7,000 allied aircraft crashed in the Dutch waters during World War II. There were enough downed planes to almost cover the entire state of New Jersey.

---

[20] Part of this section is taken from an article by David Calcutt in the Fall 2005 Newsletter of the 388ᵗʰ BG.

One Squadron, the 508th usually put up twelve B-17's for a mission and it had losses in that area, both going and coming. If we were over water and knew we were going down, ditching for us was the preferable thing to do. The B-17 had a low wing and so was apt to float for plenty of time to get out and into inflatable life rafts that all bombers carried. The B-24 was a high wing bomber so the planes body area was filled with water very quickly. We were often briefed that in the winter when we did most of our missions that if over the North Sea or channel, to bailout would be a death sentence because in that cold water the life expectancy was 20 minutes.

After the war the Netherlands started a program of reclaiming all that part of the Zuiderzee that was under water. For years of this effort, not a week went by that they did not come upon a hulk of 500 year old Spanish Armada ships, World War I planes or World War II planes. Many B-17's and B-24's have been recovered, some with human remains. One British Spitfire was buried quite deep with the flyer still in the cockpit and well preserved. In his pockets were found silver coins, identification papers and a rosary. Also in his pocket was a silver cupid from a wedding cake. He had been married 14 days before his last and ill-fated mission. The Dutch uncovered a World War I German bomber that had crashed in 1917. After 55 years being submerged, its tires were still inflated. One German fighter plane that was recovered had 63 markings on the plane's cowl to indicate that he had shot down 63 planes.

On Dec. 22, 1943, B-24H Serial No. 42-7638 of the 44th Bomb Group was heading westward for its base in England after bombing a target at *Munster*, Germany. Suddenly it was hit by German anti-aircraft shell, which disabled its engines, and it began to lose altitude. The pilot rang the bail-out bell, and four crewmen parachuted before they realized they were over water. The other six crewman decided to remain with the plane while the pilot ditched it. When the B-24 hit the waves, the impact tore off its nose, and the copilot, Lt. Charles Taylor, floated free. He held onto a life raft but soon passed out in the frigid water. Unconscious, he was rescued by some German soldiers in a patrol boat and sent to prison camp at *Stalag Luft* I for the remainder of the war. Taylor was the only member of the crew to survive. The four who bailed out died from exposure; their bodies were recovered from the Zuiderzee by the Germans and buried. No trace was found of the other five men, and they were "Missing in Action" as of Dec. 22, 1943.

The items in the museum's display are representative of the types of aircraft parts recovered by the Dutch. They were donated to the U.S. Air Force by the Royal Netherlands Air Force.

While the Dutch were pumping water from the Zuiderzee in the early 1970s, a plane with a U.S. star insignia gradually came into view. After months of research, this plane was identified as the missing 42-7638. In 1976 a project was initiated by the Royal Netherlands Air Force to recover the plane, and during the operation, the bodies of the five missing men were found in the wreckage. On request of the next-of-kin, their remains were returned to the U.S. for burial, more than three decades after they had failed to return from a combat flight.

AUGUST C. BOLINO

Part X Museums and Monuments

The Knettishall Monument

In 1985 The 388th Bomb Group Memorial Committee in England was making great progress thanks to George Stebbings. He met with Mr. John Wallace, Hall Farm in Coney Weston and they inspected various sites in the locality. Any one of these chosen sites would be acceptable to the 388th Bomb Group Association. On February 5th, George was invited to the Coney Weston Parrish Council to discuss our memorial. The Chairman advised him to approach the Burough Council (Bury St Edmunds) for planning approval, which was done.

Chuck Zetteck, who drew the plans of the memorial visited England where he met with Stebbins to look over the sites. At this same time Bob & Shirley Cooperman would also visit England to review the sites before going to Holland for their 40th Anniversary Celebration of the Food Drop to the people of Holland. This was from April 27th to May 5th, 1985. All these came to fruition.

On May 16, members of the 388th Bomb Group Association, gathered in Cambridge. The next morning, they traveled by bus to Coney Weston in a drizzling rain and were amazed to see the roads lined with automobiles and people standing in the rain smiling and waving to the returning Yanks. The buses dropped them off at St Mary's Church. They filed into the church followed by as many British as could crowd in with the remainder standing out in the rain to hear the service over a public address system. Major Kohl, an Air Force Chaplain from Lakenheath, spoke of the contributions of the 388th Bomb Group to the war effort, and in remembrance of those who gave their lives.

THE 8TH AIR FORCE WON THE WAR IN EUROPE

Following the service, they filed out of the little stone church and joined the procession of English and Americans to the memorial site, next to the road that once led up to the group headquarters. In the center of a concrete pad stood the 4 feet x 6 feet memorial. When all had assembled in a large semi-circle around the area, the dedication ceremony conducted by Reverend Taylor began. We stood quietly under the shelter of umbrellas and heard messages of thanks and remembrance from Reverend Taylor, Major Kohl, and from our own Colonel Henggeler. The Memorial was then unveiled by Pat Ryan revealing a B-17 bursting through a broken chain of Axis oppression. It was truly a Fortress for Freedom. The black polished granite slab also bore a "missing man" formation of Square H B-17s to honor those killed in action, and some vital statistics on the 388th operations from *Knettishall*. On the pavement in front was a precisely oriented airfield layout as it was in 1943-45 with a dedication message also in black granite.

Americans and British laid wreaths at the base of the memorial as the crowd applauded. The weather dampened the clothes but not the spirit of those attending. That evening, we had dinner in Cambridge with our British friends followed by coffee and a slide show of World War II *Knettishall* pictures presented by George Stebbings.

The Knettishall Memorial, Knettishall, England

On July fourth 1994, The Memorial group arrived at the *Knettishall* for a short visit. The Rector from St. Mary's Church led the service with David Calcutt reading the scripture. They honored all those who died in service. Then the group moved up the hill to the flight line. John Wallace, who donated the ground and farm that comprises part of the old base, welcomed the group. Ed Huntzinger introduced the English Memorial Committee and all 388th Bomb Group Association Officers. Later the group went on a tour of the old base area with George Stebbings, Percy Prentice, David Calcutt, Brian Chandler and Peggy Garnham acting as guides. They pointed out location of the barracks, mess halls and the remains of the original runways, the revetments and the generator building.

In 2003, with the help of Janet Pack, Editor of the newsletter, I led a group of 47 veterans back to "A Day at *Knettishall*." Our trip included visits to *Cambridge*, The Duxford Museum and *London*. On May 23, we gathered to re-dedicate the Memorial that honors our war dead. Committee Chairman David Calcutt began by leading us on a guided tour of Thetford Station, where many of us had traveled over the years. As we pulled up to the Memorial we were greeted by the local citizens who came to thank us for saving England. The British had been in the war since 1939, and they remembered that Hitler had stood on the cliff of France and declared that he would soon be in *London*.

After the Star Spangled Banner and God Save the Queen, I spoke briefly, "Ten years from now, there will be very few of us left. But people will still see this memorial, and I hope that they will remember what we did here, and they will say we were indeed gallant warriors."

The 388th Collection at Hillside Farm

This collection was started by Owner David Sarson, with volunteers Percy Prentice, Alan Tebble, Simon Frost and Paul Soames to help with any construction problems. The airplane components, which require much space, have been moved to a second area. The original Nissen hut was expanded to allow for the

THE 8TH AIR FORCE WON THE WAR IN EUROPE

display of uniforms and other memorabilia.

The Collection has limited visiting days, but David makes it known that any 388th members and their families will always be able to visit the exhibit. Be prepared to stay and chat a little while – they have plenty of questions!

The Collection continues to grow. One day recently 600 persons visited, both British and American. They were particularly interested in the historic items, most of which were donated by the 388th veterans.

On May 25, 1989 Janet Pack and her mother visited the collection and they were escorted to the Memorial Day ceremonies at the Cambridge American Cemetery by David Calcutt. It is a beautiful ceremony and a well-organized memorial service. It is difficult to forget the emotions of this peaceful place.

George Stebbings represented the 388th in the laying of wreaths around the monument, and David took them to Duxford to visit the American Air Museum. It is a magnificent tribute to American aviation!

Since its doors first opened to the public in 1994, thousands of American and English visitors have toured the 388th Collection at Hillside Farm. It is located on the grounds of Hillside Farm near the English village of *Market Weston*. The 388th Collection is dedicated to the 3,000-plus American airmen who served at Station 136 during World War II. This Collection is located a short distance from the old base. It is housed in a former Station 136 Nissen hut.

Many 388th BG Assn. members have donated their memorabilia, photos, uniforms and equipment to the Collection where the items are displayed in sincere honor to the men who fought from Station 136.

This impressive collection of memorabilia and artifacts tells the story of our bombardment group during its stay at Knettishall. An annex to the original Nissen hut which houses the main collection features not only an original Wright-Cyclone engine, but also remnants of planes lost over England and Continental Europe. English residents assist with the displays and special open days, and are always on hand when vets and their families visit.

The 388th Collection at Hillside Farm
Photo © Evelyn Simak (cc-by-sa/2.0)

The Sarsons do not charge admission to the Collection, and guests are welcome to stay as long as they like. They are also treated to personal tours of the old base area, where David points out former locations of the headquarters and other operations buildings, squadron housing units and crash sites of planes such as "Hard Luck" and "Blitzin Betsy." Ask any of our vets and their families who have come to see the 388th Collection, and they will happily tell you how they have been treated like visiting royalty.

Operating on a shoe string budget, largely out-of-pocket and through small donations, the Sarsons have managed to pay for annual insurance and security to protect this precious collection.

All this they have done without ever having to ask for help of the 388th Association's help. But now help was needed, because an expert in museum preservation informed David Sarson that the effects of the damp English weather are beginning to take their toll; and that if the Collection is to continue in perpetuity immediate steps must be taken.

First, the Nissen hut and its contents had to be de-humidified – a process that would require one month and necessitate the rental of a special unit. After the initial de-humidification had been accomplished, a permanent, continuously operating unit was obtained to maintain the low humidity levels. The combined cost of the rented and purchased units was estimated at $2,500 ... and that's over and above the ongoing expenses associated with annual insurance, regular maintenance and expansion goals.

The de-humidifier was donated by a local citizen and the museum is now dry[21].

Preserved for All Time[22]

The following description clearly defines the mission and very reason for the existence of the 388th Collection at Hillside Farm. It depicts clearly the hard work and efforts of many, who wish to preserve the memories, history, and stories they have to share before they become extinct. Preservation of their Legacy is the mission of all who served in the 388th Bomb Group at Knettishall.

Our story begins In April of 2011 when Nelda Tatum, widow of original member Louis Allen, contacted Alan Reese about an article he had written in the Association Newsletter concerning preservation of original A-2 jackets. She had her husband's original A-2 and wished to find a new home for it where it would best commemorate the legacy and history of Louis and those who served during World War II. She believed that for a jacket that was over 60 years old, it and the artwork on the jacket, were in amazingly good condition.

After several conversations with the veterans of the War, she realized that the jacket was a significant piece of history that must be preserved. The initial thought was to raffle or sell the jacket. The funds would then be split equally between Nelda, who was experiencing hard economic times and a recent diagnosis of

---

[21] This section was written by Jan Pack Singer, Newsletter Editor, in the summer of 2003.
[22] This article appeared in the Fall 2011 Newsletter of the 388th Bomb group Association.

colon cancer. While the 388th BG Association. is not in the habit of buying artifacts or memorabilia, arrangements were made with Rae to purchase the A-2, along with some other items which would be displayed in the Hospitality room.

What was to follow is testimony to the mission of the 388th Bomb Group Association. A preliminary letter was sent to the Board members and the story was shared with anyone who would listen, outlining the newly found opportunity and seeking suggestions of how best the jacket may be raffled or sold to raise funds. James Morrow, liaison to the Mighty 8th Museum in Savannah, checked to see if there was an A-2 jacket in the 388th's display at the museum. There was not.

Several months later a 388th member and his family, who wishes to remain unnamed, had heard about the jacket, and Rae's personal circumstances. They made an $800 donation for the A-2 jacket with a request that 1/2 of the proceeds be donated to Louis's widow in memory of all who served in the 388th Bomb Group. The family further requested that the jacket be donated to the Mighty 8th for our display so that another part of history and the story of the 388th Bomb Group may be "preserved for all time."

The National Museum of the U. S. Air Force

This museum dates to 1923, but it was not until 1927, when it moved to then Wright Field in a laboratory building that it was really a museum. In 1932, the collection was named the Army Aeronautical Museum and placed in a WPA building. In 1948, the collection remained private as the Air Force Technical Museum, but in 1954, the Air Force Museum became public and was housed in its first permanent facility. Many of its aircraft were parked outside and exposed to the weather. It remained there until 1971, when the current facility opened. Not including its annex on Wright Field proper, the museum had more than tripled in square footage since 1971, with the addition of a second hangar in 1988, a third in 2003, and a fourth in 2016. The museum adopted a new name for the facility in October 2004. The former name, United

States Air Force Museum was changed to National Museum of the United States Air Force.

A large section of the museum is dedicated to pioneers of flight, especially the Wright Brothers, who conducted some of their experiments at nearby Huffman Prairie. A replica of the Wrights' 1909 Military Flyer is on display, as well as other Wright Brothers artifacts. The building also hosts the National Aviation Hall of Fame, which includes several educational exhibits.

The museum has many pieces of U.S. Army Air Forces and U.S. Air Force clothing and uniforms. At any time, more than 50 World War II-vintage A-2 leather flying jackets are on display, many of which belonged to famous figures in Air Force history. Others are painted to depict the air planes and missions flown by their former owners.

The staff of the museum has very high standards for the restoration and quality of care of loaned assets. When it was determined that other museums do not have the resources to properly care for an artifact, it is sent to Ohio. This was the case of the famous Boeing B-17 Flying Fortress, "Memphis Belle."

The American Air Museum in Britain

Over half a million U.S. airmen were based in the United Kingdom during World War II. The American Air Museum is a tribute to their bravery, a memorial to the 26,000 U.S. airmen who gave their lives, and a great source of education and information for future generations about the important role of U.S. air power.

On 17 August 1942, twelve B-17 Flying Fortress bombers of the 97th Bomb Group took off from Grafton Underwood, *Northants*, to attack targets in occupied France on what was the first US heavy bombing mission flown from the UK. Sixty years later, Duxford, itself a former Eighth Air Force base, has proudly commemorated the achievements and sacrifice of the men of the Eighth Air Force.

From 1942 to the end of the war in 1945, the Eighth Air Force operated B-17 Flying Fortresses and B-24 Liberators on daylight bombing operations against Germany and Nazi-occupied

Europe. At peak strength, the Eighth Air force could dispatch more than 2,000 four-engine bombers and more than 1,000 fighters on a single mission. For these reasons, the Eighth Air Force became known as the "Mighty Eighth." In October 1942 Duxford became one of the first Royal Air force airfields to welcome USAAF personnel and in April 1943 the airfield was fully handed over to the United States Eighth Air Force. By the end of the Second World War, the P-47 Thunderbolts and P-51 Mustangs of Duxford's 78th Fighter Group were credited with the destruction of 697 enemy aircraft, thus making a significant contribution to the ultimate Allied victory.

The American Air Museum is located in Duxford, England, 48 miles from London. A famous historic site and fighter base of the 8th Air Force during World War II, Duxford is not the leading center of historic aviation in Europe. Duxford has an active airfield attached to its museum complex, and one of the best collections of historic aircraft in the world – many of which are still flown today. Duxford attracts about 400,000 visitors each year, many are veterans, family groups and students on educational tours – all benefiting from the story of the airfield and its collection.

The Museum was designed by the world renowned architect Sir Norman Foster. It is one of the most impressive museum structures in the world with a dramatic 295-foot-wide glass front, a great domed concrete roof, and raised walkways from which to view the historic American aircrafts.

Among the legendary aircraft in the Museum that were flown by Americans are the B-17 Flying Fortress, the B-29 Super Fortress, the P-47 Thunderbolt, the B-25 Mitchell, the P-51 Mustang and the F-86 Sabre.

The American Air Museum was another milestone in Duxford's history. The British were deeply honored to welcome President George H. W. Bush, 41st President of the United States, and His Royal Highness the Prince of Wales to the American Air Museum for the occasion. Their presence ensured a great deal of media coverage including CNN which broadcast part of the ceremony live across the US and around the world.

They were delighted to see that so many of our American supporters were able to join them for the historic event and it

THE 8TH AIR FORCE WON THE WAR IN EUROPE

meant a great deal to the staff and volunteers who worked so hard in preparation for the big day to meet them, the people who have supported the American Air Museum so loyally over the years. Their focus then shifted to *Air Space,* the exciting redevelopment of Hangar 1, which will be the subject of much coverage in *Duxford News* over the next few years[23].

On the 60th anniversary of the Museum a Re-dedication Ceremony followed months of demanding work, which included the removal of the spectacular glass frontage of the American Air Museum to incorporate two stunning new additions – the Lockheed SR-71 Blackbird spy plane, the only one of its kind on display outside the United States, and the Consolidated B-24 Liberator, restored by Duxford's conservation staff over the past two years. Additionally, other exhibits have been re-displayed and re-organized to complement the new layout.

It is particularly appropriate that this ceremony took place 60 years after the arrival of the US 8th Air Force in East Anglia. Prior to the ceremony, President Bush and The Prince of Wales were each given a tour of the American Air Museum, the former escorted by HRH the Duke of Kent, Patron of the American Air Museum. Of particular interest to Mr. Bush was the Grumman Avenger torpedo bomber, painted to represent the aircraft he flew during his time spent as a naval aviator in the Pacific theatre. The President paused to see his name upon the aircraft and no doubt to reflect on the past.

He must have remembered his interview on Washington D.C. Public Radio one Saturday morning, when George H. W. Bush discussed his life as a Prisoner of War on ChiChijima Island. Each Saturday one of the guards lined up all the prisoners and a Colonel pointed at one of them, who was taken indoor to the kitchen. According to Bush, that American was killed, his liver was removed and fried and was eaten by the Japanese officers. It would difficult to forget such an inhuman act.

The start of the ceremony was signaled by the roar of three approaching Royal Air force C-130 Hercules, from No. 47 Squadron, RAF Lyneham, closely followed by two pairs of United States Air Force F-15 Eagles from nearby RAF Lakenheath. After

---

[23] Some of this history is taken from the *Duxford News*, November 2002.

this display, the 41st President took center stage, genuinely impressed by what he had seen. During his speech, President Bush said of the American Air Museum, "Today marks the culmination of the efforts of so many. This is clearly a place where history still lives and breathes and the atmosphere gives a real sense of stepping back in time."

The President's words were followed by a Prayer of Rededication led by The Venerable (Air Vice Marshal) Ronald D Hesketh, Chaplain in Chief of the Royal Air Force.

The Prince of Wales echoed the former President's sentiments when he spoke of next year's 100th anniversary of the first Wright brothers' flight and that the exhibits at Duxford were testament to the achievements of the last century. The Museum is truly an Anglo-American venture. It is not just a static reminder of an era long since past, but a living exhibit to the enormous technological advances in the field of powered flight over the last century." He went on to say "The Museum is a fitting memorial to the thousands of American airmen who flew from the UK 60 years ago and never returned, for those of us born after the last war, it is a chance to salute you." Both guests of honor paid tribute to the commitment and support given to the American Air Museum by veterans, Founding and Sustaining Members and staff. The Prince of Wales added that the AAM would not have been possible without the ·'generous help of our American friends."

In 2011 the Museum acquired a B-17 which needed a lot of work before it could be exhibited. The restorers decided that they could save a lot of money by taking the airplane apart and bringing it inside through the fire exit, instead of removing the glass wall. Once inside they could re-attach the parts. They began in mid-April, with the inner wings and trailing edges being the first elements to be moved. Once transferred the trailing edges were reattached to the main plane.

The fuselage was moved back through the fire-exit on 16 May, exactly 363 days after it had been painstakingly removed, squeezing it under the TBM-3 Avenger and round the B-29. Building on the experience of the removal, the conservation team were able to reduce the time taken to return the fuselage to its rightful place and set it back on her original gear. During the following weeks the remaining sections, including the engines, outer wings and all other components were reattached, and the reassembly was substantially complete.

By the summer of 2012 it was finished and it was put in her place of honor where she was ready for the visitors to see her restored, almost as good as new. The Museum executives were grateful to all our members for their support in completing this work, especially the conservation staff and volunteers for their skill and expertise in bringing this significant project to a successful conclusion.

All future generations who visit the American Air Museum and its aircraft will be reminded of the Allied victory in World War II, and the impact that U.S. air power has had in insuring peace around the globe.

The American Air Museum in Britain has an American address also: it is 510 Eleventh St., SE, Washington, D. C. 20003.

The National World War II Museum

The National World War II Museum was created to honor all the Americans who fought together to defeat Germany and Japan. It also honors those on the home front who accepted rationing and who worked long hours to support the U. S. armed forces.

This Museum is one of the world's foremost institutions dedicated to telling the complete history of America's role in World War II and beyond as the effects of that great conflict continue to shape our world. It was originally conceived as a place to tell the story of the European D-Day invasion of June 6, 1944, but the planners faced a strong demand for expanding its mission to encompass the entire scope of World War II, including all theaters of war and the Home Front.

Founded by the late historian Stephen Ambrose, the Museum is carrying on with support of numerous prominent Americans, including President George H. W. Bush (who served in World War II), Tom Brokaw, Steven Spielberg, Tom Hanks and many members of the US Senate and House of Representatives.

The Museum continues to raise millions to build the Liberation Pavilion and to help finance construction of the newly expanded Museum, These plans call for World War **II** exhibits and artifacts. The expansion would comprise more than six acres over four city blocks, with 300,000 square feet of building space. A central parade ground will set the stage for ceremonies and presentations, a space for visitors to reflect and for the community to celebrate our veterans.

There would also be the Museum's Honor Roll as a unique tribute honoring those who participated in World War II, whether in battle or on the Home Front. Names would be displayed on a kiosk prominently located near the entrance to the Museum where all visitors will see it. All names will also be listed in a searchable database on the Museum's website, so all Americans may view these names, even if they cannot visit the Museum in person.

The Mighty 8th Air Force Museum

This is a fantastic museum located at Pooler, GA. near Savannah. The exhibits there are huge, and they have some very good artifacts. The POW exhibit and the exhibits of different groups and wings are also great. They have excellent docents who will give you great details you can't get from any of the plaques. What they don't have is a place to look up members that served in 8th Air Force in WW2.

There is one exhibit that confounds most visitors. It is a red British telephone booth. Why is it there? The answer is simple. The young British women believed (wrongly) that they could not get pregnant if they had sexual relations in a telephone booth.

On the outside there is a wall with many photographs of crews. When the Museum opened I went there to put a photograph of the crew of our Bomber "Wolf Wagon."

The Museum's latest project is the restoration of the B-17 Bomber "City of Savannah," which was obtained from the National Air and Space Museum (NASM) in Washington, DC in 2009. Visitors can watch the volunteers restore the bomber, who

THE 8ᵀᴴ AIR FORCE WON THE WAR IN EUROPE

have donated over 12,000 hours. This particular bomber was part of a very circular route to Savannah. It was part of the Black Hills Aviation in South Dakota, then it was exchanged at National Air and Space museum for two surplus navy P-2s. Then it was transferred again to the Davis-Montham Air Force Base, where it was stripped of paint and placed on exhibit at the Pima Air Museum. In 1984 it was flown to Dulles International Airport, where its future was uncertain.

By 2015 the restoration was nearly complete. All parts that were needed for the restoration have been obtained and the ball turret and nose turret were installed and are now operational. The only turret not fully completed was the top turret, but it was finished in time for the scheduled dedication ceremony.

The "City of Savannah" dedication ceremony took place on January 28, 2015. The son of pilot Ralph Kittle was present for the ceremony. Representatives from the 388th Bomb Group Association asked if they could participate, but other groups were not involved.

Vladimir Lacina, a citizen of the Czech Republic, contacted the National Museum of the Mighty Eighth Air Force and asked if it could help him obtain information about the crew of the 388th Bomb Group's "City of Savannah," which crashed in Czechoslovakia on March 5, 1945. Mr. Lacina and some of his friends who live near the site of the crash wish to erect a memorial to those crew members on March 5, 2015, the seventieth anniversary of the crash.

The Research Center Director of the Mighty Eighth Museum referred Mr. Lacin to Jim Morrow. He made contact with me for information on the crew of the "City of Sa*vannah.*"

Morrow got in touch with Mr. Lacina and did provide him with some useful information. Morrow contacted Irwin Boxer, nose gunner on the "City of Savannah," and he tried to locate the son and daughter of J. E. Watkins, navigator of the "City of Savannah." But there were no living survivors of the crew[24].

---

[24] See Morrow's statement in the Fall 2014 issue of the 388ᵗʰ Group Newsletter

AUGUST C. BOLINO

B-17 at Eglin Air Force Base

I ran across a newspaper article about the B-17 that was being restored at Eglin Armament Base. It all began when two German fighter planes fired on pilot Joe Coyner's disabled B-17 as it made its way back to England from a bombing raid on *Berlin*. "These fighter planes came down behind us, riddled the plane and set it on fire," Coyner recalled. He crash-landed his blazing B-17 near the Belgian coast. All 10 crewmen survived, but bullets or shrapnel had injured three.

"I remember hearing (German soldiers) clicking their rifles, thinking it was all over," said Jim Ghearing, the plane's waist gunner. It was April 29, 1944. The Germans took the Americans as prisoners of war. For all of the next year they struggled to survive in prison camps.

On Friday, four of the ex-POWs gathered with about 80 others from the 8th Air Force's 388th Bombardment Group for the dedication of a restored B-17 Flying Fortress nicknamed "Gremlins' Hideout." That plane is displayed at the Air Force Armament Museum.

Sandy Sandler of Marco Island, then a 19-year-old navigator, was the youngest officer on Coyner's plane -- and the only Jew. As a POW, he was frightened, because he was Jewish. The other members of the crew were held in solitary confinement and interrogated for 24 hours. Sandler was interrogated for 48.

His captors tried to break Coyner, who lives in Chattanooga, TN. "They used to put him up to the window and told him: 'There are your buddies. You can be with them if you tell us what we want to know," Coyner said. They also threatened him several times by telling him that they were going to send him to a concentration camp.

"The thing that saved me was we were captured as a crew," Sandler said. "If we had parachuted and come down separated, I would never have been heard from again."

According to the Geneva Convention, the Germans kept the officers separate from the enlisted men. The officers leaned on one another for support. That camaraderie got them through near

THE 8TH AIR FORCE WON THE WAR IN EUROPE

starvation and forced marches through blizzards.

"The worst part was the lack of food," said ex-bombardier Donald Wiley. "We all weighed about 100 pounds when we got out," Ghearing said.

"The Red Cross kept us alive," Coyner added, showing a pin he made in prison with solder from food cans. The pin depicts clipper wings, signifying the crash and a ball and chain denoting imprisonment.

"I fell and hurt my legs, and some guys I didn't even know carried me for two weeks," Ghearing said.

In February 1945, the B-17 crew wound up together in a prison camps at Nuremberg when the British bombed that city. They watched bombs exploding next to the camp for several hours, and wondered if a stray would come their way.

On April 29, 1945, exactly one year after their capture, Gen. George S. Patton's troops liberated Coyner's crew along with most of the other POWs at Moosburg. When the entire crew met again, they laughed and joked about their experiences, and they acknowledged they were lucky to be alive. They were grateful to Coyner. "None of us other guys would be here today if he wasn't flying that airplane." Sandler said[25].

Eglin was located near Pensacola Florida, although it was an Armament Air Force Base. It took many months to restore the outside of the rundown B-17, but the inside was in terrible condition.

When I attended a meeting of the 388th Bomb Group Association, I learned that Colonel Corn, who was in charge of the project, lacked many parts. A few months later, my wife and I went to visit Seattle, her birthplace. While there, my sister-in-law told me that there were some World War II items for sale at the downtown thrift shop. I headed downtown, and when I entered the store I saw something I knew. It was a navigator's seat from a B-17. I bought it and I held it on my lap flying home. I contacted the

---

[25] Gail Boxrud, "Restored B-17 stirs memories," *Northwest Florida Daily News,* Saturday, February 20, 1993.

Colonel and told him about my purchase. He said, "That is one thing we never could find." I shipped it to him the next day.

In early 1992, Wayne Dell, Executive Director at Eglin, wrote to Ed Huntzinger thanking him and the members of the 388th Bomb Group Association for the most recent contribution of $1368.75. He added that the B-17 was relocated to the Schriever Plaza.

Months Later we were at a meeting in Orlando, and I said to my wife, "We should drive to Eglin to see the B-17. She agreed grudgingly, because it was over 400 miles. It took us all of next day to find the Air Base, and when we arrived we drove right by the Flying Fortress that was on a concrete pad.

I told the officer inside that I was a navigator on a B-17 and I had not been in one for about forty years. He said the bomber was closed and no visitors could go inside. I was disappointed, but I did not see my wife who went inside. She came out with the Colonel, who was carrying a bunch of keys. He unlocked the nose and got me a ladder to climb into the plane.

It was shocking. The entire nose was full of trash and there were miles of wires hanging everywhere. I climbed down, and I asked the Colonel, "What is your plan to complete the restoration?"

He looked sad when he replied, "We simply cannot raise the amount of money we would need to finish the job, so we are just going to leave it outdoors."

I thanked him for allowing me to go inside and we drove away.

The Danish Memorial

In 2001 Mike Baker and David Calcutt were invited to Denmark to share in their celebrations on the 4th of May to commemorate the end of five years of German occupation in 1945. And during the next year they were invited back again. On Friday evening, May 3, they renewed friendships with the Danish and English people, and on Saturday they all assembled around the Memorial Stone to honor the crew of 15 Squadron, RAF Stirling "MacRohert's Reply," which crashed at that spot on May 18, 1942, with the loss of eight lives.

On Sunday Baker and Calcutt made their way to *Brahesholm*, to the memorial stone at the site of the crash of the 388th BG B-17. Only the tail gunner, Andrea Alcarese survived. The crowd of about 200 assembled. Simon, our host, and Colonel Mike Anderson from the American Embassy, spoke at the Memorial and wreaths were laid, followed by a trumpeter playing *The Last Post*. A lady we did not know told us that every time they ploughed the field small parts of the aircraft came to the surface.

They next assembled at the town hall in *Glamsbjerg* for another reception, and the Mayor showed some parts of the B-17, but we also learned that both British and American planes had crashed in that area. We then went to *Bellinge*, where we visited another 388th B-17 crash site. Since last year a "Fortress for Freedom" plaque has been erected beside the Memorial Stone.

The U. S. Air Force Memorial

This Memorial, which is in Arlington, Virginia was incorporated in 1992, and President Clinton approved it in 1993. On July 30, 1997 Congressman Gerald Solomon of New York, a marine veteran, introduced a bill to prevent its construction. It was not acted on, but on December 28, 2001 President George W. Bush directed the Defense Department to make available 3 acres of the Naval Annex for a location of the Air Force Memorial.

When it was completed it consisted of three spires 201 to 270 feet high. They are of stainless steel. The fourth spire is not visible, because it represents the missing man in a formation. There are two inscription walls which are 56 feet long and 10 feet high, and in front of it are four 8-foot bronze statues that represent the Air Force Honor Guard.

The North Wall shows the names of Air Force Veterans who have earned the Medal of Honor. One name was removed from this wall. It was Billy Mitchell who received the Congressional Gold Medal.

The Memorial was dedicated by President George W. Bush, who was a pilot in the Texas Air National Guard. It was designed by James I. Freed, and it was built with $25 million of private funds. His design was approved by the national Capital Planning Commission. The major part of the Memorial is the five tapering fins that are the five-pointed Air Force star that rises from a concrete platform that is 50 feet high.

The location of the Monument turned out to be historical by accident, because it is very close to the Fort Myer parade ground from which in 1908 Orville Wright took off on a short flight which resulted in the first military purchase of an airplane.

Air Force Memorial, Washington, D.C.

Chapter Thirty Five
The Air Force Academy

Because there were academies for the Army and Navy, it was understandable for the Air Force to want one. Support for this academy rose when the National Security Act of 1947 established a separate Air Force. At that time up to 25 percent of personnel at West Point and the Naval Academy could obtain their commission in the new Air Force.

In 1950, Secretary of Defense James Forrestal told Dwight Eisenhower, of the Service Academy Board, who was then President of Columbia University, that the needs of an Air Force Academy could not be met by the two existing academies. Following his recommendation, Congress in 1954 passed legislation to begin construction of a new academy.

By 1959 there were 306 cadets enrolled. Cecil B. DeMille designed their uniform, while the cadets chose the falcon as their mascot. Some of these early cadets died in the Vietnam War. On October 7, 1975 President Gerald Ford signed legislation to admit women to the Academy, who had a much higher dropout rate than the men. One possible reason is that the altitude is at 7258 feet.

The Bronze Model of a B-17

On May 23, 1996, I received a letter from Catherine Parish, of the U.S. Air Force Academy telling me of the plans to build "A monumental bronze replica of the famous B-17 aircraft" which would join four other war birds already in place in the distinguished 'Study Hall' Sculpture Garden at the USAF Academy. Those planes already in place include the P-38, P-40, P47, and P-51. The B-17 will have an approximate wing span of 9 feet, and sit upon a beautifully polished granite base. When completed, the plane and base would weigh approximately 3 tons.

I telephoned Ms. Parish, and she told me that if the 388th Bomb Group Association would donate $450 towards the construction, the name of our group would be put on the plaque that would list the sponsors. I did not know why I received this letter, because I was not an officer of the 388th Bomb Group Association at that time, so I wrote to Bob Simmons telling him of the forthcoming project. He said he would take it up at the next Board meeting.

When I heard nothing for a year, I decided to send a personal check to the Academy. When she received my letter and check she told me that because I am an individual and not an association, I could put any name on the base of the model.

I answered, "I want the name of the 388th Bomb Group,' and she said firmly, "And so it will be.'

The May 23, 1996 Press Release

Soon after, she sent me the latest Press Release "Our Final Mission," which told me that funds are being solicited to allow men and women throughout the world to honor the B-17 Flying Fortress. A monumental bronze replica of the famous aircraft will join four other Warbirds already in place in the distinguished "Study Hall" Sculpture Garden at the USAF Academy. The project manager and administrator of the B-17 Memorial Fund, Maurice Thomas, who was also a B-17 pilot and past president of the 305th B.G, announced that the plane will be unveiled in the spring of 1997. It is his desire to eventually have all of the main WWII aircraft represented in the "Garden."

"The creator of the Sculptor Garden, Robert Henderson, was feverishly busy over the past several years creating planes from the WWII era. "It is an honor," he said, "to recreate these magnificent aircraft while representing the men and women who designed, maintained, and flew them. They dominated the sky during their collective primes,"

THE 8TH AIR FORCE WON THE WAR IN EUROPE

Henderson said. "Thanks to the sacrifices that were made by them and others during WWII, I have the privilege of doing what I love to do. We are definitely lucky to live in this great country."

"The process involved in making one of these awesome bronze statues is no simple task. To begin, Henderson had to contact the original designer and manufacturer of the plane, or in this case, Boeing, to request original blueprints. A wooden model of the plane was then constructed from scratch. From this wooden model, "molds" were made which will serve as the basic framework of the bronze casting. The B- 17 will be comprised of over 100 different bronze pieces. A rough statue of the plane took shape after all of these pieces were welded together.

This is where the fun began. A series of grinding, sanding, and filling procedures gave the monument a very realistic appearance. From there, Henderson's attention to detail spared nothing. Every rivet, every seam, every bump from the actual plane were meticulously copied to give the final version of the B-17 its striking appearance. The plane was then coated in a patina finish which enabled it to withstand anything that Mother Nature could muster for decades to come. This whole process took approximately 12 to 24 months. The B-17 model has an approximate wing span of 9 feet, and it sits upon a beautifully polished granite base. When completed, the plane and base weighed approximately 3 tons."

"The B-1 7 project was completed on schedule. Fund raising for the project is an ongoing endeavor. According to Maurice Thomas, there are still spaces left for those who want their name inscribed on the monument, however, due to overwhelming demand, the space is disappearing."

When I was elected President of the 388 Bomb Group Assn in 2001, I suggested that we go to Colorado Springs for one of our reunions, but there seemed to be no interest. When I was elected President again in 2008, I again suggested that we go the Air Force Academy to see our B-17 model. The

Board of Directors chose instead to go to Salt Lake City and Lexington, Kentucky.

At last the group chose Colorado Springs for our 2011 meeting, and I was elated that I would finally see the bronze B-17. When we started to tour the place, we first went to the chapel of the Academy. As we were leaving, I told our guide that there was a Flying Fortress that I would like to see. She said, "What's a Flying Fortress?" and then she added, "We have no time for that because we are on a tight schedule to go to the Garden of the Gods for lunch."

I was not to be denied. I told her, "Many persons in this group flew B-17s in World War II," and I told her that, "I am going to find the B-17 on my own."

She said that I could not do that, and then she said, "Wait," as she telephoned someone, and then she added, "You can take twenty minutes to see it."

As my wife and Jan Pack and I walked towards the Sculpture Garden, other people joined us. We first saw a model of the B-29 which was not a part of the original plan, and behind it was the B-17. It was on a tall granite base and seemed to be flying. It was a magnificent replica of the planes we had flown. About a foot above the ground there was the plaque listing the donors. There I found the 388th Bomb Group Association and just below it indented on the next line was the name of the Fortress in which I had flown 30 missions – "Wolf Wagon." I thought to myself that I would send this article to my six grandchildren, and I hoped that someday they will visit this place and reflect on what their grandfather had done in World War II.

THE 8ᵀᴴ AIR FORCE WON THE WAR IN EUROPE

Part XI The 388th Bombardment Group Association (H)

This association was formed in 1947 by Edward Huntzinger and three other Floridians. It is a 501 (C) (3) non-profit organization. This application was filed with the U. S. Secretary of State where it was processed and sent to the Internal Revenue Service. IRS can revoke the non-profit status if there are violations of Federal laws. Donations to any non-profit group are not taxable as long as the group adheres to the mission statement.

Huntzinger and his associates proposed some rules that the Group should follow: The first is that the United States should be divided into three areas: East, Midwest and West, and the meetings should be scheduled in that order. In addition, they wrote that the group should not go back to a place until 10 years had expired.

What is the mission of the 388th BG Association? The objective as stated in the bylaws is "To preserve for all time the history, friendships, memories and incidents of the members of the 388th Bombardment Group (H) during World War II. This objective has been modified since the late 1940s when the association was formed. Our duty is to insure that the memories of what the original members endured during World War II will be available 100 years from now, or 500 years or 1000 years?

Our first Association meeting was at Valley Forge, Pennsylvania. It was well attended, with 406 being at dinner at the Saturday evening banquet. It was there that we learned about Lt. Daniel's experience over Hamm, Germany. As he told us, "We prepared for the bomb run. I unsnapped my flak suit on my left shoulder. I let it flop down so that I could snap one side of my parachute on the harness. Just a few minutes before bombs away, Lt. Randles called and asked if I would check to see if the bomb bay doors had opened properly as he was getting a negative symbol. I stood up in the radio room, turned around and opened the door to the bomb bay and saw that they looked properly opened. At that time there was a terrific explosion, both of my legs flew up in the air and everything went black. Then I was tumbling through space, and I just missed being hit by another B-17. I looked down to snap the other side of my chute on. It was lying across my chest in a perfect position. I was groggy, but I did feel it snap, so I pulled the rip cord and the chute opened. It was full of holes from flak. I found myself hanging sideways as there was only one snap holding the chute.

It was about 55 degrees below zero at that altitude, and I felt that my helmet and gloves had blown off during the explosion. I covered my ears with my hands and both were very cold. At that time I could see holes and blood on both legs of my flight suit. I knew that my wounds were serious. On the way down I could see four other chutes below.

I drifted through some broken clouds and landed about 20 miles from the target. I just missed a big oak tree, farm house and barbed wire fence by kicking my legs and landed hard. As I landed my left leg broke about 4 inches and sounded like a rifle crack.

As I landed, farmers came running out of the house, women fought for the parachute.

I tried to get my first aid kit, because I wanted to give myself a shot of Morphine for pain. As soon an oxen cart arrived and they lifted me up, put me on the hay in the cart and then a long painful ride to a bombed out town to a hospital. Catholic Sisters were the nurses. They gave me a shot, cut off my pants leg, made a plaster cast and I went to sleep. Later, when I was in the operating room, a German SS Officer tried to remove two rings from my fingers, but I was stronger than he and kept closing my hands. He was enraged, and pointed at me and shouting at the doctor. Later the doctor told me that the SS Officer ordered him to cut the rings from my finger and he told them that he was a doctor not a butcher.

I awoke later in a small room with Lt. Reith, also badly wounded and S/Sgt. Saunders who had a big black eye. Later that night, we were transferred to the *Eichelborn Lazzarette* hospital and Lt. Al Soo, our Navigator was also in this hospital. S/Sgt. Saunders was in the hospital a short time, Lt. Soo about two

THE 8TH AIR FORCE WON THE WAR IN EUROPE

months, then sent to P.O.W. Camps. Lt. Reith and I were there for 4 ½ months of nightmare, while the British bombed all night and the Americans bombed and strafed all day.

Chapter Thirty Six
A Special Meeting

The 26th Annual Reunion of the 388th Bomb Group Association was one the biggest ever, because it was in Seattle, Washington and it was the 50th Anniversary of the first flight of the B-17. It was at the Madison Hotel.

Members came from all units of the Bomb Group. There were Crew Chiefs, Armament, Sub-depot, Headquarters, and many crews. These were also some of the Original Staff Personnel, including General Chet and Irene Cox, Colonel B. C. and Lorraine Reed, Gil and Ginny Goodman, Andy and Elsie Chaffin. There were three members from Alaska and from 38 other states. California was first and Florida second in early registrations.

Stewart and Sue Evans came from Bury St. Edmunds, England and on Sunday, July 21st. Ian Hawkins of Stowmarket, England, the author of "Munster: The Way it Was." This is his poem:

He knew her very well
A grand old fighting bird
The B-17 Flying Fortress
Flown by the "Gutty" 43rd
We knew her very well
A grand old fighting bird
The B-17 Flying Fortress
Flown by the "Gutty" 43rd
We inherited her from the 19th
She had been through fire by then
She had the marks of battle
With flak holes in her skin

THE 8TH AIR FORCE WON THE WAR IN EUROPE

We quickly learned to love her
And soon became her slave
We flew her many missions
Before many had learned to shave

They called us "Kenney's Kids"
We had no military skill
All we knew what to do
Was fly and bomb and kill
We soon became known as "Ken's Men"
The Fortress' stature also grew
We saw her many war wounds
And marveled that she flew
We flew her from Mareeba
Iron Range and Jackson Strip
A mission over the Owen-Stanleys
Was a test for man and ship

Sometimes she couldn't make it
And the jungle claimed her crew
But she had many namesakes
And once again she flew

When she became too war-weary
And could do battle no more
She was replaced by her fighting sister
The Liberator B-24

    It took them 24 hours to get to Seattle from *Diss*, England. They visited the Boeing plant in Everett. The Boeing Management Association staged a gala dinner and show.
    Our Guest of Honor was George Stebbings, who arrived with his wife Margaret. It was at a dance on Friday evening in the hanger at Boeing Field that Chuck Zettek came by to meet with George Stebbings. Every one of our four squadrons was well represented. Jack Hollister, who lost an eye on one of our missions, came by to say hello. He was president of the Air Force Sergeants Association, which was meeting at another location.

AUGUST C. BOLINO

Chapter Thirty Seven
What Does "Legacy" Mean?

The 388th Bomb Group (H) Association has always adhered strictly to its objective, "To preserve for all time the history, friendships, memories and incidents of the members of the 388th Bombardment Group (H) during World War II, by publishing a quarterly newsletter and endeavoring to hold periodic reunions of our fellow members."

In 2005, Wayne Daniels made contact with the leaders of the Hill Fighter-Bomber Wing. It promised to sponsor the 2007 Annual Meeting at Hill. When nothing was done for months, the Sneads offered to conduct that meeting in the State of Washington, where they resided. They had managed several meetings in the past. At that point Henry and Betty Curvat offered to hold the 2008 meeting at the Marriot Hotel in Ogden, Utah. Their program was two days at the base.

I joined the discussion. I suggested that we consider changing the meeting place to Colorado Springs for the following reasons:

1. It contains the U. S. Air Force Academy

2. The Peterson Air Force Base is there. It is a leading missile defense base 3. There is the new 9-foot bronze wing span model of the B-17, which has the 388th symbol added to the base.

The association has always refused to compromise its identity by aligning itself with like organizations. In 2006 it refused to hand over its membership list to the powerful Mighty Eighth Historical Society. It has also refused to participate in reunions sponsored by this organization, which combine all entities of the former Eighth Air Force. In 2006, the Association's board of directors also declined a proposition from the 452nd BG Association that the two groups merge.

THE 8ᵀᴴ AIR FORCE WON THE WAR IN EUROPE

On March 23, 1953, nearly eight years after the 388th Bomb Group (H) ceased to exist, the 388th Fighter-Wing was established. It was designated the 388th Fighter-Bomber Wing on November 5, 1953 and was inactivated in December 1957.

In May 1962, the former 388th Fighter-Bomber Wing was reactivated as the 388th Tactical Fighter Wing. It was inactivated less than two years later, in February 1964. It was activated again in March 1966, and re-designated the 388th Fighter Wing on October 1, 1991.

After 2004, efforts were exerted to form a link between the 388th Bomb Group Association and the 388th fighter wing, and to foster the concept that the modern-day Air Force unit is the legacy of the World War II bomb group. This idea came originally from Wayne Daniels, who flew three missions for the 388th Bomb Group when he was shot down. In a few years several persons who had contributed mightily to the success of the Bomb Group Association resigned their membership.

The argument seemed to rotate over a definition of the word "legacy." I looked up the word in five encyclopedias, and they all indicated that "legacy is anything of the past." This means that a fighter Wing created in 1962 cannot be a legacy of a group that was terminated in 1945. We began to see the effects of this argument when beginning with the 2011 reunion at Colorado Springs, posters of current fighter jets outnumbered images of B-17s on the walls of the hotel hospitality rooms where reunion attendees congregate.

Some of the requirements mentioned above were not met when the Group voted to go to Salt Lake City at the 388th Fighter Wing twice in three years. It seems to have ignored one important fact: The 388th Bomb Group (H) and 388th Fighter Wing were two distinct entities, having only the number 388 in common.

My Goodbye Letter As President

In 2001 I addressed the membership for the last time as President: "I want to say some good-byes and a hello. The first goodbye and thank you is for Bit Snead for doing what the Brits call "yeoman's service" as Secretary. Equally important and deserving of our plaudits is the team of Bob Simmon/Janet Pack Singer as editors of our newsletter. Janet is young and vigorous enough to do the many things we used to do 25 years ago. My final goodbye is to Larry Curtis. By this time he probably knows the meaning of the lyrics of that spiritual 'Nobody Knows the Trouble I've Seen.' It's okay, Larry; you did a great job in Duluth."

My hello is to my friend of more than 35 years, Jim Cotton, the incoming President. I know he will keep the 388th one of the best in the 8th Air Force.

I want to leave you with some information about our bombing missions. I live about five or six miles from the National Archives at College Park, MD. I spent a lot of time getting copies of the missions I flew. I learned that the 388th records are contained in Record Group 18, Stack Area 190, Row 58, Box Nos. 1287-1299. These box numbers are for April to August 1944.

I telephoned David Giordano of the Military Textual Reference Section (phone: 301-713-7250). He said you can request up to five missions at one time for mission reports. You will need to provide him with the dates and destinations of the missions. They will research this for you and send you an estimate of the cost of duplicating the file folder at $.50 per page. Each file folder is one mission. My experience indicates that each mission would cost $3-$5 to duplicate. Send your requests to National Archives at College Park Modern Military Records NWCTM 601 Adelphi Road, College Park MD 20740-6001.

Chapter Thirty Eight
Historically Speaking

Dick Henggeler has brought a wealth of information on the 388th Bomb Group. He has accumulated a vast library of reference materials. He now contributed a regular article in each Newsletter concerning our history.

On his first, regular column he explained his objectives. As he wrote, "One of my most important duties has been to create a definitive list of the men, crews, missions and aircraft of the 388th. The database website (www.388bg.org) provides easy access to this information. The data are constantly being updated, corrected and expanded on a daily basis.

At the same time, he established the 388th Research Library. It contains reference material related to the 388th. Most of this information was received through donation or purchases from e-bay. So far the library contains the following sources:

31 Books
73 Manuscripts
15 Videos
4 Audio Tapes
170 Newsletters

In addition to this, the library contains folders for each mission, crew, and crash. Various letters, official or unofficial documents (Xeroxed), emails, notes etc are collected in these folders.

A major part of the library is the photo collection, which is a combination of actual photos and digital copies. This website contains the following:

110 Aircraft photos
180 Crew photos
634 Individual photos
22 Mission photos

Other photo-related items of the library are document photos. The National Archives has the original Clearance Cards that show the crew members for each mission (we have over 9,000 of these photographed). Also the Air Force Historical Society has the operational papers for the group (we have 2 of the 25 months photographed)[26].

---

[26] 388th BG Newsletter, Winter 2010

THE 8TH AIR FORCE WON THE WAR IN EUROPE

Chapter Thirty Nine
Some Correspondence

A Sweet Letter from a Daughter

This letter was published in the July 2000 issue of the 388th Bomb Group Newsletter following her visit to the 8th Air Force Heritage Museum in Savannah. It was written by the daughter of John S. Harrison, who was a top-turret gunner on a 388th B-17.

Our last day in Savannah has come to a close. Packing is finally finished for an early morning flight home. The few hours remaining to sleep before wake-up call will be very welcome. Mom is already at rest. She did quite well this weekend, but the tiredness from all the activities and from being away from her own familiar environment was evident tonight. The last light is off and I am anxious for that sense of delirium that comes before our minds are no longer aware of time and space. I lay my head upon the pillow ready to surrender consciousness. Instead of the anticipated numbness of mind and body, tears begin to trickle down my cheeks.

All that I have experienced these past three days seems to be crashing in on me. I am being bombarded with all I heard, saw and felt. The trickle is beginning to turn into a steady flow. A mini rivulet wetting my hair and pillow. I can no longer breathe easily and try to restrain my sobbing. I am trying not to make any sounds that will disturb Mom's peace; a peace that seems to have come to her at fleeting moments these past few nights.

I am not quite sure why this sadness has come upon me so suddenly and unexpectedly; perhaps because tomorrow I return to my small secluded universe. There will be no more tales to awe me from a generation of brave men that survived a time of horror to plant the seeds of my generation of baby boomers. Perhaps the catalyst was our visit to the wonderful 8th Air Force Museum. Each exhibit drew me more deeply into events of years I never knew. I was overwhelmed with feelings for an event I could never fully comprehend. I listened intently to each presentation which led up to the coup-de-grace, the film about the B-17. That's the aircraft you flew in Dad. The Flying Fortress.

The movie began with loud noises and bright lights. The focal point was from a top turret. That's where you were Dad. I never really knew too much about your position until now. As the movie continued I was struck by how young the crew was. My son, your grandson, is older than those boys. They all entered the cavity of that cold metal giant with the unabridged courage of seasoned men. The top turret gunner stood on a platform that turned 360 degrees with only a plastic bubble to protect his head. What a terribly vulnerable position. How could he possibly defend himself, his crew members, and his aircraft from other boys in foreign aircraft attacking from all directions? I was mesmerized and tried not to blink for fear of missing something.

The fighting continued on and on. There was constant chatter of warnings among the boys as each one manned their own station. I watched and listened in amazement, trying to catch a glimpse at each overhead screen. The noises grew louder and louder, almost deafening. Then came an illuminating red flash. I waited for the next tactic to occur. But there was nothing. I held my breath for what seemed like an eternity. My brain finally registered what had happened. "Gone!" Everything was gone.

The boys, the chatter, the B-17. Just gone. How could that be? That aircraft was supposed to be a 'Fortress,' protecting those within its walls. I told myself to take a breath. I wanted to cry, but I hold back the tears. How dare I let even one of them loose. This was not my war, not my pain, not my grief, not my memories relived. That all belongs to the men sitting around me.

I felt as though I intruded on something almost sacred. That could have been you. Gone. How lucky I was you made it home from that nightmare. How unfortunate I never realized it until more than 17 years after your death with your own private war with

THE 8TH AIR FORCE WON THE WAR IN EUROPE

cancer. You died as you lived; quietly and without fanfare.

I overheard one of the men at the reunion say that people called all of you who served in the war heroes. He replied that you were all just men. At the time I didn't give too much thought to either statement. After seeing the film, I strongly disagree with him. Most of you left home as boys, were forced into manhood, and if lucky, returned home as heroes. Some skipped the manhood portion of their short lives altogether and went from wide-eyed boys to fallen hero.

The past few days have made me miss you terribly, Dad. I have been thinking back to the few months before you died. Life was a little simpler for me then and I was able to help Mom take care of you. I didn't realize it at the time but that was one of the greatest blessings and privileges of my life. I hope I helped ease your way down that path you traveled with such uncomplaining dignity. On one visit from your sister she called me your princess. I remember thinking what a funny thing for her to say. I never thought of myself as anybody's princess and you would never have called me that.

You were a man of few words but I knew you loved me. How sad it makes me when I speak of you to my children and they don't always remember. You would like them both. They've grown to be very special people. Your legacy lives on through your Grandson in his innate goodness and sense of humor, and in your Granddaughter in her aloofness and introspective demeanor. I hope someday they have an awareness of what a gift their lives and freedom are thanks to you and all the other heroes of previous generations. I also hope someday they can experience and appreciate the museum and have their hearts touched as mine was.

The tears are still flowing as my thoughts turn to this evenings dinner dance. The band played "Off We Go Into The Wild Blue Yonder" and everyone in the ballroom stood. I had goose bumps. I was surrounded by heroes from near and far.

I was deeply moved by those who had journeyed from England and France to share in this weekend. Those wonderful people fought the war on their homelands and came to pay homage to the men of another because they remember and are grateful. All share a common brotherhood. I feel more bonded to my heritage thanks to being a part of all of this. Thank you Dad. Thank you men. I hope you all realize how special you are. The many ways in which I have been touched while here will stay with me for a very long time.

Let me borrow a line from Shakespeare, "Good Night Sweet Prince."

The Story of "Tom"

The April 2000 Newsletter of our Bomb Group featured this story of leaving the war.

During World War II, sixty-eight B-17 s from the 8th Air Force landed in Sweden. One of these 68 aircraft -- 42-31163-- was among the 504 B-17s and 226 B-24s that set out to bomb *Berlin* on March 6, 1944. Damaged already over western Germany, the aircraft began to lose speed. But "Chuck" Wallace and his crew still continued to their assigned target, and released their bombload. Now being a sitting duck for German fighters, they ducked into clouds. Number 2 engine had been shut down. Soon the engine problems were compounded by ice forming on the wings. There was no way that they could reach Knettishall, their base in England. The course was set north, to get out of German territory. They began to lose altitude, and at one time the order to bail out was given. But a troubling engine restarted, so the order was rescinded. They continued on three engines, out over water, and made landfall.

What country was this? German occupied Denmark? Or was it Sweden? There were electrical trains traversing the countryside. They spotted a town, and an airfield. On the field was a B-17. So this must be Sweden! The crew had already thrown guns and heavy equipment overboard, as well as the Norden bombsight. They fired an emergency cartridge, circled the town, and lined up for landing. After touchdown, a Swedish officer galloped up on a horse, pointed a gun at the cockpit window, and said: "Welcome to Sweden"!

After a military interrogation the crew was interned in *Rattvik*, in the province of *Dalarna* in central Sweden. So were

THE 8ᵀᴴ AIR FORCE WON THE WAR IN EUROPE

several other crew members from other B-17s and B-24s that had been forced to emergency land in Sweden.

Out of the 68 B-17s, seven were converted to passenger configuration, to serve in the Swedish Air Lines ABA, Swedish Intercontinental Air Lines SILA, and the Danish Air Lines DDL.

Ingemar Melin of *Trelleborg* in southern Sweden, provided a picture of the 42-31163 as it looked before and after the conversion. The Swedish authorities registered the B-17 as "Felix", as a tribute to Lt. Col. Felix Hardison, Air Attache at the U.S. Legation in Stockholm, SE-BAM was christened "TOM". The four other B-17s in the service of ABA and SILA were named "JIM" "SAM" "TED" and "BOB to honor the American crew that had manned them.

From January 1945 "TOM" served ABA with distinction, and opened up the Stockholm - Paris route on May 18, 1945, a week and a half after VE-day. Some weeks later, "TOM" flew to Athens, Greece via Rome.

On December 4, 1945, after having served 1094 hours in the service of ABA, in preparation for landing at the Bromma airport in Stockholm, in dense fog, "TOM" flew into the terrain and crashed near Stallarholmen, 25 miles due west of the airport. Six crewmembers were killed.

This is dedicated to all the brave men of The Mighty 8ᵗʰ Air Force, and to the six Swedish crewmembers who perished on the final journey of aircraft 42-31163.

"The Little Girl"

I was a young school girl of 12 years and my father was a Grocer and supplied food to the canteen at Honington Base, 364 Fighter Base. I would ride along in the van with my dad on school holidays to help carry any goods! On December 1945 he took me to a Christmas Children's Party in the hangar of the Base.

I was so excited, my mum fit me in a new dress and did my hair. G.I.'s were waiting at the big open doors to pick the child they most wanted to share Christmas with. I was one of the oldest at 12 years old. I thought nobody would be choosing me and that I would have to go back home with my parents.

Then suddenly this young G.I. approached my mum and dad and handed a photo to them, then he took my hand and led me to the table, loaded down with food of all sorts and decorated with balloons.

All these G.I.s had contributed to this table for the British kids. At the end "Father Christmas" had a huge sack full of presents to each child to take home. We were all so spoiled on that night. It was a child's dream.

Jimmy (James T.Ainsworth) took me back to my parents and he asked them, "Could you bring her to a special dinner Christmas Day at the Sgt. Mess? My parents said yes quickly. Being the only child there, I was so thoroughly spoiled once again, I came home with boxes full with tins of turkey, fruit, sweets of all sorts and Oh Henry Bars of Chocolate with nuts, which became my favorite chocolates. I don't remember sharing these!

Jimmy went back to Marshall, Texas, and married Melba on August 10th, 1946. Melba wrote me until 1952 and then our correspondence dropped off. Her life became very busy with four children. It was then that I went to America to our special American Tenant's for their daughter Karen's wedding in Abilene, Texas. I was speaking to a guest Mary Bell, and saying it was my biggest wish in life to be able to meet up with Jimmy & Melba Ainsworth. I wanted to "thank" Jimmy and to let him know that he would never be forgotten and that he was her first American boyfriend. Amazingly she said "I work in the Sheriff's Office and I'll find Jimmy," and she did.

Walking down the stairs at Midland Airport, there he stood with his granddaughter, Cara, to greet me. We recognized each other immediately. (Sadly Melba wasn't there, she had a heart attack the previous Christmas, and James T. Ainsworth died on May 10, 2012.

A Tree and a Friend[27]

Like other World War II bomber bases in East Anglia, Knettishall is difficult to find. And like other bases, most of its

---

[27] This story appeared in the June 2013 issue of the 8th Air Force News.

THE 8TH AIR FORCE WON THE WAR IN EUROPE

buildings, hangars, runways, and Nissen huts are long gone; the land that once supported the huge flying fortresses was returned to its pastoral state. But Knettishall, former home for the 388th Bomb Group, is distinctive, and in its simplicity is worthy of a visit as any former base. In its serenity and quietness punctuated only by the sounds of pheasants and other birds, and breeze rustling the trees over the now overgrown terrain, it tells a story and provokes memories for veterans who once lived there, flew its runways and faced death on an almost daily basis, that no plow or wrecking crews can ever erase.

While on sabbatical leave in England in 1995, I visited several former Eighth Air Force bases as part of a text-book on the air war that I am writing. I had not included Knettishall on my list of visits due to the fact that is was so difficult to locate and the fact that I expected to find nothing of significance remaining from its days of glory. Then, as part of my pre-visit contacts I called George Stebbings, a "Friend of the Eighth", who had devoted his life to this patch of land that was once his boyhood home. After a brief conversation with George I was hooked. There was more to Knettishall than I had suspected. George has never forgotten the days he watched the base constructed from the farm land adjacent to his home, and most importantly the many men who were stationed there and befriended him as a lad of 14, literally adopting him as one of their own. George's eyes welled up as he recounted the many different airmen he knew personally--some who transported back to 1943-45, and he can see the faces of hundreds of men who walked or rode up the path that once led to their waiting planes and the uncertainty of the day's mission. Then he vividly describes the scene as you walk with him through the tangled brush that now covers the once bushy path.

At the end of the path now all is quiet; the scenes of war are long gone. But a glance to the left reveals a poignant reminder of George's description of what was once a beehive of activity. There is the stump of an old beech tree, and a closer look reveals many names and initials carved into the trunk by countless crews in the frightful days of 1943-45. Suddenly the visitor can see--not a deserted field--but hundreds of men carving not only their names, but they managed to take him along on B-17 training flights, and some who never returned from their missions.

George has adopted the remnants of the once proud base, and with the help of other interested residents in the area, has built a most striking memorial to the 388th Bomb Group at the entrance that once led to the base headquarters and flight line. George is very proud of this memorial, as well he should be, and is always delighted to show it to visitors, especially former residents of the base.

At the end of the path now all is quiet; the scenes of war are long gone. But a glance to the left reveals a poignant reminder of George's description of what was once a beehive of activity. Then George takes you to the large flat farm land that was once the main runway; the point of departure for so many bombing missions. At first glance the visitor sees nothing more than a cultivated field. But George then points out a huge earthen mound covered with trees and vegetation. The mound was placed there by the land owner as a "living runway," a special memorial to the many airmen who took off from that very spot with their lethal cargo destined for Hitler's fortress Europe. The striking scene reminds today's visitor that instead of a field of war Knettishall now represents in its serenity and the greenery on the living runway not death but life; life as enjoyed by individuals in the post-war generations who are the beneficiaries of the sacrifices of the 388th Bomb Group and others like it scattered throughout East Anglia.

By the time I left George's presence I realized that the visitor to England does not necessarily need to see the monuments and castles of England to appreciate the grandeur of that country. A trip into the countryside of East Anglia and a day with George Stebbings will leave you, in the simplicity of an overgrown path, a beech tree stump, and a living runway, with a vision of perhaps the most significant era in Britain's long history; an era when a group of Americans created their own "castles" in the form of bases such as Knettishall, and made it possible for free men today to visit the England of the centuries[28].

---

[28] Written by Donald E Wilson, PhD; Professor, Dept. of History, Samford University Lt. Col. USAF (Ret.).

THE 8ᵀᴴ AIR FORCE WON THE WAR IN EUROPE

After 56 years – The Puzzle

In 2001 I was president of the 388th Bomb Group Association. For the Spring issue of our newsletter, Bob Simmon, the editor, received a puzzling story by Ron Stone about the death of his uncle. He wrote I was 8 years old the last time I saw my uncle, Navigator, Lt. Herbert Lakow. On a Sunday evening in 1943 the family was listening to the big Zenith console, as all families at that time were probably doing. The phone rang and I heard my Mom (Herb's sister) exclaim, "Where are you?"

Suddenly, we forgot about The Shadow or Jack Benny and the family piled into our car and we headed out to Floyd Bennett Field in Brooklyn. Herb's B-17 had, in the course of ferrying to the UK, been forced down by a faulty engine. What a sight to this kid. A battle-ready B-17, all engines roaring and my uncle in full flight gear. An awesome sight then and a lasting memory now.

It is at this point in time, 56 years after the end of World War II, I find myself finally completing the circle and documenting the trail from that Sunday evening in 1943 to this year of 2001. With apologies to Mr. Paul Harvey, I would like to share with you now, "the rest of the story."

I remembered, vaguely, a crew member visiting our home and meeting with Grandma and my Mom. He told of Herb's devotion to his team. I seemed to remember the name *Stuttgart* and a "fact" that he was shot down and killed while not on his own plane. Over the years, having inherited all of Herb's personal affects sent from his base at Knettishall, UK, I began the task of restructuring the last months of a young man, who like so many, never saw his 25th birthday. I was without the knowledge of any direct identification sources which would be a starting point in my effort of final closure.

It was a fund-raising letter that pointed me toward a response from the 8th Air Force. Subsequently I was aided by the Association representing the 388th, which was comprised of the very group of men who flew and died with 1st Lt. Herb Lakow.

I made a call to Col. Robert Simmon, Sr. (Ret), out in Cabot, AR. He led me to books, sent me photocopies of crew lists and provided addresses of potential contacts who might have been with Herb in his last days. There it was --Hanover, Bonn, later over Lille and Merville, followed by Wattek and Brussels, finally Meulans and a Black Sept. 6th raid over *Stuttgart* where so many young men and so many Flying Fortresses met their heroic end.

With the information I was able to provide from Herb's flight logs, Bob Simmon and I found that three men, all gunners brought in from a B-24 outfit, had made it out of Herb's plane after being attacked head-on (seemingly usual strategy for that time). They had been blown free after the explosion and finished the war in a POW camp. I confirmed that one man, Ed Rogowski, had passed away in the past few years but that both Bill Herman of Pittsfield, MA and Charlie Herald of Indianapolis, IN were both okay.

It was with much apprehension that I dialed first one and later the other. It turned out that neither knew then Lt. Lakow but provided an important part of the missing puzzle. They had just transferred on to this particular mission and were not really familiar with all of their fellow crew members, BUT did remember that their plane's navigator was too sick to fly that morning and that another navigator took over. The story about Herb not being on his own plane started to make sense.

I thanked Bill and Charlie for giving me their time, recollections and so much more. I would like to think that my uncle, after 56 years, put these two men back together again after they saved each other from their doomed plane and together were imprisoned in Stalag 17B for the duration of the War.

Was there a person out there who could truly say, "Yes, I knew Your Uncle Herb?" Here was a man who was the lead Navigator over *Woensdrecht* and *Meulans*, and yet I could not find that one key person who knew him. That is until I read and then reread the Fall/Winter 2000 issue of the 388th newsletter, specifically the article concerning the reunion of the members of the Gunn crew.

Commander Francis (Hank) Henggeler was reminiscing with other members of the 563rd, recalling in part that on the morning of September 6, 1943, a young navigator approached him seeking permission to replace a navigator who was sick that day.

Henggeler had said "are you sure? You know it's not a milk run."

After sending this young Lt. back to his pilot, Capt. Bob Bernard, to see if he could indeed switch planes, he was told that it would be OK. It was, and as they say, the rest was history

I contacted Commander Henggeler at his home in Kansas City, MO. After introducing myself, I asked one simple question, Was the navigator too sick to fly that morning and that another navigator took over. The story about Herb not being on his own plane started to make more sense.

To those that made up The Mighty 8th, the 388th and the 563rd, my generation that followed you extends our deepest thanks for what you provided our country and promises that your courage will never be forgotten. I want to wish you, your families and your "Buddies" a happy and a healthy New Year.

A very special "Thanks" to Bob Simmon, Hank Henggeler, Bob Bernard, Charlie Herald and Bill Herman who made this holiday season a great deal more special for me, the last living relation who remembers the roar of those engines and a goodbye wave from that Navigator in full flight gear.

Signed Ronald Stone, 60 E. 8th Street, New York, NY 10003.

A Letter from the Boss to First Lt. Julian M. Carr

Dear Julian,

Most of your birthdays, I imagine, have been celebrated at home, among family and friends, in an atmosphere of peace and security that none of the world knows today. We accepted these things as a natural way of life, being a people that disdained war and prized the fellowship and affection that accompanied such simple events, as birthdays.

You cannot be with your family and no one regrets that fact more than I and, at the same time, no one is prouder of the manner in which you and your fellow soldiers are celebrating your birthday this year. You are here in this theater of war because Hitler and his associates have decided that there was too much sentiment in the world. They thought that nations that placed importance on such human qualities would be "push-overs" for a "goose-stepping gang" that was dedicated to hatred and destruction.

We are here to prove that the Nazis and Fascist are wrong; that birthdays and home and family are good things. We are here to see to it that the right to enjoy these things and to live our lives as we will, as free men, shall be preserved for us and for those to come after us.

You are celebrating this birthday in an atmosphere of war that is also an atmosphere of optimism for we have Hitler on the run. You, as one of the allied soldiers who are participating in this big push, have reason to be proud of the way you spend this birthday. The gift you are helping to give the free world in this war in one that men will never forget. You can be sure of that and happy in that knowledge.

The best birthday that I can make with you is that you continue to function in the same splendid manner that you have in the past. I am honored to have men like you under my command. I know you will join me in a toast to your loved ones at home with the promise that you will be celebrating your next birthday at their side. Happy birthday, Julian.

Signed William B. David, Colonel, Air Corp Commanding

Return To Knettishall
By Walter Mayberry, waist gunner, Ellis Crew, 560th Squadron

Tonight, on the edge of this small English village I stand, looking over familiar scenes that flood my mind with memories of things long past. Before me - now, distorted shapes in the gathering darkness - stands a row of barracks, quiet and deserted; shelters that once knew the voices of many men, walls that knew their dark and lonely hours and shared their happiness and their sorrows; walls that once listened to tales of home, of war.

Once friendly places now empty, deathly still and stark in the misty night. Underfoot, I tread the paths that felt the step of GI shoes and heavy flying boots; paths that seem to sense the feeling of footsteps known long ago, now overgrown and

THE 8TH AIR FORCE WON THE WAR IN EUROPE

reclaimed by the creeping grass.

Before me I see long ribbons of white stretching off through fields of English countryside; seemingly endless strips that once felt the weight of a thousand warplanes, heavily laden with men -- and death for those who trembled below-- strips now deserted and, like the paths, slowly being reclaimed by the foraging weeds.

The quietness now presses in on me in violent waves as if it would suddenly burst forth in an eruption of all the familiar sounds I knew. There, suddenly, in front of me, out of the darkness, I hear the noise of a hundred giant engines thundering in the morning air. I hear the quiet voices of men talking, soon to go off into the dawn in the gigantic metal birds.

Out on the strip I see a thousand khaki-plad warriors in endless rows, marching to the heart-stirring strains of martial music, their colors whipping in the cold wind. As I stand there transfixed, all of it is gone as suddenly as it appeared, and I am alone again with the quiet and darkness. I breathe a lonely sigh, for all these things are gone, never to return, only to live in dark recesses of the mind, brought forth again in moments of wakefulness.

As I turn for a last look at the darkened spot, I see again, for a fleeting instant, those silver giants taking to the air for the last time, in the darkness of dawn. I hear the vibrant sound of their roaring engines straining to raise them airborne. I hear the low murmur of voices saying last minute 'good lucks,' and the thunderous roll-call of men long gone before.

I hear the music and the sound of their marching feet mingled with the engines' full-throaty roar echoing down the dark corridors of time. As these shapes disappear into the dusk of years, I feel a great sorrow, the sting of tears -- and lift a heavy hand in final salute.

Walter Mayberry was shot down over Nurnberg on his tenth mission and was held as a POW in Stalag 7. He wrote this on July 28, 1948 at his home in Harrison, Arkansas.

Bibliography

- 388th Bomb Group. *562nd Bomb Squadron patch.* Scan. www.388thbg.info/photos. Web. 24 April 2018.
- 384th Bomb Group. *Grafton Stained Glass cropped.* Photograph. www.384thbombgroup.com. 17 Oct 2004. Web. 24 April 2018.
- 388th Bomb Group Association. *Knettishall Memorial.* Photograph. www.388thbga.org. Web. 24 April 2018.
- Anderson, Christopher J. *The Men of the Mighty Eighth: The U.S. 8th Air Force, 1942–1945 (G.I. Series N 24).* London: Greenhill, 2001.
- Astor, Gerald. *The Mighty Eighth: The Air War in Europe as told by the Men who Fought it.* New York: D.I. Fine Books, 1997.
- Bowman, Martin. *8th Air Force at War: Memories and Missions, England, 1942–1945.* Cambridge, UK: Patrick Stephens Ltd., 1994.
- Bowman, Martin. *Castles in the Air: The Story of the Men from the US 8th Air Force.* Walton-on-Thames, UK: Red Kite, 2000.
- City of Savannah. *Fortress Will Be Christened Today.* Photograph. savannahb17.hwythunder.com. Web. 24 April 2018.
- CindyN. *Planes of Fame P-38.* 2009. Wikipedia Commons. Source: Own work. https://commons.wikimedia.org/wiki/File:P38 Lightning.jpg. 4 April 2009. Web. 24 April 2018.
- Costlow, Jeff. *The World War II Memorial, Washington, DC.* 2005. Photograph. Wikipedia Commons. Wikimedia Foundation. Public Domain Image. 30 Dec 2005. Web. 25 April 2018.
- Maurer, Maurer. *Air Force Combat Units Of World War II.* Office of Air Force History, 1961, republished 1983.
- Freeman, Roger A. and Winston G. Ramsey. *Airfields of the Eighth: Then and Now.* London: After the Battle, 1978. Republished 1992.

- Freeman, Roger A. *The Mighty Eighth: Units, Men and Machines – A History of the US 8th Air Force*. 1970. ISBN 0-87938-638-X.
  - Revised as *The Mighty Eighth: a History of the Units, Men and Machines of the Us 8th Air Force*. Cassell & Co., 2000. ISBN 1-85409-035-6.
- Freeman, Roger A. et al. *The Mighty Eighth War Diary*. London: Jane's Publishing Company, 1981.
- Freeman, Roger A. (Ed.) *The Mighty Eighth in Art*. London: Arms & Armour, 1995.
- Freeman, Roger A. *The Mighty Eighth in Colour*. London: Arms & Armour, 1991.
  - New Edition as *The Mighty Eighth: The Colour Record*. London: Cassell & Co., 2001.
- Freeman, Roger A. *The Mighty Eighth War Diary*. 1990. ISBN 0-87938-495-6.
- Freeman, Roger A. *Mighty Eighth War Manual*. London: Jane's Publishing Company, 1984.
- Freeman, Roger A. *The Mighty Eighth: Warpaint and Heraldry*. London: Arms & Armour, 1997.
- Goshimini. *P-51D 44-11153 NL451TB Kimberly Kaye 150502*. 2015. Wikipedia Commons. Source: own work. https://commons.wikimedia.org/wiki/File:P-51D_44-11153_NL451TB_Kimberly_Kaye_150502.JPG. 8 May 2015. Web. 24 April 2018.
- Lambert, John W. *The 8th Air Force: Victory and Sacrifice: A World War II Photo History*. Atglen, Pennsylvania: Schiffer Publishing, 2006. ISBN 0-7643-2534-5.
- La Bruno, Victor. *ME 410 Hornisse with BK 5*. 1943. Wikipedia Commons. Wikipedia Foundation. Public Domain Image. 10 August 2009. Web. 24 April 2018.
- McLachlan, Ian and Russell J. Zorn. *Eighth Air Force Bomber Stories: Eye-Witness Accounts from American Airmen and British Civilians of the Perils of War*. Yeovil, UK: Patrick Stephens Ltd., 1991.
- McLaughlin, (Brigadier General) J. Kemp. *The Mighty Eighth in World War II: A Memoir*. Kentucky University Press, 2000.

- Miller, Kent D. *Fighter Units & Pilots of the 8th Air Force September 1942 – May 1945. Volume 1 Day-to-Day Operations – Fighter Group Histories.* Atglen, Pennsylvania: Schiffer Publishing, 2000. ISBN 0-7643-1241-3.
- Miller, Kent D. and Nancy Thomas. *Fighter Units & Pilots of the 8th Air Force September 1942 – May 1945. Volume 2 Aerial Victories – Ace Data.* Atglen, Pennsylvania: Schiffer Publishing, 2001. ISBN 0-7643-1242-1.
- Office of Air Force History (1983) [1961]. Maurer, Maurer, ed. *Air Force Combat Units of World War II (PDF).* Washington, D.C.: U.S. Govt. Print. Off. ISBN 0-912799-02-1. Retrieved 4 October 2007.Ramsey, Winston G. [Editor]. *Airfields of the Eighth.* London: 1978.
- Quadell. *B-17_Flying_Fortress.* 2004. Wikipedia Commons. Wikimedia Foundation. Public Domain Image. 7 April 2006. Web. 24 April 2018.
- Scutts, Jerry. *Lion in the Sky: US 8th Air Force Fighter Operations, 1942–1945.* Cambridge, UK: Patrick Stephens Ltd., 1987.
- Smith, Graham. *The Mighty Eighth in the Second World War.* Newbury: Countryside Books, 2001.
- Steijger, Cees. *A History of USAFE.* Voyageur, 1991. ISBN 1-85310-075-7.
- Strong, Russell A. *A Biographical Directory of the 8th Air Force, 1942–1945.* Manhattan, Kansas: Military Affairs – Aerospace Historian, 1985.
- United States Army Air Force. *Beech AT-7 – N40 Kelly Field TX.* 1943. Wikipedia Commons. Wikimedia Foundation. Public Domain Image. 22 Dec 2015. Web. 24 April 2018.
- United States Army Air Force. *Emblem of the USAAF 388th Bombardment Group (World War II).* 1944. Wikipedia Commons. Wikimedia Foundation. Public Domain Image. 11 July 2009. Web. 24 April 2018.
- Unknown. *Dolittle Toyko Raiders.* 1940s. Official United States Airforce Website. Photograph. 24 April 2018.
- Unknown. *General of the Air Force Henry H. Arnold.* Before 1949. Photograph. Wikipedia Commons.

Wikimedia Foundation. Public Domain Image. 21 Sept. 2013. Web. 24 April 2018.
- U.S. Air Force. *Cutaway drawing of a V-1 showing fuel cells, warhead and other equipment.* 2008. Wikipedia Commons. Wikipedia Foundation. Public Domain Image. 25 May 2008. Web. 24 April 2018.
- Varhegyi, James. *Air Force Memorial DC, US.* 2015. Photograph. Wikipedia Commons. Wikimedia Foundation. Public Domain Image. 25 May 2015. Web. 25 April 2018.
- Werrell, Kenneth P. & Robin Higham. *Eighth Air Force Bibliography: An Extended Essay & Listing of Published & Unpublished Materials.* Manhattan, Kansas: Military Affairs – Aerospace Historian, 1981 (Second Edition 1997, Strasburg, Pennsylvania: 8th Air Force Memorial Museum Foundation, 1997).
- Woolnough, John H. (Ed.) *The 8th Air Force Album: The Story of the Mighty Eighth Air Force in WW II.* Hollywood, Florida: 8th AF News, 1978.
- Wolny, W. *Preinvasion bombing of Pointe du Hoe by Ninth Air Force bombers.* Photograph. Wikipedia Commons. Wikimedia Foundation. Public Domain Image. 26 August 2015. Web. 24 April 2018.
- Woolnough, John H. (Ed.) *The 8th Air Force Yearbook: The current Status of 8th AF Unit Associations, 1980.* Hollywood, Florida: 8th AF News, 1981.
- Woolnough, John H. (Ed.) *Stories of the Eighth: An Anthology of the 8th Air Force in World War Two.* Hollywood, Fla.: 8th AF News, 1983.

About the Author

August C. Bolino joined the U.S. Army Air Corps in 1942 and completed his navigation school flight training at Selman Field in Monroe, LA in October 1943. He was assigned as a member of a Boeing B-17 "Flying Fortress" combat crew at the 388th Bomber Group at Knettishall, East Anglia, England, where he flew 30 combat missions including two on D-Day, June 6, 1944. He received the Distinguished Flying Cross and the Air Medal.

After being discharged from the military, Bolino enrolled at the University of Michigan under the GI Bill, where he obtained an MBA degree in finance. In 1957, he finished his Ph.D. in economics at Saint Louis University. He began his teaching career at the University of Washington in Seattle and moved to Idaho State College (now University) and Saint Louis University.

In 1963, he was appointed chief of the division of economic analysis of automation in the office of Manpower Automation and Training to the U.S. Department of Labor in Washington, D.C. In 1964, he served as assistant to the U.S. Commissioner of Education in the Department of Health, Education, and Welfare. In 1978, he was elected Vice President for Research of the Ellis Island Restoration Commission while teaching full-time at the Catholic University of America in Washington, D.C.

When Ellis Island closed, the US government tried to rent or sell it without luck. After hiring a leading architect, they decided to tear down all thirteen buildings to make a picnic area. When Bolino was asked his opinion, he said, "Look up. There is a second floor to the Great Hall that was never used. Make it into a Family History Center."

This is now the most popular place on the Island. Bolino received a commendation from the US House of Representatives, along with a plaque installed near the center bearing his name and the year.

Other titles by August C. Bolino

My Life (2016)
An 1872 Case of Murder in Utah Territory (2014)
Men of Massachusetts (2012)
The Kid and the Clipper (2006)
Brother Brigham's Trial (2002)
Thomas Angel, American (2001)
From Depression to War (1998)
The Ellis Island Source Book (1990)
A Century of Human Capital by Education and Training (1989)
The Watchmakers of Massachusetts (1987)
The Ellis Island Source Book (1985)
Career Education: Contributions to Economic Growth (1973)
Manpower and the City (1969)
The Development of the American Economy (1966)
The Development of the American Economy (1961)

www.ingramcontent.com/pod-product-compliance
Lightning Source LLC
Chambersburg PA
CBHW071308110426
42743CB00042B/1215